THE CORN BELT ROUTE

A HISTORY OF THE CHICAGO
GREAT WESTERN RAILROAD
COMPANY

THE CORN BELT ROUTE

A HISTORY OF THE CHICAGO GREAT WESTERN RAILROAD COMPANY

H. ROGER GRANT

1984

NORTHERN ILLINOIS UNIVERSITY PRESS · DEKALB, ILLINOIS

Library of Congress Cataloging in Publication Data

Grant, H. Roger, 1943–
    The corn belt route.

    Bibliography: p.
    Includes index.
    1. Chicago Great Western Railroad — History.   I. Title.
HE2791.C653G72   1984   385'.065'77   83-17461
ISBN 0-87580-095-5

Copyright © 1984 by Northern Illinois University Press
Published by the Northern Illinois University Press,
DeKalb, Illinois 60115
Manufactured in the United States of America
Design by Joan Westerdale

For ELEANOR L. DINSMORE (1908–1973)
"Dinny" knew the CGW and why I liked it at an
early age.

CONTENTS

PREFACE

THIS history of the "Corn Belt Route," the Chicago Great Western Railroad (CGW), offers the first in-depth account of this late Midwestern carrier. While professional historians have mentioned it in passing, and railroad "buffs" have produced several works about it, the road has otherwise been ignored. Why this has happened is not absolutely clear. Perhaps the wholesale destruction of thousands of irreplaceable records by disgruntled employees at the time of the CGW's merger with the Chicago & North Western and the widely scattered nature of remaining documents have deterred scholars. More likely, the Great Western's size has made it unattractive as a writing project. In recent years big railroads like the Atchison, Topeka & Santa Fé; Illinois Central; and Louisville & Nashville have all received well-deserved corporate biographies, but the more modest roads, like the Chicago Great Western, have been slighted. In my estimation, this has been a grievous omission. The once dynamic, 1,500-mile Great Western had a colorful past and contributed mightily to the transportation industry. Indeed, competitive innovation commonly sprang from this smaller, less robust carrier. While a firm like the giant Pennsylvania experienced steady ossification, the Great Western did not.

Begun as a speculative venture by that imaginative and energetic Minnesotan, A. B. Stickney, the Chicago Great Western grew to be much more than its creator first anticipated. From its 1885 origins as a 110-mile pike running from St. Paul to the Iowa line, the road quickly gained access to the nation's greatest rail center, Chicago, and shortly thereafter to St. Joseph and Kansas City. Later, the company entered Omaha. By reaching these strategic gateways, the CGW became a significant property.

Although constructed at a late date in an intensely competitive region, the Chicago Great Western fought long and hard to make a profit. Initially, it relied heavily on bargain-basement charges and efficient operations. While regulatory constraints and a change of ownership ended its reputation as a "rate cutter," the company remained dedicated to flexible and innovative practices: it had little choice. Its life continued to be hectic, with powerful neighbors and increasing rubber-tire competition after World War I. These factors help to explain the CGW's most widely celebrated "first"—hauling loaded truck trailers on flatcars, i.e., "piggyback" service.

Like most businesses, the Corn Belt Route experienced its darker moments. Two receiverships and an episode of horrible mismanagement scarred it. Though employees took considerable pride in considering themselves members of a large, happy "family," nasty labor spats did erupt. An exceedingly bitter and at times violent strike hit in 1922; more serious trouble came in 1953.

The Great Western closed out its life in a fashion true to its heritage of innovation and no-nonsense operations. The tenure of William N. Deramus III from 1949 to 1957 and that of his hand-picked successor saw employment of the latest state of the art technology and the most economical methods. A lean work force moved longer and fewer freight trains along a Spartan yet modern physical plant. But the merger mania of the early 1960s radically changed the road's situation. If it were isolated by its friends and rivals, management believed, the company would surely wither and die. Thus, the CGW found a mate, the Chicago & North Western, and it officially joined that corporation on July 1, 1968.

Since the Chicago Great Western operated in a region crowded with carriers, various observers have either argued for or at least accepted the point of view that it should never have been built. This seems faulty logic. When Americans had only the railroad to break their isolation from one another, every mile of track was needed. Even when the automobile age dramatically changed the transportation picture, the Great Western still served a vital purpose: it gave generally good, dependable service at reasonable prices. As already suggested, the company achieved a remarkable record for its pioneering efforts. Undeniably, the CGW was an asset to its territory, as the pages of this book will reveal.

My interest in the Corn Belt Route springs from several sources. Admittedly I like trains and have ever since my earliest childhood. Although I grew up in Albia, a southern Iowa community served by the Chicago, Burlington & Quincy; Minneapolis & St. Louis; and Wabash, I also spent time in Carroll, Iowa, on the Chicago & North Western's main line across the state and on the Chicago Great Western's "West End." The former road's streamliners thrilled me, but the latter's long freights, pulled by those ubiquitous F-3 units with their attractive deep red paint scheme, caught my fancy. And there was something about that company's name—Chicago

Great Western—that sounded mighty and wonderful. I vividly recall dashing from my aunt's basement office in the old Carroll County Courthouse to the Great Western's tracks when the distinctive blasts of the locomotive's airhorn announced the train's approach to downtown. My fascination for flanged wheels did not end here, and graduate school ignited a strong interest in the progressive era, that great period of uplift and reform that swept America at the turn of the century. Statements by Great Western founder A. B. Stickney attracted my attention. Apparently he was a maverick among his peers for suggesting that the government regulate railroad rates in a meaningful fashion. I assumed that Stickney, and certainly his company, had been studied by at least one professional historian; I soon discovered that I was wrong. The story of this man and his railroad remained to be told.

• • •

I am indebted to the numerous people who assisted me in the preparation of this book. The emerging manuscript benefited immeasurably from the wise counsel and pertinent criticism of William N. Deramus III, Don L. Hofsommer, D. Keith Lawson, Albro Martin, F. Stewart Mitchell, Daniel Nelson, Richard C. Overton, and David C. Riede. Similarly, scores of former Great Western personnel, rail fans, and others interested in the firm have contributed greatly to this project. I wish to acknowledge my special gratitude to Charles W. Finch, John Hawkinson, William L. Heitter, John Hancock, John Hodson, William S. Kuba, William J. Lenoir, James L. Rueber, V. Allan Vaughn, and W. A. Vaughn. The staffs of numerous institutions also gave me valuable assistance. They include: Allen County Historical Society, Lima, Ohio; Association of American Railroads, Washington, D.C.; Baker Library, Harvard University Graduate School of Business Administration, Cambridge, Mass.; Chicago & North Western Transportation Company, Chicago, Ill.; Chicago & North Western Historical Society, Hazel Crest, Ill.; Chicago Historical Society, Chicago, Ill.; DeGolyer Library, Southern Methodist University, Dallas, Texas; Goodhue County Historical Society, Red Wing, Minn.; Illinois State Historical Society, Springfield, Ill.; Interstate Commerce Commission, Washington, D.C.; Iowa State Historical Department, Division of Historical Museum, Des Moines, Ia.; Division of the State Historical Society, Iowa City, Ia.; James Jerome Hill Reference Library, St. Paul, Minn.; Kansas City Southern Railway Company, Kansas City, Mo.; Kansas State Historical Society, Topeka, Kan.; Library of Congress, Washington, D.C.; Minnesota Historical Society, St. Paul, Minn.; National Archives, Washington, D.C.; Newberry Library, Chicago, Ill.; Olmsted County Historical Society, Rochester, Minn.; Regional History Center, Northern Illinois University, DeKalb, Ill.; State Historical Society of Missouri, Columbia, Mo.; State Historical Society of Wisconsin, Madison, Wis.; and the West Chicago Historical Society, West Chicago, Ill. I want to thank, too, the Faculty Research Committee of the University of Akron for two generous travel grants and the American Historical Association for awarding me an Albert J. Beveridge Grant for Research in American History. History Department secretaries Garnette Dorsey and Dorothy J. Richards saw the manuscript through every stage with incomparable fortitude and good humor. And my wife, Martha Farrington Grant, exhibited her usual tolerance and made editorial suggestions throughout the many months of writing. All these people should take credit for the good things in this publication; yet, the final results are my own, and for all errors of fact and interpretation I assume responsibility.

H. Roger Grant
Akron, Ohio

CHAPTER ONE
A. B. STICKNEY BUILDS A RAILROAD: THE MINNESOTA & NORTHWESTERN, 1883–1887

1880s: DECADE OF RAILROAD GROWTH

THE 1880s witnessed the heyday of railroad construction in the United States. More miles of track were built at this time than at any other period. As the decade dawned, the American rail network stood at 93,267 miles; ten years later it soared to 163,597, an impressive 43 percent gain. While track-laying gangs toiled mightily throughout the country, they did extensive work in the upper Mississippi River valley: Minnesota added 2,315 miles; Iowa, 2,956; and Illinois, another 2,363. This represented percentage increases of 73.4, 54.7, and 30.0, respectively. Although already extensively settled, these three states also experienced a population boom. Minnesota grew by 521,053; Iowa gained nearly 300,000; and Illinois acquired more than 700,000.[1]

More railroads and more people seemed to be the keys to future prosperity. In some instances, the former helped to blaze the way for the latter; the iron horse could alone shatter the isolation of a region or locality. And if an area were already inhabited, an expanding rail network meant increased agricultural, industrial, and commercial advances, for steamcars rather than steamboats were usually the only effective means of intercity transportation. Thus, the public needed virtually every mile of railroad. Citizens hungered for the new service, knowing that it would give them an enormous injection of economic strength. A Chicago merchant said it best: "Railroads are the magic carpets that bind the Republic. . . . [They] . . . are the only mode of travel between most points. They give life to those they serve."[2]

While the advent of railroad use signaled long-term progress, the popularity of this form of transportation had another explanation. Since the days of the Granger agitation in the 1870s, residents of the upper Midwest, in particular, had desired increased railroad competition. With an arrogance characteristic of the "Gilded Age," the established companies commonly "abused" consumers. Anti-industry feelings, therefore, developed over a variety of perceived evils. While service-related problems annoyed and even angered patrons, other grievances troubled them much more deeply. "Watered stock," tax-dodging, and rampant bribery worried many. But the foremost concern centered on discriminatory freight charges. The conventional wisdom of the day held that carriers existed to plunder rather than to serve. Even the most casual observer realized that rates for the "short" haul were usually greater than for the "long" haul. While government regulation, even national ownership, might solve the problems associated with the late nineteenth-century railroad enterprise, the public firmly embraced the long-standing notion that more lines would surely help to remedy their transportation difficulties. And sometimes they were right.[3]

By the waning years of the century, residents of Minnesota, Iowa, and Illinois got their wish for more railroads. They enjoyed a magnificent transportation network, the envy of many elsewhere. Indeed, the railroad map of the three states began to resemble a plate of wet spaghetti. While a variety of short lines served the region, several trunk roads — the "Big Four" — gained dominance. The Chicago, Burlington & Quincy (CB&Q) tied Chicago with Omaha and by the late 1880s, the Twin Cities. It also covered southern Iowa and northern and western Illinois with a plethora of branch lines. The Chicago, Milwaukee & St. Paul (CM&StP) likewise connected Chicago and Omaha and the Twin Cities, and its branches blanketed eastern Iowa and southern Minnesota. The Chicago & North Western (C&NW), including its affiliate, the Omaha Road, was yet another Chicago to Omaha and Twin Cities carrier. It also possessed an extensive network of feeder trackage in northern Illinois, western Iowa, and southern Minnesota. Last, the Chicago, Rock Island & Pacific (CRI&P) owned a fourth Chicago to Omaha route and through subsidiaries reached the Twin Cities. The Rock Island, too, sported a substantial number of auxiliary lines within the boundaries of the three states. Thus, the "Big Four" covered the upper Midwest like a morning dew. But increased competition did not always foster the better service and lower rates that consumers expected.

Considering the extent to which the "Big Four" served Minnesota, Iowa, and Illinois, construction of still another carrier that linked Chicago and the Twin Cities and later other sections might seem foolish. Yet the building of such a road was fully justified. Even by the mid-1880s there were localities that had large amounts of freight and passengers to transport but were either inadequately served or not served at all. By this time, too, astute observers realized that the railroad business was becoming more and more one of long, "through" hauls. Since

A. B. Stickney, builder of the Chicago Great Western, poses for Chicago portrait photographer Henry Taylor early in the 20th century. (Hill Reference Library)

the entrenched "Big Four" failed to seal off the interchange centers of the Midwest, a company that connected two or more of these points possessed an opportunity for immediate success and a reasonable chance for long-term financial health.

ENTER A. B. STICKNEY

TAKING advantage of the conducive environment for railroad construction in the Midwest was an uprooted New Englander, Alpheus Beede Stickney, who by the 1880s called the bustling city of St. Paul, Minnesota, his home. Stickney is the individual, more than any other, who created and guided what eventually would become a spunky

1,500-mile truck carrier, the Chicago Great Western Railway Company (CGW).

A. B. Stickney (he refused to use Alpheus) was born in the village of Wilton, Maine, on June 27, 1840, son of Daniel and Ursula Beede Stickney, of old New England stock. His father — a sometime abolitionist newspaper editor and Universalist minister — farmed in rocky Franklin County. Young Stickney attended a local school and private academies in New Hampton, New Hampshire, and Foxcroft, Maine. Even before leaving home, this red-headed lad was willing to labor hard and seek business opportunities. When not working as a plowman, he toiled in a shoemaker's shop, and the money he needed to purchase a seventy-five-cent algebra book came from drying "windfalls" in his grandfather's apple orchard and selling them at two and one-half cents a pound.[4]

At eighteen, Stickney left home to seek his fortune. Initially, he seemed most interested in a legal career. He "read" law for Josiah Crosby, a Dexter, Maine, lawyer; but because of financial difficulties he interrupted his studies with several stints as a schoolteacher. Then, in 1861, Stickney gained admittance to the bar. The beckoning opportunities of the Minnesota frontier prompted the young barrister to leave his native state for the thriving St. Croix River community of Stillwater where he both served as superintendent of schools and hung out his shingle. Although Stickney eventually left education, he continued his legal practice until 1869.[5]

Stickney's new interest became railroads. After all, the area in which he now resided had experienced an explosion of rail projects following the Civil War; this enterprise, more so than the law, seemed to hold the promise of great adventure and possible wealth. As did most young men who selected railroad careers during the days of peak rail expansion, Stickney held a variety of positions before establishing himself as head of the Minnesota & Northwestern (M&NW), the principal predecessor of the Chicago Great Western, with which he stayed until his retirement in 1908.

Upon making his decision to enter railroading, Stickney moved to the nearby Minnesota capital, where he began an active business life. First, he spearheaded a local syndicate that used a federal land grant in Wisconsin to open a rail line from the lumber-rich St. Croix River valley to Lake Superior. He even personally supervised the building of the initial section, the North Wisconsin Railroad, from Hudson to New Richmond, a rather remarkable undertaking considering that his training was in law and not in civil engineering. Next, Stickney became involved with the infant St. Paul, Stillwater & Taylor Falls Railroad (which, like the North Wisconsin, later became part of the Chicago & North Western system). During much of the 1870s, he served as that company's vice-president, general manager, and chief legal counsel. Then, in 1879, St. Paul's leading railroad figure, James Jerome Hill, offered him the superintendency of construction on the rapidly expanding St. Paul, Minneapolis & Manitoba (the core of the future Great Northern). A year later, Stickney wore another hat: general superintendent of the western division of the Canadian Pacific, a firm with which Hill was deeply involved financially and emotionally.[6]

A. B. Stickney's work in the rough and tumble environment north of the border would soon test his friendship with Hill. As the Canadian Pacific pushed westward from Winnipeg through the empty prairies, several high-ranking employees of this company apparently exploited opportunities to reap handsome profits from townsite speculation. Stickney was one so accused. The affair cost the chief engineer his job, but Hill accepted Stickney's word that he was not involved in any such conflicts of interest. Hill's positive intercession not only kept Stickney on the Canadian Pacific's payroll but surely strengthened their common bonds.[7]

Returning to St. Paul in 1881, Stickney found employment with the Minneapolis & St. Louis (M&StL). At that time, the "Albert Lea Route" was emerging as an important road in southern Minnesota and northern Iowa. While an M&StL official, Stickney oversaw the building of the subsidiary Minnesota Central. This little pike took shape during 1882 between Red Wing and a connection with the

M&StL at Waterville. (A year later, the Minnesota Central became the Wisconsin, Minnesota & Pacific [WM&P], a property that the CGW would later acquire.) Although an apparently valued lieutenant, Stickney resigned in 1883, probably because of his personality—he was "a lone wolf"—and his burning desire to head his own railroad.[8]

THE MINNESOTA & NORTHWESTERN TAKES SHAPE

THIS shrewd Yankee soon spearheaded a most promising venture, the revitalization of the Minnesota & Northwestern Railroad Company. By 1888, this road was to tie the Twin Cities to Chicago and would operate several important branches. The M&NW was born, though, long before A. B. Stickney entered railroading or even arrived in the North Star State, and it was from this beginning that the company took its name.

On March 4, 1854, N. C. D. Taylor, Speaker of the Minnesota House of Representatives, and J. Travis Rosser, the territorial secretary, signed the charter of the Minnesota & Northwestern Railroad Company. A group of financiers, most of whom hailed from New York, Albany, and Boston, received permission to build a railroad "from a point on the North West shore of Lake Superior . . . by St. Anthony and St. Paul . . . to such point on the northern boundary line of the State of Iowa—as the board of Directors may designate; which point shall be selected with reference to the best route to the City of Dubuque." But the devastating impact of the Panic of 1857 prevented the projected road from becoming more than a dream.[9]

The Minnesota & Northwestern's incorporation papers gathered dust until the fall of 1883, at which time Stickney, joined by William R. Marshall, a St. Paul investor, acquired the unused franchise together with the 10,000 shares outstanding. Why they did so is easily explained. When Minnesota entered the Union in 1858, its newly adopted consti-

tution prohibited the chartering of railroad firms, except under a general corporation act that imposed a liability upon stockholders "for as much again as the promised amount of their shares." The original agreement of 1854 not only protected shareholders from such legal responsibilities, but it offered a considerable tax benefit: "Under the charter the company is forever exempt from all local and other taxation in Minnesota except a two percent tax on its gross earnings." Since the M&NW charter was the last pre-1858 charter available, Stickney and his partner knew they possessed a potentially valuable document.[10]

With charter in hand and with substantial financial backing from Minnesota and English investors, the new owners of the Minnesota & Northwestern began to shape its destiny. Not long after the resourceful A. B. Stickney energized the M&NW, he launched another Minnesota-chartered corporation, the Minnesota Loan & Debenture Company. This fiscal entity, which would position itself between the railroad and the source of capital, was designed to enhance the pocketbooks of Stickney and his business friends in various clever ways. While details about the Minnesota Loan & Debenture Company's financial arrangement with the M&NW are scanty, the firm apparently charged steep construction rates, extracting payment in cash, bonds, and common stock. Since the Minnesota Loan & Debenture Company was technically not a construction company, it arranged with a principal builder to undertake the actual work at the lowest charges possible. The press eventually recognized the significance of Stickney's non-railroad firm; one newspaper reported that Stickney and his associates "openly admit that they made their money in constructing it [the M&NW], and that they do not expect to make any by operating it." The Stickney strategem was hardly unusual. Few could make large profits by just operating a small Granger road.[11]

By early 1884, A. B. Stickney's "paper" railroad showed positive signs of becoming real. Foremost, it had started a track survey between St. Paul and a connection at Mona, Iowa, near the Minnesota state line, with the Illinois Central's (IC) leased road, the Cedar Falls & Minnesota. With such a southern terminus, the M&NW could gain access to Chicago and thus forge a strategic Twin Cities–Windy City route. Specifically, cars would travel from St. Paul to Mona over M&NW rails; next, they would use the Cedar Falls & Minnesota to Cedar Falls, Iowa; from there they would cross the Dubuque & Sioux City (D&SC), another IC-leased property, to the Mississippi River; after traversing the Illinois Central's own trackage to Forreston, Illinois, equipment would cover the last two laps via the Chicago & Iowa, a Chicago, Burlington & Quincy (CB&Q) affiliate, to Aurora, and then take the CB&Q main line to Chicago. Shortly before Stickney's son, Samuel, drove the first surveyor's stake at Randolph, Minnesota, about thirty-two miles south of St. Paul, the St. Paul City Council granted the M&NW access over its streets and along the river levee. Company representatives busily acquired the necessary parcels of real estate for right-of-way, station, and terminal purposes.[12]

Construction of the approximately 110 miles of trackage from St. Paul to Mona, a station 1.4 miles southeast of Lyle, Minnesota, began in September 1884 without fanfare. Crews of D. C. Shepard & Company, the vigorous St. Paul-based firm that worked closely with the Hill interests, started their grading and bridge and culvert building in the vicinity of Randolph. Soon hundreds of men carved out the roadbed along its entire route. Although the Minnesota terrain posed no major obstacles, except for the need to span the "Father of Waters" at St. Paul, it was not all level prairie. The "pot-and-kettle" sections necessitated considerable "borrow" and "fill" work. Huge quantities of steel and other supplies arrived over the M&StL's Cannon Valley Division at Cascade, a mile west of Randolph; and when the graders had finished, tracklaying gangs moved north. By May 1885, the rails lay only seven miles from St. Paul, and soon they reached that destination. Workers then turned their efforts to the southern section from Randolph to Mona. While the territory along this emerging road was populated, it lacked extensive transportation facilities. Although the line officially opened for through traffic on September 27, 1885, after completion of the 1,400-foot Mississippi River bridge, a local mixed train entered service on July 3, and a regular passenger run started between West St. Paul and Lyle on September 5.[13]

The timing of the first segment of the Minnesota & Northwestern proved ideal. A period of "business slowness" had struck the country in 1884. Material and labor costs dropped appreciably, and concerns like the M&NW, which had the financial wherewithal to exploit the situation, profited from this good fortune. Stickney noted, for example, that the cost of steel rails delivered to St. Paul had been $74.50 per ton in 1881; but the 1884 price tag was only $32.70, which also included a "guarantee from Mr. Carnegie to replace any rail that is broken or gives out during six years." These rails, furthermore, weighed sixty pounds to the yard rather than the fifty-six pounds originally intended; thus, the M&NW got better rail for less money.[14]

The opening of the St. Paul–Mona line caused considerable speculation about Stickney's intentions and of the property's ultimate fate. Since the road offered the Illinois Central access to the Minnesota capital and the Great Northwest, several newspapers and trade publications logically concluded that the Minnesota & Northwestern would join the IC's expanding network. "The Illinois Central is now a large system, and well backed financially," observed the *St. Paul Globe* in August 1885, "and, with the other large systems, must in time have its own line to the Northwest and become a direct competitor for the wheat and milling traffic. By securing this road [the M&NW] it would have a splendid line . . . , a thing it has been wanting for some time past." The *Dubuque Daily Times*, however, believed that either the Chicago, Burlington & Quincy or the Chicago, Rock Island & Pacific might swallow up the infant carrier. Since the CB&Q was at that time in the process of building into Dubuque from Chicago, the paper thought it might acquire the Dubuque & Northwestern, a local firm with a presumed Minnesota objective; and then, together with

The Minnesota & Northwestern got access to St. Paul in 1885 when it constructed the massive Robert Street Bridge over the Mississippi River. This structure led directly to development of South St. Paul. (Minnesota Historical Society)

the Stickney road, gain access to St. Paul. The Rock Island likewise hoped to reach the Twin Cities. As the rumor went, the Rock Island "will build across from one point on the Burlington, Cedar Rapids & Northern [a railroad it owned jointly with the CB&Q] to Mona." Yet, the *Daily Times* also believed that the Illinois Central longed for the M&NW, perhaps not so much to win entry into St. Paul but to force the directors of the Dubuque & Sioux City Railroad "to come down in the rental of the Iowa [lines]." The lease agreement was scheduled for renegotiation in 1887, and the IC's owners believed that they were paying too much. Thus, if the Illinois Central were to acquire the M&NW and connect it directly with its own line at Dubuque from the east, the value of the D&SC and its affiliated companies would surely drop, perhaps markedly.[15]

Such speculation made the sale of the Minnesota & Northwestern seem probable. After all, this was a time of system-building and, indeed, was fully con-

sistent with A. B. Stickney's own past. He appeared to be much more a plunger than an investor-manager. Argued one editor: "Of the many railroads he built, not one of them did he build with the intention of operating them as independent lines, but built them for speculation, and he has made money by doing so." Perhaps this was Stickney's original objective; his organization of the Minnesota Loan & Debenture Company gives additional credence to this claim. But by late summer 1885, reports began to circulate that the creator of the M&NW had no intention this time of liquidating. "Mr. Stickney built his road for the purpose of making money out of it," noted the *St. Paul Pioneer-Press*. "If he can realize more on his investment by operating the road than by selling, he will operate it. . . . Whatever are his intentions, he has no idea of selling now. His property has not been developed sufficiently for that." And the paper concluded, "He will operate the road himself, until he has secured for it connections, that will make it the most valuable piece of railroad property in this section of the country."[16]

The *Pioneer-Press* story had merit. A. B. Stickney unquestionably sought to make the Minnesota & Northwestern something more than a puny pike. For in that highly competitive Midwestern arena only a through road had much hope of financial success. He had his eyes set on America's greatest railroad center, Chicago. To achieve this objective, Stickney decided that he must first acquire the largely "hot-air" road, the Dubuque & Northwestern Railway (D&NW), for entry into Dubuque, a thriving Mississippi River community of 30,000, was seemingly a mandatory and wholly logical springboard to the Windy City. Specifically, a Dubuque line, proposed to leave the original trackage at Hayfield, Minnesota, held advantages other than simply providing Stickney with the potential for a much better property. First of all, a St. Paul–Hayfield–Dubuque–Chicago line would be forty-two miles shorter than the existing Mona route. Then, too, the M&NW did not know how long its current, "highly satisfactory" arrangement with the Illinois Central might last. Moreover, the territory through which the Hayfield–Dubuque extension would pass was well established and could provide immediate traffic. Finally, construction costs continued to remain relatively low, and Stickney still enjoyed access to pools of capital.[17]

DUBUQUE & NORTHWESTERN

In early 1883, Dubuque businessmen, led by lumber dealer George B. Burch and steamboat owner Joseph "Diamond Jo" Reynolds, began agitation for a narrow-gauge railroad (later changed to standard gauge) that would open up more fully the region north and west of their community. Although the Dubuque & Sioux City, through its subsidiary, the Iowa Falls & Sioux City, had reached the Missouri River in 1870, and, as a result, this Illinois Central–operated system brought considerable traffic into Dubuque, residents longed for another rail artery. "Dubuque must not let her sister Iowa cities outfloat her in the race for commercial supremacy." What Dubuquers had in mind for their new railroad's destination is not clear. The *Dubuque Daily Times* reported on June 17, 1883, three days before the Dubuque & Northwestern's official incorporation, that the line would run "into the valley of the Wapsie [Wapsipinicon River], thence near the northwest corner of Buchanan County, and on northwesterly through Minnesota to Van Couvers [*sic*] island, or as far as enterprise will take it." The Articles of Incorporation filed with the Iowa Secretary of State revealed a somewhat less grandiose plan: "The purpose of the company is to build a road from Dubuque, in a western and northwestern direction into and through Minnesota and Dakota to connect with the Northern Pacific." Whatever the objective, a substantial line was contemplated.[18]

Enthusiasm for the project initially ran high. Promoters took advantage of the widespread public approbation to raise $38,000 in a stock subscription drive and to win approval in November 1883 of a five percent tax on assessed real estate values that ultimately generated $265,000 to help underwrite the costs of the first segment of the line, that expensive mileage that had to be built within and immediately west of the city. Moreover, all along the first 100 miles of the projected route, other urban and rural residents expressed an intense desire not only to be reached by the D&NW; but, like their brethren in Dubuque, they showed a nearly universal willingness to subscribe liberally to company stock and to tax themselves.[19]

But the economic dislocations that befell the nation in 1884 prevented construction of the Dubuque & Northwestern. Only preliminary line surveys were completed. And the directors faced problems collecting the five percent tax, even though the law provided that those who paid the levy would receive stock in the enterprise equal to their contribution. Money was tight, and some property holders dodged the assessment. Furthermore, sources of out-

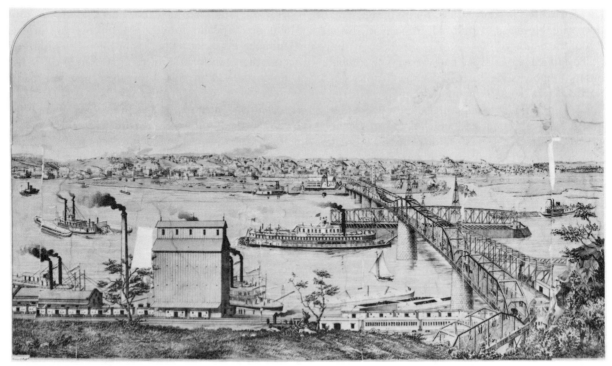

This drawing of Dubuque, Iowa, the self-proclaimed "Key City," appeared about the time the Minnesota & Northwestern arrived. The Illinois Central owned the Mississippi River bridge. (State Historical Society of Iowa)

side capital were not readily available; after all, this was a minor project that had an uncertain future. Thus, the combined impact of unpaid taxes and the depressed money market for railway securities prompted the D&NW's cautious leaders to await a more auspicious time. "Our home company is composed of several of the most responsible business men in Dubuque," the *Daily Times* reminded its readers, "and they entered upon the work with the unalterable purpose to build the road honestly and economically, or not at all."[20]

As hoped, a bright new day dawned in early 1885. Not only did the economy show positive signs of improvement, but A. B. Stickney entered the picture. The Dubuque & Northwestern would be mutually beneficial both to Dubuquers and to the Minnesota & Northwestern: local citizens would get their longed-for rail artery to the northwest, and Stickney could win access to Iowa's second largest city—one that already had made a substantial financial commitment to the project—and chances for his own line into Chicago, 175 miles to the east, increased measurably.[21]

In May 1885, the Minnesota & Northwestern and the Dubuque & Northwestern agreed to unite. "It is a most important event for Dubuque," concluded a local journalist, "and one over which every citizen has good reason for congratulation and encouragement." Dubuque businessmen understandably believed that their community's sphere of commercial influence over the surrounding territory would increase dramatically. Under the arrangement between the two company heads, the D&NW would build approximately fifty miles of line in a westerly direction from Dubuque to the hamlet of Compton, two miles east of Lamont in Buchanan County. Stickney's Minnesota Loan & Debenture Company would act as the construction agent. Once completed, the D&NW would surrender its assets to the M&NW in exchange for the latter's securities.[22]

An important step toward construction of the Dubuque & Northwestern took place during the last two weeks of July. A large crew from D. C. Shepard & Company, under contract to the Minnesota Loan & Debenture Company, arrived from St. Paul to start the eight miles of grading from Dubuque to Durango. On July 29, the first shovelful of earth was turned. Rather than rejoicing with music and speeches, Dubuquers expressed anger. The Minnesota contractor, it seems, had brought to the worksite several hundred immigrant laborers instead of hiring area workers. "Times are hard, money scarce and labor goes begging for something to do," commented the *Daily Times*. Asked the paper, "Must the demands of the laboring classes of this city be entirely disregarded when the enterprise is one that a magnificent bonus has been voted for by our citizens?" Fortunately, the D. C. Shepard Company subsequently awarded subcontractors portions of the road, and they showed a willingness to hire locally.[23]

Although the construction workers were confronted with the rocky bluffs that towered above the Mississippi River, their grading work went smoothly. By November 1885, the roadbed was ready for the iron to Durango; in fact, graders, with their teams and wheel scrapers, had started another segment, sixteen miles to Farley.[24] When the D&NW prepared for the first spike, 2,000 jubilant Dubuquers decided that this was reason for celebration. Monday, November 9, 10:00 A.M., marked the time of the first swing of the hammer. The *Daily Times* related the exciting details:

• • •

About 9:30 o'clock the bandwagon containing the Cornet Band was driven through the principal streets while the boys played several popular airs. At a few minutes to 10 the Directory [D&NW Board of Directors] . . . and a large delegation of prominent citizens and leading business men formed in line at the corner of Sixth and Main streets and headed by President Burch with the band following, marched up to where the spike was to be driven. Upon reaching the location they found a vast concourse of people already upon the scene. The whistle of the furniture factory heralded their approach, and when the assemblage caught sight of them a spontaneous and ringing shout of welcome went up. The Directors of the road, and Mayor and City Council, Senator [William Boyd] Allison, Hon. M. C. Woodruff, Hon. H. B. Fouke and many other citizens took positions upon a large platform made of ties. After music by the band, President Burch stepped forward; his face beaming with satisfaction, . . . cordially greet[ed] the great audience. . . . President Burch advanced with hammer and spike in hand to where the track was laid. As he did so, a whistle was blown at a factory close at hand, and this was the signal for the blowing of every steam whistle in the city, and as they tooted forth their brave notes of gladness, each member of the Directory in turn stepped forward and, amidst the glad acclaim of the people, struck the spike a blow, and at last it was driven home. Just as the last blow was struck, a very auspicious omen transpired, for the sun, which had been overcast with dark, forbidding clouds all morning, suddenly came forth in all its golden glory, radiating the scene and smiling down a warm benediction upon the demonstration.[25]

• • •

Much pounding soon followed. By the year's end, the eight miles between Dubuque and Durango sported ties and rail. When spring came, construction gangs turned their attention to the remaining segment between Durango and Compton. By May 14, 1886, the roadbed was finished to Farley, and the track was quickly installed. Meanwhile, the M&NW started to grade the connecting line from Hayfield to Compton. By early July, much of the roadway awaited rails; indeed, twenty miles had been completed southeast from Hayfield, leaving 135 miles to be constructed. "The road is being ballasted and put in perfect order as the tracklaying progresses," reported the *St. Paul Pioneer-Press*, "so that when the last rail is laid the line will be ready for the opening of business." With the rate of track laying at about two miles per day, the northern section opened for scheduled freight and passenger traffic to Elma, in Howard County, Iowa, on August

21. (This tiny community grew rapidly, for the M&NW soon made it the division point between St. Paul and Dubuque.) When the track gangs reached the Chickasaw County village of Fredericksburg on August 28, its inhabitants and nearby farm folk decided to welcome the iron horse with a "grand blow-out." The reason was simple. As hymn writer ("The Little Brown Church in the Vale") and local resident Dr. W. S. Pitts explained, "[The coming of the railroad] was like food for a starving man, like fresh fuel to a smoldering fire. The town awoke from its lethargy. It received the road with open arms, and man to man clasped hands and thanked God and took on new courage." That Saturday more than 3,000 joyful souls jammed the town's picnic grove, eating fried chicken, enjoying three brass bands, and listening to long-winded speeches made by "distinguished citizens." In contrast, when the rails arrived in Sumner on September 4, the next station ten miles away, residents largely ignored the event. "The Sumnerites are to [sic] busy for such doings." By early fall, the pace of tracklaying became hectic; crews working toward the proposed Delaware County meet hammered down more than three miles a day. On October 20, 1886, the final spike pierced the last tie forty-three and a half miles west of Dubuque, near Oneida. But no celebration occurred. As the *Dubuque Daily Times* noted, "No red cedar tie, no silver rail nor golden spike will be used, neither will a bottle of the ruby colored liquid be wasted upon the pilot of the first engine which crosses the juncture." The reason: "The M&NW [people] are too practical to attempt any such ceremonies."[26]

Freight and passenger service on the M&NW began immediately. Locals traveled the 253 miles between the two terminals. Then, more than a month later, on Sunday, November 28, 1886, the first through passenger train left St. Paul; the next day the maiden train departed from Dubuque. Although the initial equipment lacked distinction, in February 1887, the M&NW acquired seven "magnificent" chair coaches, five sleepers ("the interior being of cherry wood"), and four baggage cars.[27]

The Dubuque & Northwestern was officially dissolved on November 13, 1886. Four days after consolidation took effect, D&NW stockholders received two preferred and three common shares of Minnesota & Northwestern in exchange for each five of their D&NW stock. There were no complaints; the Stickney "system" seemed to hold great promise.[28]

MINNESOTA & NORTHWESTERN OF ILLINOIS

THE next major event in the saga of the Minnesota & Northwestern was its drive from Dubuque to Chicago. Months before the last spike was installed near Oneida, the Stickney road filed articles of incorporation in Springfield for the Minnesota & Northwestern Railroad Company of Illinois to satisfy the Prairie State's business code. Even before this was done on February 25, 1886, the M&NW had ordered surveying parties into the field to locate the line from Forest Home (Forest Park) nine miles west of Chicago (the M&NW planned to reach the Windy City through a trackage rights arrangement) to a junction with the Illinois Central near Freeport (South Freeport or, as the IC called it, Dunbar), a distance of approximately 100 miles. Subsequently, a route between South Freeport and East Dubuque, Illinois, would be selected.[29]

Line location for the first segment of the Illinois project posed few problems. The twenty-seven miles between Forest Home and St. Charles followed the abandoned right-of-way of the ill-fated Chicago, St. Charles & Mississippi Air Line Railroad. Organized in 1850 and partially graded three years later, this projected Lake Michigan to Mississippi River carrier never turned a wheel, although various efforts were made prior to the Civil War to build it. From St. Charles, the surveyors next selected a route in a northwesterly direction through the counties of Kane, DeKalb, Ogle, and Stephenson. Once the specific routing was established to South Freeport, field parties finished by hiking through the exceedingly

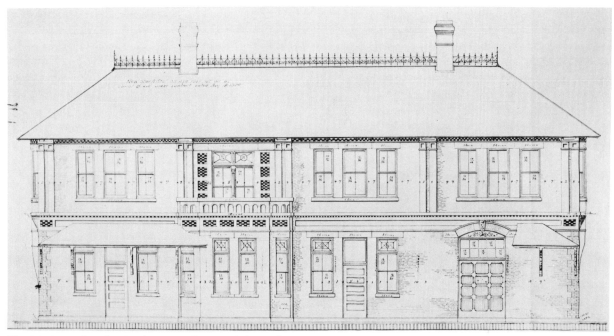

The M&NW selected a handsome yet functional design for its station at Dubuque. The first floor accommodated patrons, while the upstairs served operating and associated personnel. (William Armstrong Collection)

rugged and snake-infested countryside of Jo Daviess County to the Mississippi River opposite Dubuque.[30]

This survey laid the way for the construction that was to follow. Rather than pushing the Minnesota & Northwestern east from the Mississippi, the crews first tackled the portion between Forest Home and South Freeport. This reflected the M&NW's desire to complete as much of the Illinois line as soon as possible. By moving east to west the company enjoyed access to a section of finished grade and even usable bridge piers in the Fox River, and it would not have to encounter immediately those troublesome hills of Jo Daviess County, which meant high construction costs and slow going. Indeed, this terrain forced the company to bore what was to become the state's longest tunnel. Furthermore, with trackage rights from Forest Home to the Wisconsin Central's terminal at Harrison and Wells Sts. in Chicago over the Chicago & Great Western (later the Baltimore & Ohio Chicago Terminal) and conti-

nued use of the Illinois Central between South Freeport and Dubuque, the M&NW would possess a line far superior to the original route over the IC, Chicago & Iowa, and CB&Q and one, also, that would significantly reduce rental charges. (The IC kept its not-so-satisfactory northern Illinois route until it, too, gained direct access to Chicago. The Central did this by having a subsidiary, the Chicago, Madison & Northern, build a 112-mile line that opened in late 1888 between the Windy City and Freeport.) Without doubt, the M&NW would achieve important returns for its considerable capital investment in a relatively swift fashion: east to west movement made sense.[31]

The construction arrangement repeated the earlier events in Minnesota and Iowa. Stickney's Minnesota Loan & Debenture Company controlled the project, and D. C. Shepard & Company (shortly to become known as Shepard, Winston & Company) won the right to do the actual building, with subcontractors

Shepard, Winston & Company laborers carve out a right-of-way in the rough terrain near Elizabeth, Illinois, in the summer of 1887. This work proved to be extremely expensive. (James L. Rueber Collection)

obtaining some jobs. Under the terms of the agreement signed on June 28, 1886, between the M&NW of Illinois and the Minnesota Loan & Debenture Company, the line would be constructed to reasonably high specifications: a maximum cut of twenty-four feet would mean medium to heavy fill work in some places, and, once readied, sixty-pound Bessemer steel rails would be fastened to hardwood ties. The M&NW would pay the Minnesota Loan & Debenture Company a generous $36,000 per mile, $11,000 in first mortgage, five percent gold bonds and the remainder in common stock. (The actual cost to Minnesota Loan & Debenture Company ranged from $10,000 to $25,000 per mile, but the securities it received would be substantially discounted when sold.)[32]

Throughout the summer the necessary pregrading preparations took place. Rights-of-way, especially, needed to be acquired. Fortunately, the M&NW

engaged a skilled land agent, a Mr. Clark, described by the *Byron Express* as "a perfect gentleman" and by the *Freeport Journal* as one who "understands human nature thoroughly." Although the company paid handsomely for land parcels, "to avoid delay, litigation and unpleasantness," some farmers opposed the coming of the Stickney road, usually because it would slice their acreages. Notwithstanding Mr. Clark's skills, he and several associates even met physical resistance. A Freeport area plowman "gave them warning not to come on to his possessions and when they attempted to do so, he took a stick and knocked one of the men down, doing considerable injury."[33]

Grading commenced, however, prior to the last land settlement. Activity began in earnest near Byron, Illinois, in mid-July 1886. By July 16, carloads of horses, mules, and work equipment arrived there via the Chicago, Milwaukee & St. Paul, and soon,

Carpenters and local residents congregate in front of the unfinished M&NW depot at Stockton, Illinois, in late 1887 or early 1888. (Joseph Piersen Collection)

Workers at the Winston tunnel take a few minutes from their toil for this photograph in 1902. This "hole in Stickney's pocketbook" required extensive reconstruction and maintenance throughout its eighty-four-year history. (W. A. Vaughn Collection)

crews from D. C. Shepard & Company pitched several boarding tents in that Ogle County community. Then, on July 20, workers started to clear brush west of the town, and a Stone City, Iowa, subcontractor began erecting the bridge piers for a span across the Rock River. Within days, other laborers commenced work on the section near St. Charles. In this town in Kane County, the Fox River posed less of a challenge. Builders could get a headstart by taking advantage of the previous efforts of the defunct Chicago, St. Charles & Mississippi Air Line Railroad: "The old stone piers, which had been built in 1853 and stood like ghosts of ancient days to remind the people of buried hopes, were repaired and made to support the splendid iron bridge which the company erected at that place."[34]

Two thousand men, most of whom were husky Scandinavians and Italians, and a "sprinkling of Greeks and negroes," graded at a feverish pace between Forest Home and South Freeport, and the rails were soon in place. "Tracklaying . . . is rapidly progressing east of here," observed the Byron newspaper on November 12. "In Sycamore [between Byron and St. Charles] all the tracks have been put down and crews are laying about a mile and a half a

day, east of that place." As the year ended, the noisy, bulky tracklaying machines recently acquired by the contractor worked both east and west from Sycamore and west from Forest Home. On January 7, 1887, the Chicago Junction–St. Charles link was finished; thirty-three miles of steel had been laid in one month. Five days later, a construction train rumbled over the Fox River bridge for the first time. Near the end of January, Sycamore acquired its long hoped-for connection with St. Charles; and by February, the entire route from Forest Home to South Freeport was completed. Ballast-dumping crews immediately worked the 97.08 miles of freshly set track; and carpenters finished depots, water towers, an enginehouse at Byron, and other support facilities.[35]

Regular service came later. Local freights switched segments beginning in June, but the inaugural through-passenger run took place on July 31, 1887. That Sunday was a day for celebration at various points between Forest Home and South Freeport. At 8:45 P.M., for example, the first passenger train chugged into St. Charles from Chicago; and several hundred presumably excited residents gathered to see Engine #42 haul five cars past the recently completed depot. Reporters from the Chicago press corps claimed that this consist was "the handsomest train ever pulled out of Chicago." It surely must have been distinctive: "The coaches were of natural red cedar finish with gold lettering and the [locomotive] . . . was called 'Red Stack' because that was the color of its smoke stack." If the onlookers entered the "compartment" sleeping coach owned by the Mann Boudoir Car Company of New York, its luxurious embossed leather-covered sections, strikingly different from the traditional open-section sleepers, likely caused wonder and amazement.[36]

While the Minnesota & Northwestern of Illinois placed the finishing touches on the Forest Home to South Freeport extension, graders tackled the difficult countryside between the Illinois Central interchange and the Mississippi River. During the winter of 1886–1887, surveyors selected a nearly fifty-mile route, and grading began on March 7, 1887, just as the snows melted. Several crews from the newly named Shepard, Winston & Company pushed the M&NW of Illinois toward completion. Virtually all the roadbed was finished by September, and the shining rails were in place by early 1888. The line did not open for through Chicago to Dubuque traffic, however, until February 9, 1888, about the time that the M&NW of Minnesota officially leased the Illinois company for 999 years.[37]

Two factors explain the delay. The Minnesota & Northwestern did not build from Galena Junction to Dubuque Junction, Illinois, a distance of approximately fifteen miles. Rather, it planned to acquire running rights over the Illinois Central and the Chicago, Burlington & Northern (CB&N), a CB&Q-controlled firm that had opened between Oregon, Illinois, and St. Paul, Minnesota, in October 1886. But a squabble erupted between the IC and the CB&N about who had rights to a narrow shelf of land between Portage Curve and East Dubuque. The disagreement lasted through much of 1887, and only then was it possible for Stickney representatives to hammer out a suitable rental arrangement. Fortunately, the M&NW reached a speedy and equitable rental contract with the IC's Dunleith & Dubuque Bridge Company to use its mile-long span across the Mississippi River.[38]

Death came to thirty-one-year-old John Hill while digging the west end of the Winston tunnel. (Mark Nelson Photograph)

The more important obstacle to using the recently railed Illinois line was the one-half-mile Winston tunnel project near Rice, eighteen miles east of Dubuque. Started in early 1887, work progressed slowly, "an elephant in the hands of the Minnesota & Northwestern." Since the boring of the tunnel fascinated residents, the *Dubuque Daily Times* sent a reporter to investigate the site. He filed a depressing story:

• • •

It is next to impossible to drive the tunnel, which runs through a bed of blue clay, which can not be worked with picks, and on which blasting has little effect. . . . The tunnel, when completed, if the time ever comes when it is completed, will be the longest tunnel in the State, and as the blue clay when exposed to the air becomes a rotten shale rock, which crumbles to pieces, the tunnel will have to be strongly arched from one end to the other. The cost of the tunnel will probably exceed the cost of grading fifty miles of any part of the road.

• • •

However, the work force of 354 men persisted. The "sandhogs" dug from both portals around the clock; they even sank a shaft through the top to speed the process. Obviously, the entire enterprise was dangerous. Scores were injured, and one Finnish immigrant laborer was killed. Naturally, the tunnel was expensive; the total cost exceeded $600,000. Although the work gang finished in late January 1888, and trains rolled over the entire line by about March 1 (the date on which the M&NW's lease with the Illinois Central expired), the bore caused constant problems; it would be extensively reworked in 1902, 1918, and 1947, and would need repeated repair. The railroad eventually added a sophisticated fan system, since the intense heat and smoke of slow-moving trains turned crewmen into "boiled lobsters." Indeed, the Winston tunnel proved an expensive and bothersome mistake. The alternative of making the site an open cut was hardly a better idea; the road, according to one wag, "would have to purchase most of the land in Rice township to dump the waste clay onto." Hindsight reveals, instead, that the M&NW should have run the line through nearby Galena, a route, in fact, that the engineers initially had selected.[39]

M&NW EXPANSION: THE REALITIES

THE Minnesota & Northwestern's St. Paul to Chicago line was not its only trackage. Before the road lost its identity to the Chicago, St. Paul & Kansas City in December 1887, the emerging, albeit infant, M&NW system contained two additional segments, one to be built, the other to be purchased.

While the omnivorous Stickney molded the Minnesota & Northwestern into a respectable Midwestern trunk carrier, he also briefly headed another comparable regional road, the Central Iowa Railway (CIRy), subsequently the Iowa Central and, after 1912, part of the Minneapolis & St. Louis. When Stickney joined the CIRy in 1885, this Marshalltown-based firm owned slightly more then 500 miles of track but lacked entrance into any major metropolis. The company connected the Iowa towns of Mason City on the north with Albia near the Missouri line on the south. At Oskaloosa, twenty-four miles northeast of Albia, the CIRy's second principal stem covered the 190 miles east to Peoria, Illinois. Several minor branches completed the company's network. Since the Central Iowa utilized the Chicago, Milwaukee & St. Paul for access into the Twin Cities, Stickney logically decided to divert that traffic by forging a link between the M&NW and the CIRy. Construction started in the early part of September 1885 on a 20.2-mile branch from Lyle, Minnesota, to Manly Junction, Iowa, near Mason City. The work went swiftly, and the segment opened three months later. Minnesota & Northwestern trains, however, did not appear; rather, Stickney leased the property to the Central Iowa. Yet this trackage shortly carried M&NW equipment. Stickney lost hold of the CIRy in February 1890, and the lease was abrogated; once more the Central Iowa returned to Milwaukee rails to reach St. Paul.[40]

During A. B. Stickney's tenure with the Central Iowa, he did more than physically link it with his Minnesota & Northwestern. For a few years this imaginative railroader used the CIRy to reroute traffic around the congestion of Chicago. By directing freight cars, even Pullmans, from St. Paul through Mason City and Oskaloosa to Peoria and interchanging with the Indiana, Bloomington & Western (a future component of the New York Central), he created an eastern route to Indianapolis and Columbus. Stickney also "concocted" a direct link to St. Louis and Kansas City. At Givin, Iowa (near Oskaloosa), trains switched from the CIRy to the Keokuk & Des Moines (a CRI&P affiliate) and then interchanged with the Wabash at Ottumwa for Moberly, Missouri; there they diverged either east over that company's rails to St. Louis or west to Kansas City. Boasted the M&NW in May 1887, "OUR ST. LOUIS AND KANSAS

CITY LINE IS FASTER BY THREE HOURS THAN OUR COM-PETITORS, AND OUR ... EASTERN ROUTE UNEQUALED BY ANY OTHER LINE." Unquestionably, Stickney sought to capture the greatest possible share of the region's long-distance movements and knew the advantages of through connections.[41]

Besides building the Manly branch, the Minnesota & Northwestern absorbed an ailing Iowa short line, the Dubuque & Dakota (D&D). The road owned sixty-three miles of trackage: a forty-one-mile main line that ran west from Waverly, the seat of Bremer County, to Hampton, Franklin County's capital, and a twenty-two-mile branch that went northeasterly from Waverly to a connection with the M&NW at Sumner. When the D&D officially fell into Stickney's hands on January 19, 1887, area residents recalled the road's rather complicated past. Eight years before, the D&D had risen phoenix-like from the ashes of Iowa's "Lost Railroad," the Iowa Pacific (IP), a firm remarkably similar in many respects to the Chicago, St. Charles & Mississippi Air Line.[42]

The Iowa Pacific Railroad Company formally began its life on October 24, 1870, when a group of eager Hawkeye State promoters, led by General Caleb H. Booth and Platt Smith of Dubuque and John F. Duncombe of Fort Dodge, filed articles of incorporation. These railroad enthusiasts decided to undertake construction of a trans-Iowa line. Reported the *American Railroad Journal:* "[It] is intended to run from Dubuque to the Missouri River at Onawa." Strangely, Dubuque already enjoyed direct access to the "Big Muddy"; in the same year as the IP's birth, components of the Illinois Central would reach Sioux City, less than forty miles north of the Iowa Pacific's proposed western terminus.[43]

Surveyors located much of the Iowa Pacific's line in 1871. Rather than hammering their first stakes in Dubuque, field personnel selected the Clayton County hamlet of Elkport as their starting point. This was where the IP would meet the proposed Chicago, Dubuque & Minnesota Railroad (built as a CM&StP predecessor) for a connection to Dubuque. The intended route passed westward through Volga, Wadena, Randalia, Sumner, Waverly, Shell Rock, Clarksville, Allison, Hampton, Belmond, Clarion, Fort Dodge, Rockwell City, Sac City, Ida Grove, and Mapleton. Once the line was determined, land agents acquired much of the right-of-way; some was donated, and several local governments voted the standard five percent tax.[44]

During 1872, graders carved an extensive travelway on the fertile Iowa prairie. Before the contractions caused by the Panic of 1873 forced suspension of construction, more than 100 miles of roadbed had been readied in Fayette, Bremer, Butler, Franklin, Wright, and Webster counties; furthermore, the company signed a contract for the grading of another fifty miles between Fort Dodge and Sac City. Dozens of bridges awaited rails, and crews had actually completed thirteen miles of track between Waverly and Clarksville.[45]

As the depression deepened, Iowa Pacific bonds became worthless, and the road was sold on a mechanic's lien. Not only did the IP's backers despair, but most inhabitants along the graded route fretted about the seeming loss of their financial investments. They worried, too, about the future of their farms and communities, for without the "iron horse" their isolation would continue.[46]

Then, as the economy rebounded during the formative months of the Rutherford B. Hayes administration, the possibilities of a railroad operating over the Iowa Pacific's weed-covered grade improved. The Illinois Central saw value in the abandoned project, if for nothing else than to protect its Iowa interests from an unfriendly competitor. Company treasurer J. B. Dumont told vice-president William K. Ackerman in July 1877 that "I have always feared this Iowa Pacific more than any other competing line and I think it will be a mistake not to secure it now if possible."[47]

The Illinois Central subsequently exerted its influence over a reconstituted Iowa Pacific. The IC's leased carrier, the Dubuque & Sioux City, guaranteed the construction bonds issued by a "second" IP, the Dubuque & Dakota Railroad Company, and J. B. Dumont later became its president. (Several Iowa Pacific backers also participated in the D&D's

The crew and a few friends pause on board engine #1 of the Dubuque & Dakota Railroad as it passes through Allison, Iowa, in July 1879. The poor quality of the infant road's track is evident. (James L. Rueber Collection)

ownership and management.) Formally incorporated on August 23, 1878, the D&D was to operate a ninety-four mile route from Randalia (Fayette Junction) to Belmond.[48]

Work began quickly. Dubuque & Dakota employees repaired the rusty Waverly-Clarksville fragment and pushed the track to Dumont, thirty miles west of Waverly, by July 19, 1879. As the year ended, the D&D had finished laying its fifty-six pound English-made steel the thirteen miles northeast from Waverly to Tripoli, and then it shortly spiked down the remaining distance into Sumner.[49]

The Dubuque & Dakota never finished either the Hampton–Belmond or Sumner–Randalia portions because of financial problems — the failure to win local tax support (some voters earlier had approved a five percent levy for the Iowa Pacific and understandably resisted a double tax for the D&D) and the unwillingness of the Illinois Central system to increase its pecuniary commitment. The D&D lost the Hampton–Belmond segment by condemnation in 1882 to the Iowa Central & Northwestern (Iowa

Central), which then railed the twenty-two miles of roadbed. The Sumner–Randalia section, however, never saw track, and the right-of-way reverted back to the original property owners. The Illinois Central adamantly opposed completing this line. IC executives feared that if the D&D were to reach Randalia and tie into the Burlington, Cedar Rapids & Northern, then the D&D might fall into the hands of that competing carrier. Since the Illinois Central already enjoyed a useful connection with the D&D at Waverly, the Randalia addition would mean little.[50]

By the time A. B. Stickney won control of the Dubuque & Dakota, it was barely covering its expenses. Yet it served "magnificent and prosperous country" and several "live" communities. The physical condition of the sixty-three mile carrier was awful; its light rail, for example, regularly sank into the unballasted roadbed during wet weather. Recalled one Butler County resident, "[Its] time schedules were as uncertain as a political platform." Apparently, the D&D richly deserved its nickname, the "Damn Doubtful."[51]

But Stickney saw potential in the Dubuque &
Dakota. If rehabilitated, it might become a valuable
feeder line for the Minnesota & Northwestern, and
eventually it did. The M&NW founder at this time
also headed the Central Iowa; thus, the D&D
nicely bridged the M&NW at Sumner with the
CIRy's main line and Belmond branch at Hampton.
Stickney struck a deal with Dubuque & Sioux City
president Morris K. Jesup and the other principal
owners in December 1886, "a surprise to the best
posted men in railway circles." Most observers
thought that the Illinois Central would retain its
influence; indeed, the IC leadership seemed ap-
palled that Jesup let Stickney take the D&D. Observed IC vice-president Stuyvesant Fish in late
1886, "If rumor is correct, the D&D, on which
over $750,000 of the money of the D&SC ... has
been spent, has recently been secretly sold to ...
Stickney, whose system, ... when in working
order, [will] greatly injure the D&SC unless there is
new blood put into that organization."[52]

M&NW EXPANSION: THE DREAMS

ALTHOUGH the Minnesota & Northwestern acquired potentially valuable trackage in Iowa with
the acquisition of the Dubuque & Dakota, simulta-
neous plans for additional mileage in Minnesota
came to naught. Stickney pressed as early as the
autumn of 1885 for a survey of the easiest grade and
shortest possible distance from St. Paul to Duluth.
At the head of Great Lakes navigation, this booming
Lake Superior port community of 30,000 experienced steady growth and battled with the Twin
Cities for the economic control of the northern Wisconsin, Minnesota, and Dakota hinterland. Certainly, such a 180-mile line to Duluth was fully
consistent with the M&NW's charter; practically, it
would provide access, of course, to a promising
terminal. One reason, in particular, why this route
appealed to Stickney is that it would "afford a sum-

mer outlet in that direction for the cattle and hog
business."[53]

Rumor of a major extension toward the rich
wheat lands of western Minnesota and central Dakota coincided with the St. Paul–Duluth line location work. The idea was for the M&NW to leave
the Duluth extension at about the midpoint and to
run to the west past Mille Lacs to an undisclosed
point in Dakota Territory. Although the road conducted three separate surveys to Lake Superior,
nothing came of the scheme. Intense pressure from
Hill's Great Northern and construction activities
elsewhere stymied both proposals. The Duluth and
the Dakota suggestions were harbingers of a host of
"paper"-only additions to the Stickney system.[54]

THE M&NW MATURES

BY the time the Minnesota & Northwestern relinquished its assets to the Chicago, St. Paul & Kansas City, it governed a nearly 500-mile three-state
network; and the property was respectable for that
time. Observed one enthusiastic on-line editor:
"Everybody that has [taken] a ride on the M&NW
says that it is the smoothest new track they ever
rode over." For recently built trackage, this seemed
accurate.[55] In one colorful footnote to the road's
earliest days, the *Waterloo Courier* reported an unofficial "race" between the Stickney road and the
Illinois Central. The quality of the track and
roadbed is graphically revealed:

• • •

From Dyersville, for five miles east, the track of the
M&NW runs parallel and within a short distance of
the Illinois Central's track and gives a splendid opportunity for racing. The [IC's] "Clipper" train going west leaves Dubuque at 5 P.M., and a [sic]
M&NW train leaves for the west at the same time.
Wednesday evening, both trains reached the point
where the tracks approach each other at the same
time, and from there to Dyersville one of the most
exciting races on record took place. . . . The distance

The workhorse locomotive of the Minnesota & Northwestern and other contemporary railroads was the 4-4-0. The Stickney road used this type of engine to power both freight and passenger runs. (Alco Historic Photos)

was made at the rate of a mile a minute and both trains maintained the same relative positions, neither gaining on the other. Both trains were crowded and the passengers took great interest in the race and one enthusiastic passenger waved his hat so vehemently that it flew out of his hand.[56]

• • •

While an engineer might have been able to run a passenger train briefly at sixty miles per hour, the M&NW was no high-iron speedway. Recalled station agent J. H. Manley of Dyersville, Iowa, who joined the company in 1886: "The road in its infancy was very rough with an unsettled bed, low joints and was continually out of line. . . . Derailments from defective track were almost daily occurrences. Injuries to trainmen and others were very frequent and on account of the numerous accidents in this vicinity I always kept a stretcher and a supply of first aid remedies on hand and they proved very beneficial."[57]

Regardless of physical condition, the Minnesota & Northwestern showed immediate signs of financial health. Its first annual report, released in late October 1886, revealed gross earnings of $414,528 and a net income after taxes of $143,408. As for actual profits, "it requires," said Stickney, "$124,350 to pay fixed charges, leaving a surplus of $19,058." And the trend continued. The M&NW's subsequent financial statement (June 30, 1887) showed earnings from all sources reaching $873,498, with a net income after taxes of $266,702; and its surplus nearly doubled. The balance at the close of the fiscal year totaled $36,631.[58]

There were various reasons for the M&NW's positive financial developments. For one thing, business thrived. The company's twenty- to thirty-car freight trains with their thirty-three foot long, 40,000-pound capacity boxcars hauled sizable quantities of agricultural and manufactured products; and travelers selected its trains with increasing regularity. Indeed, the M&NW's 1,546 employees were kept busy operating the rolling stock of forty-four "standard" and "mogul" locomotives and 2,001 freight and passenger cars. Patronage became especially brisk in those communities that previously lacked adequate outlets. At Wasco, Illinois, the first station west of St. Charles, for instance, local dairymen began shipping sixty cans of milk to Chicago daily, and the volume increased steadily. The road's competitive rates likewise drew customers. For example, large quantities of barbed wire, produced in DeKalb, Illinois, went over the M&NW from Sycamore to St. Paul. "The freight rates are so much better [than the ones charged by the Milwaukee and North Western] that the expense of hauling by team six miles [to the station] is more than covered."[59]

Stickney's road had to seek traffic aggressively, however. While it enjoyed short-haul monopolies in communities like Wasco, these situations were limited and not enormously profitable. Even though the M&NW directly led to the founding of nearly a score of settlements along its main line, none emerged as important trade centers. Since the company faced fierce competition between St. Paul and Chicago (four roads already served these gateways), it logically exploited available options — acquiring additional trackage, devising "foreign" road traffic arrangements, and cultivating on-line businesses.[60]

The South St. Paul Stockyards soon emerged as the M&NW's leading and ultimately most famous revenue producer. Stickney knew about the Northern Pacific's unsuccessful efforts in the late 1870s to erect an extensive stock facility in North St. Paul to serve the western range cattle industry. Believing that the idea had merit, he purchased, in 1882, cheap land near the Mississippi River five miles south of the capital city, where he built a modest stockyard "with the ostensible purpose of feeding and resting stock shipped and driven into market by Minnesota farmers." When the M&NW started its southward push, Stickney succeeded in expanding this enterprise. He leased the property to Swift & Company in the fall of 1885, who in turn immediately sold the lease to the New Brighton Stock Yards Company of North Minneapolis. This firm's South St. Paul Yards & Packing Plant quickly failed, however, and in 1886, Swift regained control. Under this management, the volume of livestock increased dramatically, thereby helping producer, packer, and railroad.[61]

Rate-cutting, however, soon emerged as the Minnesota & Northwestern's principal way of boosting volume. In fact, it became its hallmark. From the first, A. B. Stickney wanted rate adjustments. He especially sought lower through charges. But this was largely impossible until the M&NW ran the St. Paul–Chicago line under its own corporate banner. (When this occurred, the road slashed freight costs between the two terminals, at times from thirty-three to forty-two percent.) Other competing roads strongly resisted what they called "demoralization of rates," and they continued to support actively regional traffic associations — "pools" — to prevent such happenings. Stickney, though, flatly refused to embrace any "gentlemen's agreement." The M&NW head publicly blasted pooling, for these arrangements permitted carriers to set steep charges on local movements and commonly established "unreasonably stiff tariffs" for the longer, competitive hauls as well. Similarly, pooling caused enormous consumer unrest, an alarming development in Stickney's mind. Railroads should avoid any "public-be-damned" attitude and actions.[62]

Stickney's rate-slashing served several purposes. More than anything else, no doubt, it tended to increase the volume of traffic and, theoretically, profits, too. As a struggling new carrier, the M&NW needed to familiarize shippers with its services, and bargain-basement rates did that superbly. Yet, this astute iconoclast saw his rate-making policies as a function of his overall view of business practices.

Although industry critics bitterly attacked him for causing havoc, Stickney cogently argued that his notions would not cripple the railroad enterprise. He did not believe that goods and people should be hauled at or below cost, but at a fair profit. Since the very nature of technology insured carriers a virtual transportation monopoly, there existed an enormous volume of traffic to be divided; earning capabilities were considerable for every road, even between the most competitive points. What Stickney wanted then was an *orderly* rate structure based on costs. Competition should center on service and not on charges. If this format were followed, the M&NW head foresaw healthy companies and a diminution of consumer protests. The latter, in Stickney's mind, was especially critical. Public unrest might lead to far-reaching unwarranted regulations, even dreaded government ownership. Obviously, such actions would hamstring the industry, perhaps even destroy it.

A. B. Stickney's activities as a rate reformer suited his personality. He enjoyed a fight, and he relished the limelight. Unlike most of his colleagues, Stickney wanted to be the center of attention; in fact, he might be called a "publicity hound."

Locomotive builder Cooke & Company of Patterson, New Jersey, took this photograph of M&NW #12, sans headlight, an unusual 2-4-2 style engine, designed for switching chores. (Alco Historic Photos)

With tensions growing between shippers and carriers, the public, particularly the reform-oriented press, applauded the builder of the Minnesota & Northwestern. He seemed genuinely sensitive to consumer concerns, not only about rates but about safety, too. One editor noted that Stickney ordered that heating stoves used in the wooden passenger equipment be enclosed in iron cases so that if a wreck occurred, the chance of a train fire was lessened. The M&NW was the first area road to adopt this potentially life-saving practice.[63]

The press also liked Stickney's conduct as an employer. The *Dubuque Daily Times* praised him for "recognizing the peculiar conditions that characterize the railroad man's life while away from home, especially the tendency to evil associations." The newspaper then cited the company's construction of a workers' clubhouse at Elma. "The structure is substantially built of brick, and will contain bath rooms, reading rooms and other home-like comforts. . . . The rooms will be free to the men, and will be kept open day and night." Whether paternalistic or not, Stickney got the favorable attention that he sought.[64]

By 1887, the Minnesota & Northwestern was

ready for major changes. Its name, for one thing, was to be altered, a logical act since the corporate title did not suggest the geographical area served. "It is not uncommon to hear Railroad men about St. Paul wondering that the name of the M&NW is not changed to the Chicago, Minnesota and Northwestern," observed the *Northwestern Railroader*. "The larger name would certainly better describe the road in its present shape." Stickney opted instead for the Chicago, St. Paul & Kansas City, for this banner would aptly reveal the road's soon-to-be extended nature. The railroad was to go to St. Joseph and Kansas City, to be reached by the acquisition of another small firm, the Wisconsin, Iowa & Nebraska, and by construction of additional trackage.[65]

While his contemporaries probably gave the matter little thought, A. B. Stickney was in the process of forging a truly intraregional company. He stood in the vanguard of industry change, for at this time, localized carriers characterized much of the era's rail patterns, just as interregional ones would dominate a century later. Stickney had the good sense to realize that future prosperity lay with trunk lines that linked such vital, thriving gateways as Minneapolis, St. Paul, Chicago, and Kansas City.

CHAPTER TWO
THE CHICAGO, ST. PAUL & KANSAS CITY AND THE FORMATION OF THE CHICAGO GREAT WESTERN,
1887–1892

THE railroad map of the Midwest changed significantly in 1887, for A. B. Stickney's conquests continued. This hard-driving entrepreneur not only renamed the Minnesota & Northwestern but also acquired a strategic Iowa short line, the 144-mile Wisconsin, Iowa & Nebraska (WI&N). Stickney then extended this road at both ends, first between Waterloo and Oelwein, Iowa, and subsequently from Des Moines toward Kansas City, Missouri. The combined and expanded property, appropriately called the Chicago, St. Paul & Kansas City (CStP&KC), soon looked to be a spirited trunk route that promised to make Stickney "one of the greatest American railroad kings."[1]

THE DIAGONAL

As the decade of the 1880s began, the Iowa capital of Des Moines, located at the juncture of the Raccoon and Des Moines rivers, appeared destined to emerge as a premier city of the American heartlands. Its population had mushroomed since it won the grandest of all political plums in 1857, when it was designated as the state capital. The capitol building itself, which was started in 1873, tangibly symbolized the seemingly boundless future of this Polk County metropolis of 22,408 citizens. This massive Romanesque structure, with its great central dome and four corner domes and its location on an eastside hill, soon dominated the skyline and became an object of general pride and wonderment.[2]

Des Moines attracted more than just visitors; it naturally captured the attention of railroad builders. Although the capital city enjoyed its location on the Chicago–Omaha main line of the Chicago, Rock Island & Pacific and claimed several other carriers as well, the community lacked direct access to either the northeastern or southwestern sections of the state. Recognizing the potential profit in such a construction venture, a group of Iowa sponsors, headed by Marshalltown banker Dr. George Glick, organized the Des Moines, Marshalltown & Northeastern Railroad in 1880 to link the capital city with the thriving county seat towns of Marshalltown and Waterloo, the terminating point of which would be at a connection with the Chicago, Milwaukee & St. Paul, probably the Mississippi River village of McGregor in Clayton County. While the firm began conducting a route survey and discussed raising local subsidies, it soon disappeared, giving way shortly to a company that held largely the same ambitions, the Wisconsin, Iowa & Nebraska. In fact, Dr. Glick and his associates joined this successor enterprise.[3]

Officially incorporated on December 1, 1881, the

Wisconsin, Iowa & Nebraska sought to build diagonally across the Hawkeye State from McGregor through Waterloo, Marshalltown, and Des Moines to Nebraska City, Nebraska, where it would meet the Burlington Route (Burlington & Missouri River Railroad in Nebraska), a system that was about to reach Denver, Colorado. The WI&N would surely generate business from several sources: the bustling and often inadequately served communities along its intended line; bridge traffic, especially Wisconsin lumber; and, most important, coal from the extensive fields of Marshall, Jasper, and Polk counties.[4]

In autumn, 1882, the builders' dreams started to be fulfilled. "By the first of October the fifty miles of grading between [Marshalltown] and Waterloo will be finished," happily announced the *Marshalltown Times-Republican*. "The surveys are completed south [to Des Moines] and a number of subsidies voted, and the grading contract will be let immediately. . . . From Waterloo to Brush Creek, in Fayette County, a distance of fifty-five miles, the surveys are completed and subsidies all voted. From Brush Creek to McGregor, . . . a distance of only thirty miles remains to be settled, and agents . . . are now working there."[5]

The reason that the WI&N (commonly called the "Diagonal" because of its catercornered route), rather than the Des Moines, Marshalltown & Northeastern, seemed a viable proposition rested with the make-up of its financial backers. The latter had attracted local investors with limited resources and expertise, while the former gained support from experienced outside capitalists, most notably Robert T. Wilson, head of the New York investment firm of R. T. Wilson & Company. This financier would succeed in winning British approval for the project, a task made less difficult because the operation could generate substantial revenues immediately.[6]

The Wilson syndicate soon created a construction arm, the Iowa Improvement Company, to complete and operate the new railroad. Throughout 1883, crews shaped additional miles of grade. Initial track-laying commenced at Marshalltown and extended northeastward. By early March, the company's "substantial" sixty-pound steel rails spanned the sixteen miles to the Tama County town of Gladbrook. On April 23, residents of Hudson in Black Hawk County, thirty-eight miles from Marshalltown, welcomed the arrival of the Iowa Improvement Company's work train, and regular freight and passenger service began to this point in August. By October the Diagonal operated nearly fifty miles of line and had track laid to within five miles of Waterloo. Also, another dozen miles southeast from Marshalltown toward Des Moines were finished, and the remaining forty-five miles to that city awaited steel. Then, gangs pushed both ways from the capital city and the earlier railhead, closing the gap on November 28, 1883. Shortly thereafter, the Diagonal dispatched a daily passenger train over the ninety-four miles between Des Moines and Hudson, along with regular freight runs. Although the carrier was completed four miles further to the northeast, to a point called Wilson's, that section lacked service. At this location the Iowa Improvement Company stopped working, due to winter weather and wrangling with Waterloo residents about how the road should enter their city.[7]

Final construction began in 1884. Workers first extended the line eight miles from Wilson's north to Cedar Falls where it interchanged with both the Illinois Central and the Burlington, Cedar Rapids & Northern. This segment formally opened on June 22, 1884. After considerable negotiation, the company completed the four miles from Wilson's (soon known as Wilson Junction) into Waterloo by late summer. In addition to the Des Moines–Waterloo stem and the Cedar Falls branch, the road also ran about three miles of spur track from the main line at Valeria in Jasper County into adjoining coalfields along the Skunk River.[8]

Although the Wisconsin, Iowa & Nebraska never completed further mileage, it conducted extensive projections, such as selecting a Waterloo to McGregor route. The *Iowa State Register,* as early as April 1883, reported that a grade had been located west from Des Moines to Council Bluffs, closely paralleling the Rock Island: "While a reasonably

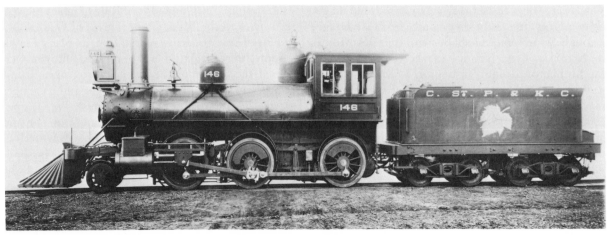

A Cooke & Company official photographer shot this view of CStP&KC #146 (2-6-0), resplendent with the newly created "Maple Leaf" logo. This mogul-type locomotive pulled mostly freight trains. (Alco Historic Photo)

good line . . . , much of the country to be traversed is pretty rough." But, the surveyors continued their tasks, and that spring they fixed a route to the road's originally stated objective, Nebraska City — one that touched Winterset, Greenfield, Red Oak, and Sidney, and, in all probability, an equally "rough" line but with less direct competition. Perhaps more work would follow. The *Red Oak* (Iowa) *Express* noted that a Salina, Kansas, promoter planned to seek a connection from Nebraska City through southwestern Kansas ultimately to Old Mexico; and his road, presumably affiliated with the WI&N, would undoubtedly win immense shipper support, since it would be "independent of the railroad pools."[9]

While the Nebraska–Kansas–Mexico road was nothing more than a grandiose "hot-air" proposition, the Des Moines to Missouri River plan contained substance. Communities on the Nebraska City survey eagerly sought the Diagonal; some voted the customary five percent tax assistance or offered various other inducements. The proposed 135-mile link seemed essential: the region lacked direct access to the capital city and the other points along the WI&N's projected route; furthermore, most southwest Iowa communities faced transportation monopolies, and many languished on isolated branches.

Similar reasons also made the McGregor–Brush Creek–Waterloo line appear viable.[10]

The explanation for the failure of the Iowa Improvement Company to complete its property from McGregor to Nebraska City is open to speculation. The national business slump of 1884, which disrupted numerous construction plans, probably caused the Wilson group to abandon any serious notions of new-line projects. Instead, the Diagonal's expansionist impulses might be channeled in a different fashion. Both the local Iowa newspapers and the railroad trade press published rumors that suggested a less costly course of action. According to these sources, the Iowa Improvement Company would take over a flimsy, narrow-gauge route, the 111-mile Des Moines, Osceola and Southern, which linked the Iowa capital with the North Missouri coal camp of Cainsville. If acquired, this road could be widened and perhaps extended to St. Joseph or Kansas City. But before the sale could be arranged, the Osceola road collapsed, and the bond- and lienholders could not reach a mutually acceptable price with the immediate parties involved.[11]

Before the Wisconsin, Iowa & Nebraska could conveniently return to either its Nebraska City or McGregor extension plans, or commit itself to the Des Moines, Osceola & Southern, brighter possibilities arose. As with the original segment of the Minnesota & Northwestern, once the Diagonal became a functioning concern, rumors began about its future. While Wilson at first said that the property would be "operated as an independent road," several entrenched companies eyed it carefully for possible merger. The Illinois Central and the Milwaukee seemed the most interested. Both knew that the WI&N would flesh out their own growing Iowa networks at the expense of their rivals, and they certainly read the balance sheet with interest. In the WI&N's report for the fiscal year ending June 30, 1885, the road generated $214,695, with a net income after operating expenses and taxes of $35,896. Even during this "soft" economic time, the firm's eleven locomotives hauled considerable volumes of coal, lumber, and general merchandise; and, more important, the traffic potential looked strong.[12]

What specific offers, if any, the owners of the Iowa Improvement Company received are unknown. It is evident, however, that A. B. Stickney also viewed the developing pike as an intriguing proposition. The Minnesota & Northwestern head inspected the Diagonal during the summer of 1885, even though his own railroad was still in the gestation period. Stickney apparently liked what he saw, and the road's backers must have found his plans similarly attractive, for as the *Railroad Gazette* revealed, "negotiations are in progress for a sale or lease of this road to the M&NW." Shortly after the Stickney visit, officials of the Iowa Improvement Company prepared for the sale when they formally transferred the railroad to the WI&N, which they themselves owned.[13]

The overall financial structure of the Wilson enterprise differed dramatically from Stickney's Minnesota & Northwestern. Except for local subsidies, the Diagonal's promoter-owners used their own funds to construct the two million dollar property. The reason for its having a mortgage-free line likely centered on its sponsors' strong commitments to the most conservative and, hence, locally popular approach. Indeed, small roads of the period sometimes adopted this strategy.[14]

By having the Wisconsin, Iowa & Nebraska own the railroad after September 16, 1885, thus removing the Iowa Improvement Company, the syndicate could easily convey its holdings to the soon-to-be-formed Chicago, St. Paul & Kansas City Railway Company, "a corporation . . . organized to build a railroad from Dubuque to Kansas City." This transfer occurred in the spring of 1886. Robert Wilson assumed the presidency, and the board of directors contained both former Iowa Improvement Company and WI&N backers and various officials of the Minnesota & Northwestern, including A. B. Stickney and his son Samuel. While not merged with M&NW, the CStP&KC claimed a cozy relationship. This closeness soon became even more evident when the road let a contract on June 5, 1886, for a connecting twenty-six mile link between its terminus at Waterloo and the M&NW at Oelwein. The trackage opened the next June. The Wilson carrier now abandoned its earlier mortgage-free policy and proceeded to borrow heavily against its assets to underwrite its programs of expansion.[15]

About the time that the contractor, J. N. Foye & Son of Manchester, Iowa, placed the finishing touches on the Waterloo-Oelwein segment, the CStP&KC and the M&NW moved toward a legal union. Beginning July 1, 1886, the two roads adopted a common management. This arrangement led to a formal consolidation that December, when minority stockholders of the M&NW exchanged their certificates on a share-for-share basis for securities of the CStP&KC. Still, the M&NW and the M&NW of Illinois corporate shells remained, with Stickney and his investor friends holding most of the stock. Since the M&NW's mortgage totaled $16,000 per mile, against the $20,000 per mile on the rapidly growing CStP&KC, the Stickney and Wilson parties agreed before the merger "to inscribe the Minnesota & Northwestern with a second mortgage at the rate of $4,000 per mile (but not exceeding $2,000,000), to make the debt on either property uniform, and such second mortgage powers duly vested in the Chicago, St. Paul & Kansas City Company, for the benefit of the amalgamated concern."[16]

REACHING ST. JOSEPH AND KANSAS CITY

BEFORE the banner of the Chicago, St. Paul & Kansas City officially flew over the Minnesota & Northwestern, the former Wisconsin, Iowa & Nebraska line pushed speedily toward the Missouri River. While its path would not be the "diagonal" initially intended and subsequently surveyed, St. Joseph and ultimately Kansas City (more promising places than Nebraska City) were to be reached.

Prior to the building season of 1887, Shepard, Winston & Company, principal contractors for the Minnesota & Northwestern, secured the right to construct about 100 miles of the CStP&KC from Des Moines to the Iowa-Missouri line. Soon, literally thousands of men and animals tackled the hilly countryside. With the primitive building tools and equipment of the day, the "borrow and fill" jobs were Herculean. "The earthwork on this section is very heavy," the railroad duly reported, "averaging 37,000 cubic yards per mile against 12,000 to 15,000 on an average prairie road." The movement of so much dirt was necessitated by the desire to maintain a maximum one percent grade, which ultimately would mean considerable fuel savings and speedier train movements. By October, Shepard, Winston & Company had completed most of the right-of-way and bridges; and track itself extended south for fifty-seven miles, ending near Talmage, a junction on the CB&Q's Chicago–Denver main line. Rails reached Knowlton in Ringgold County a month later.[17]

Even before completion of its contract with the Chicago, St. Paul & Kansas City, Shepard, Winston & Company won the privilege of finishing the extension sixty miles from the Missouri line to St. Joseph. By the end of 1887, workers completed most of the pre-tracklaying chores, and rails ran as far as Andrew County. When the 150 hands arrived in Savannah, the county seat, on Saturday, January 7, 1888, they received their most boisterous reception.[18] The *Democrat* vividly described the long-remembered event:

• • •

At four o'clock in the afternoon the cannon on the hill belched forth, announcing that the first rail had been laid in the corporate limits. . . . The church and school bells were then rung and the steam whistle at the mill turned loose, and amidst the booming of cannon, ringing of bells and screeching of steam whistles the enthusiasm was great. In a few minutes old and young could be seen rushing to the north part of the city where the road enters, and in a short time the hill was crowded with people who braved the terrible cold weather, not merely to satisfy an idle curiosity but to show to the Diagonal folks that we appreciate their road and feel highly elated over its completion into our city. At night a banquet was given by a number of our citizens to the gentlemen connected with the road which was highly enjoyed by all present.[19]

• • •

The city of St. Joseph became the next goal. After a winter delay, track gangs reached this vital transportation gateway in late May 1888, but CStP&KC trains did not immediately enter it. The Kansas City, St. Joseph & Council Bluffs Railroad, a Burlington affiliate, refused to grant the Stickney road trackage rights through the city. The row was eventually settled, although it delayed the opening of the line until August 1888.[20]

Kansas City, only fifty miles "as the crow flies" from St. Joseph, proved more difficult to reach. Rather than running a direct line into this teeming trade center of 132,716, management thought it would be cheaper to build only a portion of the distance and then rent the remaining trackage. So on March 3, 1890, Stickney interests incorporated, under Missouri law, the Leavenworth & St. Joseph Railway Company (L&StJ). Specifically, the plan was to reach Beverly, Missouri, four miles from Leavenworth, Kansas, with its own rail, then secure rights over the Rock Island to the east bank of the Missouri River, rent the Leavenworth Bridge Company's crossing, and lease Rock Island and Union Pacific tracks between the west end of the bridge to a nearby connection with the Kansas City, Wyandotte & North-Western Railroad for the final stretch into Kansas City.[21]

The Leavenworth & St. Joseph completed the twenty-three mile Bee Creek (St. Joseph) to Beverly line in December 1890; and the first train rumbled over it on February 1, 1891. "It was the Sabbath, and a large and profane crowd was aboard." The next day, the CStP&KC officially leased the L&StJ, and through service over the sixty-eight-mile route to Kansas City began. "When the train . . . arrived at Leavenworth," wrote a *Kansas City Times* reporter, "[it] was greeted by 3,000 people who crowded on . . . and filled all the available space. . . . The train then pulled out very slowly through the mass, while the air was full of cheers and yells. At every station and farm house the people got out and waved their handkerchiefs and table linen."[22]

In building the Des Moines–St. Joseph extension, the Chicago, St. Paul & Kansas City managed to miss every county seat and town of importance except Savannah, Missouri (1890 population of 1,288). Why this apparently foolish routing strategy developed is a matter of speculation. The rough terrain may possibly explain their having avoided several county seats, particularly Winterset, Iowa, a town that had earlier voted a five percent subsidy for the WI&N. One explanation rests with the CStP&KC's probable desire to minimize confrontation with the Burlington Route; it crossed what the latter road considered its sphere of influence—southern Iowa and northern Missouri. The dispute over access to St. Joseph graphically illustrates the tensions that characterized railroad building in a competitive area. Another reason centers on cost. Not a particularly strong road financially, the CStP&KC knew that if a community did not grant adequate concessions, real estate acquisition expenses might soar to ruinous levels. A final factor, perhaps foremost in the minds of the Stickney people, was the idea that the carrier could ultimately benefit by *avoiding* established settlements. Since poor roads and slow-moving vehicles limited range, ambitious merchants and their rural clientele would naturally gravitate toward a new railroad. Once the line was built, these places would depend totally upon the CStP&KC for their transportation needs.

This, in fact, happened. Villages like Hanley, Lorimor, Arispe, Shannon City, Maloy, and Athelstan in Iowa and Sheridan, Parnell, and Ravenwood in Missouri quickly appeared. When the line was extended through Ringgold County, Iowa, the hamlet of Goshen simply relocated itself to CStP&KC rails and took its nickname, Diagonal. As with the original construction, the company did not enter the townsite business, relying again on farmers and speculators to subdivide land into commercial and residential lots.[23]

THE UNBUILT CStP&KC

ONCE it reached St. Joseph, the Chicago, St. Paul & Kansas City did little further construction. In 1889 crews did install a four-mile branch from the main line at Eden in Dodge County, Minnesota, to Wasioja. Like the Valeria, Iowa, stub, this extension was designed to tap local mineral deposits, in this case burgeoning stone quarries.[24]

Still, the CStP&KC contemplated major building projects. Even though the company was becoming known for eschewing branch lines ("It is a road constructed on the principle of having only main lines operated"), reports that circulated in the early 1890s suggested that the Stickney regime was about to embark upon three important additions, two of which fell into the feeder-line category. Totaling approximately 265 miles, rails were to connect Peru in Madison County, Iowa, thirty-four miles southwest of Des Moines, with Omaha; Savannah, Missouri, with Omaha; and Sheridan, Missouri, with Tarkio, Missouri.[25]

The Peru to Omaha projection seemed most likely. Following south of the Rock Island's Des Moines–Omaha main line and closely paralleling several Burlington branches, this 110-mile artery would give the CStP&KC competitive Chicago to Omaha trackage. Four hundred and ninety miles in length, it would be only five miles longer than the shortest of the already existing five routes between the two gateways. As with the Des Moines–St. Joseph extension, the Peru project would mean considerable earth work and would also likely skirt the few significant population centers.[26]

The other plan to reach Omaha involved pushing 115 miles northwest from the Des Moines–St. Joseph line at Savannah through the Nodaway, Tarkio, and Nishnabotna river valleys. This territory was known for its exceptionally fine livestock, a commodity that would surely move in large quantities over the CStP&KC's rails. Residents seemed anxious for this addition. As the *Tarkio Avalanche* explained, "So far the railroad interests here have been wholly controlled by one company [Burlington], and hence the shippers have not been to any extent able to secure reasonable freight rates. With this line piercing our country, our people will be enabled to compete with those of other localities who reap the advantages of opposing lines." Not only did this general area suffer from little competition, but some sections were nearly a day's journey away from the existing steamcars.[27]

The final project was merely designed to connect the mainstem (St. Joseph Division) at Sheridan in Worth County near the Iowa line with Tarkio, seat of Atchison County. This forty-mile extension would likewise tap the rich bluegrass country of northwest Missouri. Like the Savannah–Omaha proposal, the area either depended largely on Burlington branches or simply lacked convenient railroad service.[28]

Details of these three projects are obscure. It is apparent that the CStP&KC conducted the line location surveys. In the case of the Savannah-Omaha extension, the Stickney people organized the St. Joseph & Tarkio Valley Railroad Company in June 1890, capitalized at $1 million, to build the first forty-five miles from Savannah through Fillmore and Graham to Tarkio. Although "the people along the proposed route are enthusiastic for the road and will no doubt grant the right-of-way willingly," this proposal and the other two died on the drawing boards. The most probable explanation for this re-

lates to the drastic contraction of English investment funds that followed the October 1890 failure of Baring Brothers, a London-based investment house crippled by heavy losses in Argentine securities.[29]

During the formative years of the Chicago, St. Paul & Kansas City, other "paper" projects emerged. While company officials may well have given them serious consideration, more often than not these proposals were products of booster types who longed to have additional rail outlets. In April 1888, for example, a group of Algona, Iowa, residents told Stickney that they would pay for the grade and bridges on a thirty-two-mile line from their Kossuth County seat southeast to Belmond, located on the loosely affiliated Central Iowa, which connected at Hampton with the old Dubuque & Dakota.[30]

About the same time, the *Oelwein Register* quoted the local station agent, who firmly believed that "there is little doubt now that the Waverly branch [Dubuque & Dakota] is to be extended to Sioux City in the spring." As with subsequent tales of Omaha lines, the notion of a Sioux City extension became merely one of similar rumors that foretold such construction. Although Omaha would eventually be reached, Sioux City never saw Stickney's presence.[31]

Repeated talk of a Rockford, Illinois, line developed during the 1880s and continued for some time. The idea seemed sound. This Winnebago County seat of 23,584 claimed a growing and diverse industrial base and could be easily reached. Between Stillman Valley, four miles east of Byron on the CStP&KC's Chicago line, and Rockford lay nine miles of the crumbling remains of the never-completed Rockford Central, started twenty years earlier. The *Rockford Star* knew (certainly hoped!) that the Stickney property "is going to send a spur to this city [and it] is settled beyond a doubt." The company did not enter this city, however, and the community accepted life with the Burlington, the North Western, the Milwaukee, and the Illinois Central. These roads obviously would not have welcomed any newcomer into an already crowded market.[32]

LIFE ON THE CStP&KC

For those places reached by the Chicago, St. Paul & Kansas City, however, the quality of transportation appeared generally satisfactory. The *St. Joseph Gazette* caught the popular conception of the road, or at least the one its owners wanted to cultivate: "The Chicago, St. Paul & Kansas City will never, in all probability, outlive the appellation Diagonal. A better term would be air line, for while it crosses all the States it traverses diagonally, it takes the shortest possible line between the termini. Mile after mile is traversed without a curve. It passes over or under most of the roads it meets, thus avoiding all danger from collision. Its road-bed is substantially constructed, its rails heavy steel, and its motive power the best. . . . " Even if all this journalistic adulation is to be believed, the press did give occasional glimpses of a less than perfect railroad. The *Dubuque Times* revealed that life aboard a CStP&KC passenger train might prove unnerving: "Passengers on the CStP&KC Monday night train from Des Moines relate a great experience. In the first place the baggage master was green and several traveling men were obliged to check their own trunks. After the train had fairly got started, the whole train was aroused by the screams of a woman, whose husband was giving her a whipping by way of discipline. In the smoking car room soon after, two Irishmen engaged in a knockdown fight, and to cap the climax, when the train reached Dubuque, the colored porter of the sleeping car had disappeared and could not be found."[33]

The CStP&KC valiantly tried to cultivate the best possible public image. It kept its rolling stock in good repair and attempted to be an "on-time" passenger carrier. As for freight movements, one employee recalled, "We had quite a reputation for running fast trains. If you ran slow you got fired." A soon-to-be-common hallmark of the road—innovation and self-promotion—showed in 1891 when it

Typical of the advertising employed by the Chicago, St. Paul & Kansas City is this page from the Minneapolis Industrial Exposition program for 1888. A. B. Stickney's brief control over the neighboring Iowa Central is evident in the "system" map. (Don L. Hofsommer Collection)

issued the first transportation brochure for the great Columbian Exposition to be held in Chicago two years later. Concluded the *Kansas City Times*, "It may be a little premature, but it is enterprise, and enterprise of this sort makes the road worthy of the name it bears—The Kansas City." Since the firm also was known variously as the "Minnesota," "Northwestern," "Diagonal," and even "The

Stickney," it asked the nation's ticket agents in 1889 to participate in a contest to design a trademark. They eagerly responded. More than 2,000 submissions flooded the company's St. Paul headquarters; and early in 1890, the winner was announced: a Wabash Railroad employee from Fort Wayne, Indiana, earned $100 in gold coin for his design of a sugar maple leaf on which the system's lines were depicted as veins. Soon the CStP&KC placed this snappy logo on its public timetables, passes, and advertisements; and the former nicknames gave way to "The Sugar Maple Leaf Route" and then simply "The Maple Leaf Route."[34]

Shortly after the Chicago Great Western absorbed the Chicago, St. Paul & Kansas City, passenger engine #113 (built for the CStP&KC by Cooke & Company in 1889) stands in Chicago's Grand Central Station awaiting a run to the west. The tender still sports CStP&KC markings. (W. A. Vaughn Collection)

STICKNEY'S SEARCH FOR ORDER

ONE factor that contributed immeasurably to the widespread public approbation of the Chicago, St. Paul & Kansas City was A. B. Stickney himself. By the early 1890s, the founder of the Maple Leaf Route became obsessed with establishing predictable and equitable rates, and thus he became a darling of the reformers.

It seems that as railroads grew, so did the need for government control. While from the 1870s on, various state regulatory commissions, particularly those in the upper Mississippi River Valley, had sought to squelch unfair rate charges, a conservative United States Supreme Court, in its 1886 decision in the *Wabash, St. Louis & Pacific Railway Co.* vs. *Illinois* case, severely damaged these past achievements. Specifically, Illinois authorities had found the Wabash guilty of violating their law that prohibited rate discrimination; the company had charged more for a shorter haul from one in-state community to New York than it did for a longer one. The high court, however, reversed this decision on the basis that the shipment in question could not be regulated locally because the Constitution gave exclusive jurisdiction over interstate commerce to federal officials. Public outcry at this decision helped to push a Senate anti-discrimination proposal through the legislative proc-

ess. After all, approximately 75 percent of all rail traffic fell into the category of interstate commerce. The subsequent Interstate Commerce Act of 1887 seemed to offer a greater hope. It not only prohibited rebates to favored shippers, but it curbed discrimination among commodities and, more vitally, among places. The Act furthermore created the Interstate Commerce Commission (ICC) to try to insure compliance with the new law.[35]

As subsequent events reveal, the 1887 statute, from the consumers' standpoint, was less than perfect. Although the infant Commission made a reasonably good start toward implementation of its mandate, the judicial branch soon obstructed its efforts. It would not be until the Hepburn Act of 1906 that the ICC could wield the clout needed to attempt protection of the public interest.[36]

But long before shippers made major regulatory gains, A. B. Stickney spearheaded his own personal crusade to see that his colleagues obeyed the Interstate Commerce Act and to press for federal government assumption of the rate-making function. He wrote letters, speeches, and even, in 1891, a book, *The Railway Problem,* to advance his views.[37]

Stickney's thoughts reveal no radicalism. He found totally unacceptable the increasingly popular notion, as expressed in the People's Party's famed Omaha Platform of 1892 that "transportation being a means of exchange and a public necessity, the government should own and operate the railroads in the interest of the people." Rather, the CStP&KC head agitated repeatedly for a uniform, consistent rate-making policy that, while involving government, would continue to allow the private sector to own and operate at a profit the nation's railroad network.[38]

Stickney's book carefully explained the rate bugaboo. The issue was not whether the industry or consumers were right or wrong with their perceptions of the matter. As Stickney saw it, the problem was simply to review the situation rationally. "Rates between points which are usually termed competitive are so low that the railway managers fully realize that to reduce all rates to the same level would result in speedy bankruptcy for the railways, while, on the other hand, the sufferers from unequal rates point to these low competitive rates, and cannot understand why, if the railways can afford to carry that traffic at the low rates, they cannot carry noncompetitive traffic at correspondingly low rates." The rising tide of public unrest could have been avoided, he thought, "had the managers . . . shown even a slight disposition to conciliate, and to correct some of the more glaring discriminations." This type of pronouncement hardly ingratiated him with his fellow railroad leaders. Yet most could accept his conclusion that "in order to keep railways running, sufficient revenue must be collected to pay operating expenses, and fairness requires an additional amount as compensation for the use of the capital invested."[39]

Stickney knew he had a better mousetrap. In a chapter in *The Railway Problem* titled, "Making Standard Average Rates," he lucidly argued that "if all rates are made by one authority, like Congress or a commission [presumably the ICC], to arrive at the best possible result, . . . is not so difficult." And he felt that no acceptable alternatives existed: "It is manifestly impossible to maintain uniformity in the rates through schedules made by different authorities, like State commissions or railway managements acting separately." Stickney believed that the federal government could develop with ease a national schedule based upon types of commodities hauled and average line-haul and terminal expenses. "It must be conceded that rates thus established would fit together all over the United States with mathematical precision."[40]

This Granger railroader emerged as the predecessor to that ubiquitous progressive reformer described by historian Robert H. Wiebe in his study, *The Search for Order*. According to his interpretation, the most meaningful "uplift" of the early twentieth century involved attempts by a new breed of citizen determined to remedy the disruptions produced by the emerging urban-industrial society. The solutions advanced by these so-called "modernizers" regularly involved "bureaucratization." They believed, for example, that independent regulatory commissions, staffed by bureaucratic-minded professionals, could best solve the problems posed by industrial disorder. Unmistakably Stickney fits the Wiebe mold: he blasted the "chaos of rates," and he dearly craved a predictable railroad enterprise realized through the labors of regulatory experts.[41]

Stickney's credentials as bona fide reformer, however, are open to question. Although he probably sincerely believed that his blueprint for solving the "railway problem" was needed, his carrier would also benefit considerably if rates, especially, became uniformly established and were based partially on terminal costs. Since its opening, the system had gained a reputation as a "rate-cutter," a charge that management usually denied. But these rate wars were damaging, particularly so for roads like the CStP&KC that confronted the fixed costs of recent construction. And, too, the combined M&NW–CStP&KC property relied heavily on foreign railroads and switching companies. By the early 1890s, these expenses included the lease of trackage between St. Paul and Minneapolis (10.56 miles), Dubuque and Aiken, Illinois (15.67 miles), St. Joseph and Kansas City (67.67 miles), and the Chicago (10.18 miles) and Des Moines (2.70 miles) terminals. For the fiscal year 1891–1892, trackage and switching charges amounted to $213,008.13 or nearly six percent of its total operating expenses of $3,664,677.04. The next year they reached 8.23 percent. Moreover, the uncertainty of tariffs, as Stickney so capably argued, caused enormous ill-will among the public.[42]

Whether Stickney was a self-serving advocate of reform or not, the immediate results of his reform agitation came to naught. The types of corrective measures he envisioned had to await the progressive movement—that great national housecleaning escapade that burst upon the federal level of government shortly after the turn of the century. The Populist Revolt of the 1890s offered to Stickney's way of thinking the wrong approach—nationalization—yet it revealed superbly that the issue of the industry's relationship to society was intensely critical. Still, the Maple Leaf founder enjoyed what may be conveniently termed "self-help" assistance that his fledgling carrier badly needed.

REORGANIZATION

Soon after the CStP&KC began operations in 1887, its financial health weakened. Obviously, an infant company could expect seriously constricted earnings when its fixed costs rose dramatically with new-line construction; but by 1889, the debt level soared well beyond its yearly earnings. Then there was the factor of rate wars that plagued roads in the Midwest, one of the great competitive battlegrounds. Tariffs were slashed enormously during the winter and spring of 1888, and the problem continued. There was also the general agricultural downswing of the late eighties that further hurt the balance sheets of regional carriers. Notwithstanding the *Oelwein Register*'s pronouncement that the company was "doing a vast business" with its "passenger and freight traffic . . . rapidly increasing," the annual reports indicated precisely its growing woes. While the road reported a modest surplus of $71,328 for the first twelve months that ended on June 30, 1887, a year later it showed a net deficit of $260,558. Red ink continued to spill; the loss reached $731,358 in 1889.[43]

The deteriorating situation forced management to

act: on August 20, 1889, bondholders were asked to forego payment of their interest earnings for a three-year period. Since the investors lacked an immediate practical alternative, they acquiesced. The next financial report must have made them happy that they had done so. Instead of a hefty deficit, the company had earned a tidy net income of $608,954. The joy, however, was short-lived; the 1891 results proved much less encouraging. Due largely to a souring economy and the failure of operating expenses, especially wages, to follow gross revenues downward, the net income declined by twenty percent. Although Stickney and his fellow officials held hope for substantial improvement, these perilous conditions warranted more sweeping action. Not only were bondholders unlikely to be as lenient, but the funded debt was simply too high. The road therefore concocted a boot-straps program that led to formation of the Chicago Great Western Railway Company.[44]

With the funding agreement to expire in 1892, there was no time to lose. The restructuring plan was to center on paring down the CStP&KC's fixed charges, "otherwise the railroad would operate in constant danger of foreclosure."[45]

The vast majority of the Maple Leaf Route's investors were British, a connection that dated back to the birth of both the Minnesota & Northwestern and the Wisconsin, Iowa & Nebraska. The latter company benefited considerably from R. T. Wilson's abilities to attract pounds sterling to the infant Iowa carrier, while the former profited from A. B. Stickney's close association with St. Paul financier Charles W. Benson. It was to be Benson and his brothers, of the London-based firm of Robert Benson and Company, who tapped considerable English capital. In time, John Saunders Gilliat of London's Gilliat & Company and William Lidderdale of the Liverpool-headquartered Rathbone and Company also became heavily involved. With this substantial British influence, it is understandable why the CStP&KC embraced a non-American model for its financial salvation—debenture stock.[46]

Through a cleverly formulated scheme, the

drafters of the revitalization plan sought to end forever the bugaboo of huge fixed charges. Specifically, they authorized the new company, capitalized at $70,000,000, to issue four classes of securities, all listed nominally as stock. While having varied privileges, some of this paper closely resembled conventional bonds. First in importance was the $15,000,000 of debenture stock, designed to pay four percent annual interest in gold. Next, the road offered an equal amount of preferred A stock that would yield five percent yearly. Then it had $10,000,000 of preferred B stock earmarked to remit four percent. Finally, common stock, totaling $30,000,000, would be issued.[47]

English railroads had long favored debenture stock but never had major American carriers used it extensively, largely because of investor resistance.[48] These securities shared characteristics of both stocks and bonds. Holders of debentures had the right to vote in annual elections of boards, but they also received a fixed rate of interest. The payments had to be made when earned, and thus the certificate served as a lien upon the property. But differing from a bond, this stock was a "perpetual" obligation not terminable after a definite time period. Obviously, the principal advantage for the company was that if revenues failed to be sufficient to pay dividends, owners of this debenture stock were entitled to absolutely nothing. As for the benefits to the stockholders, Stickney himself explained them in a pamphlet entitled, *A Western Trunk Line Railway Without a Mortgage.* "Having no mortgage indebtedness, investors may hold its first security, the Debenture stock, without fear of its interest and principal being scaled down by a Reorganization Committee and may hold its junior securities without fear of an assessment through the machinery of foreclosure."[49]

To make the reorganization more palatable to investors, the company empowered a finance committee with unusual rights. Consisting of holders of the debenture and preferred A securities, this group possessed an absolute veto of any action the board of directors might take toward issuing additional debenture stock, borrowing money, and expending

funds, except those required to cover daily operating expenses. If for any reason the committee was unsatisfied with the financial records given them by the directors, it could appoint an independent auditor to examine the books. If the board refused to pay dividends when earned, the committee could capture the treasurer's office and force the disbursal.[50]

Actual implementation of the reorganization scheme began on January 16, 1892. On that dreary winter day, a Stickney representative walked into the office of the Illinois Secretary of State in Springfield to file the necessary incorporation papers for the Chicago Great Western Railway Company.[51] The articles state that the road's purpose was to "construct a railroad from a point on the boundary line of Illinois and Indiana, to a junction with the Minnesota and Northwestern, thence to a point on Lake Michigan, with a branch to a point on Lake Michigan, near the mouth of the Calumet River." Thus, the avowed intention of the CGW was merely to link the CStP&KC (M&NW of Illinois) to the heart of Chicago. Stickney told the press that the CGW was created to find a solution to the "enormous increases of traffic" entering the Windy City. Such a statement, however, was pure fabrication. Rather, the desire to provide a convenient corporate vehicle for a reconstituted Maple Leaf Route prompted this move.[52]

Despite this, the process of amalgamation continued with dispatch. On March 22, 1892, the CStP&KC board of directors ratified the lease of its property to the Great Western; the arrangement took effect on July 1. The next day, the CGW management bought the Leavenworth & St. Joseph Railway, that portion of the Oelwein–Kansas City line that linked Bee Creek with Beverly, Missouri. Then, fourteen months later, the directors of the CStP&KC officially exchanged their assets for Great Western securities. Holders of CStP&KC first mortgage bonds received for each $1000 a combination of CGW four percent debentures ($500) and five percent preferred A ($600). Those who possessed CStP&KC general mortgage bonds obtained for each $1000 an equal amount of four percent

CGW preferred B stock. And common stockholders either paid a ten percent assessment for a mix of the four percent preferred B and CGW common or traded their certificates for half their amount in CGW common. Owners of M&NW securities got a similar arrangement.[53]

Not all parties seemed happy with the management-inspired change. Although most bondholders gave their blessings, one body of investors—the common stockholders—objected. They faced considerable shrinkage in the volume amount of their assets. In fact, one irate shareholder brought a suit to have the arrangement nullified. An unsympathetic court, however, denied the objection.[54]

Once the financial scheme was executed, backers of the Chicago Great Western expected their creation to have a prosperous life. While the catastrophic Panic of 1893 triggered five troubled years for the nation's economy and sent literally scores of railroads into their financial graves, the reorganized Maple Leaf Route endured. Unmistakably, the company's adoption of the English-inspired structure that made it a mortgage-free property with only a lien upon its income proved a wise course.

SURVIVING DEPRESSION

THE timing of the Stickney system reorganization proved ideal. Shortly thereafter, in May 1893, wholesale panic struck the country, and companies failed at an alarming rate. Railroads seemed especially vulnerable to this "prostration of business." Many had severely overextended themselves during the building sprees of the 1880s and therefore lacked the wherewithal to cope with the crisis. By the time prosperity returned five years later, much of the nation's transportation network lay in financial ruins. Nearly 200 roads had fallen into the hands of receivers; leading casualties included the Atchison, Topeka & Santa Fé, Baltimore & Ohio, Northern Pacific, St. Louis–San Francisco, and Union Pacific. But the Maple Leaf Route weathered the storm.[1]

Still, the "extreme economic dullness" of the 1890s injured the Chicago Great Western. Gross receipts of $4,011,709 for fiscal 1893–1894 slipped a year later to $3,636,098, and the net dropped from $1,128,812 to $819,349. Train operating costs had also fallen, though less dramatically. Fortunately for the Great Western, labor and material charges dipped appreciably, and management naturally exploited these favorable market conditions. "Notwithstanding small earnings," A. B. Stickney

wrote in mid-1895, "the policy of steadily improving the roadbeds and rolling stock has been pursued and even more money has been expended than in the previous year." The reasoning made sense: "one dollar expended would stand for a dollar and a half, and in some cases for more than two dollars at normal prices." Before the Panic, for example, stone masonry cost from $8 to $12 per cubic yard, but depressed conditions lowered the price tag to $4 to $6.[2]

Just as Stickney capitalized on the recession of 1884 to construct the Minnesota & Northwestern at a bargain-basement price, he now expanded the Great Western's physical upgrading during this much graver slump. Even though net earnings increased by 70.8 percent in 1895–1896 over 1894–1895 and remained steady for 1896–1897, the last year of depression, more improvement money was sought. In February 1896, the press revealed that London financiers made a million dollar loan to the CGW for five years at six percent interest. "[It] will be used to ballast the track, cut down grades, put up new bridges and culverts," reported the *Dubuque Telegraph,* "so that the engine which now hauls 650 tons between Elma and Chicago will be able to haul much more." As Stickney told the *Minneapolis Journal,* "We propose to make the CGW one of the best and safest roads in the country."[3]

The South St. Paul Shops, established by the Minnesota & Northwestern in the late 1880s, served the Stickney system as its principal repair facility until the Oelwein complex opened in 1899.

This circa 1895 photograph reveals how geography — the Mississippi River and towering bluffs — constricted the Minnesota site. (W. A. Vaughn Collection)

OELWEIN SHOPS

PART of the revitalization program focused on the soon-to-be famous shops complex at Oelwein, Iowa. By the 1890s this Fayette County community emerged as the "Hub City" of the system. Lines to St. Paul, Chicago, Kansas City, and, after 1903, Omaha radiated out of Oelwein. Named in honor of the townsite owner, August Oelwein, the village got its start in September 1873 with the arrival of the iron horse. The carrier was not the M&NW, which came in 1886, but the Burlington, Cedar Rapids & Minnesota (subsequently part of the Rock Island system), builder of a 118-mile branch from Cedar Rapids to Decorah.[4]

As early as 1887, Stickney sensed Oelwein's strategic value. That fall the company completed a minor engine-servicing facility in the village. Yet when rail service actually had begun between St. Paul and Dubuque, management selected Elma, Iowa, the midway point between the two terminals, as its divi-

sion point and erected a small roundhouse and machine shop there. Elma, however, was nearly fifty miles from the junction with the Kansas City extension, and it further lost its locational advantage when the Dubuque-Chicago segment was opened. Elma was, however, closer to the center of the system than South St. Paul, home of the company's principal repair and maintenance facility, the South Park shops.[5]

It appears that from the first, the Minnesota installation, which cost more than $300,000 when built in the late eighties, seemed badly situated. The Great Western faced the expense of transporting wrecked and broken motive power and rolling stock from such distant points as Chicago and Kansas City. (Indeed, when the depression of the 1890s struck, officials ordered more repair work performed in Oelwein to reduce costs.) Further lessening the value of the South St. Paul facilities, the physical setting itself proved unsuitable. "With the Mississippi river on one side and high bluffs on the other, . . . to extend them would be difficult and

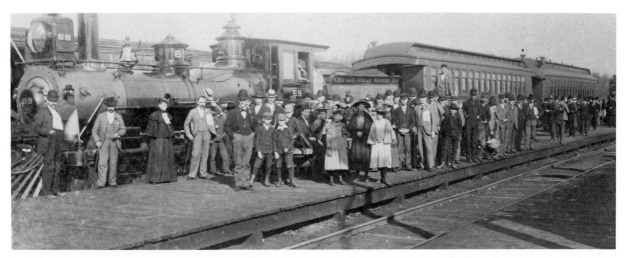

In order to promote the Oelwein Land Company's "Great Land Sale" of May 28, 1894, Oelweinites are about to board a special train for Des Moines. But the deepening depression temporarily dampened sales. (James L. Rueber Collection)

expensive." But the shops needed to be moved for more than their location and inadequacy. With widespread labor unrest occurring, sparked in part by hard times, the Stickney management envisioned the advantages of isolating a potentially troublesome work force in the tranquil farmlands of Iowa, far away from evil urban influences. The Great Northern had recently experienced prolonged worker problems at its St. Paul shops, and the CGW could ill afford similar confrontations. The company, moreover, believed that its long-term labor costs would be significantly lower in a rural milieu. The assumption, apparently, was that green country boys, likely acquainted with machinery, or at least interested in it, would flock to the site since they would be anxious to abandon the dullness and drudgery of farm work for the hustle-bustle and steady pay of railroad jobs.[6]

Understandably, already existing on-line communities eagerly sought the plum of the Chicago Great Western shops. The vast army of workers associated with their presence meant substantial growth, with a commensurate rise in land and business values and retail sales. "As an element of permanent prosperity to a village or city, railway shops are superior in value to any other manufacturing establishment, in-

asmuch as they continue to run as long as the railway runs, which is perpetual, for although men die, the railway, like the babbling brook, 'runs on forever,' " observed Stickney. "The work at the railway shops and its monthly disbursement of wages are continuous, but it is not so with some other manufacturing establishments." The public grasped fully the meaning of such words.[7]

By 1894, Elma, Sumner, Dubuque, and Oelwein entered the competition for the CGW's shops with great enthusiasm. Yet management clearly preferred the Oelwein location, and it asked residents for their financial assistance. If adequate aid was not supplied, the company planned to contact another community. To insure success, the Great Western engaged seasoned railroad land promoter E. F. House of New York City and Chicago attorney R. N. Baylies, who was also familiar with such matters, to spearhead the drive.[8]

And Oelweinites responded. Four years before the necessary funds were on hand to underwrite the project, public-spirited citizens sponsored grass-roots meetings to plan strategy. These discussions swiftly led to the formation of the Oelwein Land Company. This firm, organized formally on April 4, 1894, emerged as a joint venture between residents

A maze of machinery fills the interior of the Oelwein shops. The company correctly boasted owning state-of-the-art equipment, and it continued to modernize the facility for decades to come. (H. Roger Grant Collection)

and railroad officials to help relocate the shops. Specifically, the idea was to compensate the Great Western for the expense in leaving South St. Paul, estimated at $200,000. Since Oelwein real estate values were expected to skyrocket with the influx of workers and nonrailroad businesses attracted to this new "transportation mecca," the land company could benefit by developing the desirable residential and commercial parcels. It could then advance the railroad $200,000, and the enhanced worth of the firm's holdings would theoretically repay its financial commitment. Also, the Oelwein Land Company would deed the railroad about forty acres for the shops site itself.[9]

The Chicago Great Western readily agreed to the plan, and joy swept the village of eight hundred. As *Oelwein Register* editor A. E. Woodruff proclaimed on April 26, 1894: "OELWEIN HAS SECURED THE MACHINES SHOPS: NOW CROW! THE LONG-ANTICI-PATED AND HOPED-FOR EVENT HAS TRANSPIRED." The fact, however, that the railroad agreed to this venture did not mean that the shops would be instantly forthcoming to the site selected, which was an ad-

joining hog pasture. Although the Oelwein Land Company acquired the necessary real estate, its gala "Great Land Sale" auction held on May 28, which was attended by more than 10,000 people, many of whom traveled to Oelwein on special trains from Des Moines, Dubuque, and other parts of the system, failed to produce the anticipated sales. Furthermore, some buyers, because of the depression, could not raise the money they pledged and subsequently defaulted. Later promotional efforts fell short of generating even a portion of the hoped-for income. Legally, the Great Western could have escaped its commitment to Oelwein. Under the terms of its contract with the Oelwein Land Company, the carrier required its money by April 1, 1895.[10]

Fortunately for Oelweinites, the Great Western strongly wanted to have its principal maintenance facilities in their community. Even though Oelwein Land Company sales proved disappointing, the railroad sponsored the clearing and grading of the site during the summer of 1894. A year later it let bids for the foundations.[11]

But the Oelwein venture stalled, in spite of the

More than a dozen locomotives crowd the Oelwein Shops in this 1907 view. (Edward H. Meyers Collection)

Early in the twentieth century the Chicago Great Western constructed a "Back Shops" addition to the main Oelwein complex. (W. H. Jacobs Photograph; W. A. Vaughn Collection)

preliminary work. The depression was simply too long and too severe. The contracts for completion of the project were not signed until early 1898. By then the railroad's earnings had improved, and funds generated from issuance of $1,100,000 worth of debenture stock in January 1898 became available. Not only was the transatlantic money market tapped successfully, but sales through the Oelwein Land Company finally increased.[12]

Workers swarmed over the site in late April 1898. Their task was formidable: to erect seven structures that would contain 177,000 square feet—more than four acres—of enclosed space. The skilled employees of the Chicago-based Hoff Brothers Construction Company met the challenge; they quickly finished the foundations and started the above-ground building on June 11. A year later (April 1899) saw the completion of "Oelwein's Glory," and soon the *Register* proudly announced, "THE SHOPS ARE RUNNING!" The formal dedication took place on September 28. Coinciding with the final preparations, the process of transferring jobs and personnel from South St. Paul to Oelwein began. When federal census takers made their headcount in 1900, the "Hub City" had grown to more than 6,000 inhabitants, 1,200 of whom labored in the facilities. Town fathers expected the total population to reach 10,000, or even 15,000, by 1910.[13]

The Chicago Great Western built more than an imposing complex in an ideal location. The $450,000 investment sported an advanced design, fully consis-

tent with management's desire to embrace the most efficient and economical methods. General master mechanic Tracy Lyon teamed up with St. Paul architects C. A. Reed and Fay Berkley to devise what contemporaries considered an "unusual plan of shops' arrangement." The network of brick and mortar consisted of two long core structures: one housing the machine, erecting, boiler, and coach shops together with the general storehouse; the other containing the freight, blacksmith, and paint shops. Since the main units faced each other, a gigantic transfer table facilitated the movement of equipment between them. The designers also placed the mandatory satellite facilities in handy locations; for example, the wheel house and scrap bins abutted the freight-car shop. And the complex boasted a special building that Stickney himself ordered. As the Great Western head told the Northeastern Iowa Press Association in March 1899: "In yonder cluster of buildings stands a building separate and apart, which has no counterpart in the West. It is 50 × 100 feet and has no machinery. It will have in the lower story wash basins, sinks, lockers for men's clothing they do not wear while at work. The second story is a large assembly hall which may be divided later. This will be turned over to the employees of our shops for their comfort during their luncheon, and a place for rest and recreation while off duty. It will be christened Liberty Hall, typical of the employees of

Oelwein was home to a forty-stall roundhouse that opened in the fall of 1904. This facility employed an army of workers, including boilermakers, machinists, and engine wipers. (H. Roger Grant Collection)

the C.G.W. road." Stickney, in fact, personally paid for the "club rooms," which flourished for the duration of his tenure.[14]

ADDITIONAL IMPROVEMENTS

WHILE Maple Leaf patrons never caught more than a glimpse of the sprawling Oelwein shops as they passed through the Hub City, other improvements probably vied for their attention. With the proceeds from English financing deals and increasing revenues—net earnings for 1897–1898 reached $1,445,671, a 30.4 percent increase over the previous fiscal year, and those of 1898–1899 totaled $1,720,223, a gain of 19.8 percent—the road spent heavily on new motive power and rolling stock and continued to rework its track. Between 1897–1899, the Great Western bought forty-six locomotives, 774 box cars, 100 special ballast carriers, and dozens of passenger coaches. Throughout the late 1890s, the company kept nearly 1,200 men, eight steam shovels, twenty engines, and 350 cars busy during the construction season, reducing grades and curvatures, making bridges permanent, ballasting, adding side tracks, and replacing various station buildings.[15]

This determination to make equipment and plant

"without superior west of Chicago" continued unabated into the new century. In 1903, for example, the company spent $578,345 for thirty-six modern freight and passenger locomotives. And it regularly added heavier rail, more ballast, and longer sidings. Some of the busiest sections of the system, located on the Eastern Division or "east end," got double track. Substantial brick passenger depots and freight houses frequently appeared at trackside, further symbolizing the improved CGW. The Stickney regime, however, was not unusual with such improvements. Most other Class 1 roads extensively rehabilitated their properties after 1900. As one prominent transportation historian has observed, "America's railroads were, indeed, built *twice:* once in the nineteenth century, and again in the exhilarating era we call, with so much justification, Progressive."[16]

Repeatedly, the on-line press marveled at the improved Great Western. Attention centered on the upgraded roadbed, the nicely appointed stations, and particularly on the luxurious features of passenger trains #1 and #2, "The Great Western Limited." These magnificent trains, which entered service in July 1898, immediately captured the public's fancy. Although this "varnish" operated only between Chicago and the Twin Cities, newspapers systemwide carried thousands of column inches of copy to describe what they felt superbly characterized the "new Maple Leaf." A Missouri "drummer" penned

CGW passenger engine #63, originally CStP&KC #53, waits at the Des Moines Union Depot, circa 1893. The stag's horns on the headlight testify to a popular nineteenth-century railroad tradition, when the pride of individually assigned crews made the sheen of locomotives a personal responsibility. (DeGolyer Library, Southern Methodist University)

this account for the *Parnell Sentinel:* "Until recently the Pennsylvania Limited, out of New York to Chicago, was believed to be ideal, but so thorough is the service on the [*Great Western Limited*] with buffet cars, with their bulk heads, stained glass windows, and . . . electrical equipment, that the Pennsylvania people have ordered their renowned 'Chicago Limited' into the shops that it may be rebuilt, or rather modernized, after the cars that are in service on the CGW." He added predictably, "I think the future of this property is very great."[17]

PROGRESSIVE AND AMBITIOUS

IMPROVING the physical plant and rolling stock meant little if the Chicago Great Western could not generate a profitable traffic flow. The ultracompetitive environment of the Midwest showed no signs of weakening; indeed, such rivals as the Chicago, Burlington & Quincy, Chicago & North Western, and the Chicago, Milwaukee & St. Paul were pouring millions of dollars into their facilities. Logically, the Stickney administration continued to reveal that creative bent. The tenor of the Maple Leaf Route throughout this time supports the thesis that innovation in railroading usually emanates from the smaller, less entrenched carriers.

The Great Western proved to be progressive and ambitious. Although it never achieved the goal stated by one official in 1895 that "we intend to be the Pennsylvania Line of the West," the company tried mightily. The railroad industry commented, for instance, on such things as its agitation for a standard box car size and its operating of solid, high-speed meat and merchandise trains. It gained attention, too, for being the "first" road to "put into practical and extensive use the plan of tonnage rating [for locomotives] . . . also the Graphic system of keeping account of expenditures and revenues in all departments." The CGW's most famous single effort at creativity and the quest for greater financial security occurred in the mid-1890s when the road bought agricultural commodities for the purposes of freight traffic.[18]

This creative effort began on September 20, 1894, when the Great Western formed the Iowa Development Company, a subsidiary of the Oelwein Land Company. The affiliate quickly erected a one million bushel capacity terminal elevator in Kansas City, Missouri. Upon completion, the railroad engaged a Chicago dealer to buy the grain and pay the profits, less the usual commissions, to the Iowa Development Company, without deducting the shipping costs. In this way, growers received top dollar for their crops, and the road found a convenient device for generating considerable car loadings. The profit on each deal was the *sole* rate collected as such; published freight tariffs were thereby totally ignored. During part of 1896, the CGW carried 70 percent of all corn that moved from Kansas City to Chicago, and competitors naturally objected. They complained to the Interstate Commerce Commission, and that body ruled in February 1897 that the ingenious practice of the Stickney road violated federal law. However, as long as the Great Western followed its published grain schedules, the ICC allowed it to own its elevators. Since such facilities usually added to a railroad's profitability, Stickney spearheaded another one, the Independent Elevator Company, incorporated under Nebraska law on October 28, 1904. A year later, the fledgling firm constructed a million-bushel elevator in Omaha, and, in 1917, management decided to increase the storage capacity to 1,540,000 bushels.[19]

Aside from this kind of notoriety, the Maple Leaf also gained fame nationally for being a "rate-cutter." Stickney and his lieutenants repeatedly denied such charges, arguing that their road simply "met the competition." But as the company's Kansas City grain activities suggest, it did contribute measurably to rate instability. Indeed, throughout the period, this railroad company chopped tariffs, notwithstanding Stickney's protestations to the contrary. The carrier regularly resorted to undercover rate-reducing tactics, understandable perhaps since it constantly battled the region's stronger carriers.

A demonstration of the Great Western's tariff-making policies comes from an employee who worked in the freight auditor's office in St. Paul at the turn of the century:

• • •

[Stickney] ordered me, with several assistants, to prepare a large book itemizing all freight and passenger rates. . . . After a month of intensive work this task was completed. The volume, about 64 pages, was placed on file with the Interstate Commerce Commission, . . . and a copy was given to each of our agents and those of connecting lines.

Devious cut rates were hidden in that mass of figures. For instance, the tariff for canned goods was listed under "Peas and Other Canned Goods." Let us say the regular rate quoted by all rival roads for handling canned goods between [two points] was 45 cents a hundred weight. We would quote 15 cents (the figure we gave under "Peas, etc.") and thus would grab the competitive business. Our own local agents could not declare the lower rate, because few knew it was there. It probably would not occur to them to look under "P" for canned goods, but they

could call or write our main office for the lowest rate on a certain commodity and we would give it to them.

Our competitors realized we were taking business away from them and suspected we were cutting rates. However, they didn't know how we did it. The answer was to be found in our book tariff filed with the ICC, but at that time they did not catch on.[20]

• • •

The competitors did catch on, however, to exactly how the Chicago Great Western was capturing a large part of the meat business early in the century. In 1902, Stickney issued a circular to stockholders that told of "novel traffic agreements" the road had signed with packing companies in Kansas City, St. Joesph, and Omaha. These firms agreed to route a percentage of their output over the CGW at a guaranteed figure for a seven-year period. "The rates are a substantial advance over the rates which have heretofore prevailed." This, of course, appealed to Stickney, for it meant a predictable volume of business. The packers also knew that in inflationary times a set price held considerable attraction for them. Once more the Great Western was an industry innovator. The road, in reality, was an early proponent of "contract rates," a concept that has only recently become popular.[21]

LABOR RELATIONS

STICKNEY used other methods besides rate manipulation to keep the road competitive. For one thing, he longed for labor tranquility, and his paternalistic utterances and actions seemed to have had a positive effect. Workers liked him personally and usually trusted his judgments. And Stickney's son Samuel, the road's general manager, shared the same popularity. Also, Stickney-sponsored employee clubs, located throughout the system, were enthusiastically supported. Beginning in 1897, the Maple Leaf introduced a unique plan of corporate profit sharing. Workers could acquire the company's four

The Chicago Great Western gained national recognition for its early use of "off-lines" sales offices. The staff in Seattle, Washington, assembles for a 1903 portrait. (W. A. Vaughn Collection)

percent debenture stock (worth about $75 per share) for $10 down and $10 per month. They were told that the stock was advancing right along and employees should take advantage of this opportunity now if they wished to reap the benefits. Few availed themselves of this offer, however, and the program was subsequently dropped. It seems the laborer's long-standing suspicion of security deals, his limited discretionary income, and his inability to liquidate conveniently doomed sales. Yet, the plan probably reinforced the growing feeling among the rank-and-file that the road was a closely knit unit. In fact, the "happy-family" concept emerged as an important theme in the company's later years.[22]

Some employees, nevertheless, did object to the railroad's policies. One such occurrence came in 1894; the American Railway Union (ARU) found a band of active supporters on the Great Western. Led by the resourceful and charismatic Eugene V. Debs, this short-lived industrial union immediately took a militant stand. Much to management's horror, the Great Western's ARU members successfully shut down the road for several weeks in June to back their national union's boycott of Pullman cars. The

Debs group sought to aid workers at George M. Pullman's Palace Car Company near Chicago, who had struck that spring to protest layoffs and drastic wage cuts. When the federal government quickly shattered the ARU, labor unrest cooled on the Maple Leaf, although Debs continued to be a popular figure among hundreds of the road's operating personnel. Only a few other labor disturbances took place between the time of the Pullman conflict and Stickney's departure in 1908. With the exception of a strike by machinists and boiler-makers at the Oelwein shops between September 14–December 14, 1907, none was exceedingly long or bitter.[23]

Employees in the Oelwein complex not only enjoyed some of the finest facilities in the industry, but supervisors here showed a willingness to respond in a sensitive fashion to their complaints. The suggestions of operating people, too, were heeded. In 1897, for example, the company reorganized its operating divisions by abolishing the positions of the three divisional superintendents and replacing them with a single superintendent of transportation. The road became only the second carrier in the country to have this format. But this structure annoyed numerous workers. They felt more "at home" with the old ways; they liked the personal aspects of a decentralized divisional structure. So, the Great Western abandoned the new plan; after all, the quest for efficiency and the desire to experiment, hallmarks of the road, could be sacrificed in this case to placate disgruntled personnel.[24]

The generally pleasant, stable working conditions aided the road in attracting talented, dedicated individuals, both managers and workers. Proud employees in later years jumped at the opportunity to say that "famous" men once drew paychecks from the Great Western, two of whom stand out during these years, Ralph Budd and Walter Chrysler. Budd, a Waterloo, Iowa, native, worked in the company's engineering department between 1899 and 1902. Later, his distinguished railroad career eventually included stints as president of the Great Northern and the Chicago, Burlington & Quincy. Chrysler, a

Hayfield, Minnesota, was a busy spot on the Great Western. Nearby, the line to Manly Junction, Iowa, later Omaha, left the Twin Cities to Chicago stem. The local drayman awaits a passenger train. (James L. Rueber Collection)

Kansas boy whose love of machinery caused him to enter railroading, came to the CGW in 1904 from the Fort Worth & Denver City Railway to supervise the shops. Soon thereafter he became superintendent of motive power, but he left in 1910 to continue his career at the American Locomotive Company and ultimately in the automobile business.[25]

No different from other railroads, the Great Western employed loyal workers who, unlike Budd or Chrysler, never earned fame or fortune. At times, these unheralded souls risked their health, even their lives for the company. While some acts of heroism went unnoticed, most received at least momentary attention. The following story fortunately found its way into the historical record and represents nicely the rank-and-file's commitment to the CGW.

In mid-February 1905, blizzards pounded western Iowa. Snow drifts forced trains to wait out the inclement weather, but one Omaha-bound Great Western passenger train got hopelessly stuck between Clarion and Eagle Grove. The engineer, who dis-

covered that he could not go ahead, attempted to return to the safety of Clarion, the division point, but he soon found that too was impossible. The fierce wind quickly piled snow on top of the tender, and the struggling fireman could not keep the coal burning. So the engine crew banked the fire, drained the boiler, and fought their way back to the safety of the coaches. In the meantime, a brakeman made several attempts to walk the dozen miles back to Clarion, but each time he tried, he returned numb with cold. Fortunately, the black porter had a full box of hard coal in the lone Pullman and, after tearing off a board from a right-of-way fence, made a fire in the "Baker" heater. The crew then took the twenty-one passengers, including six elderly women, one of whom was quite ill, into the warm car. All day the storm raged. Then, as night fell and hunger became acute, the porter wrapped pillow cases around his legs and struggled to a nearby farmhouse where he got a pail of milk and three loaves of bread. Early the next morning a relief engine

The village of Ingalton, Illinois, today part of West Chicago, possessed this small depot of standardized design. A few travelers and a large load of milk cans wait for a passenger train about 1900. (West Chicago Historical Museum)

finally reached the stranded train and pulled it back to Clarion. Word of this man's valor spread rapidly, and when Stickney learned of it, he ordered him "to buy a good suit of clothes upon his return to St. Paul and have it charged to the company."[26]

BOOM AND BUST

THE Chicago Great Western's dedication to innovation and efficiency and its ability to attract high caliber, dedicated employees paid off handsomely. The formative years of the twentieth century proved to be good ones for both America and the CGW. Net earnings (gross receipts less operating expenses and taxes) remained at the stable and respectable level of about $2 million annually between June 1900 and June 1906. With acquisition of the 276-mile Wisconsin, Minnesota & Pacific (WM&P) and the 86-mile Mason City & Fort Dodge (MC&FD) in 1901, and completion of the "Omaha Extension" two years later, net revenue figures rose steadily: $1,902,631 in 1904; $2,038,618 in 1905; and $2,539,492 in 1906. As Stickney noted optimistically in 1905, "The proprietary lines [WM&P and MC&FD], being new, have not developed their full earning capacity, and it is confidently expected that during the coming year both their gross and net earnings will rapidly increase."[27]

Yet the Stickney road was about to stumble badly, for the sudden and nasty Panic of 1907 forced the company into receivership, followed by the customary reorganization. Unfortunately for the security holders, they missed opportunities to liquidate profitably before the surprise debacle.

Throughout the early years of the century, rumors circulated that some larger carrier or syndicate was about to gobble up the Maple Leaf. Its trackage had attractive features. Except for the WM&P unit, the

The DeKalb branch joined the main line at Sycamore, Illinois, and this bustling terminal with its water tower and coal chute (background) meant a sizable depot. This station was a carbon-copy of the one at Ingalton, twenty-six miles to the east; the company merely lengthened the plan. This postal card view, taken about 1905, attests to a common error in referring to the Chicago Great Western as "Chicago & Great Western." (Paul Stringham Collection)

CGW was a main, not branch line, operation. Although it did not always utilize the best route, it reached exceedingly important gateways—Twin Cities, Chicago, St. Joseph, Kansas City, and Omaha. Once the road entered the Nebraska metropolis, its value increased considerably, for it tapped a vital transcontinental artery, the Union Pacific's "Overland Route." And there was another factor which attracted outside interest: the CGW's competitiveness disturbed rivals. One newspaper editor said it well: "Its vigorous management is hot competition for the more conservative roads and they would be glad to pay Stickney and his crowd of capitalists a large sum to step out of the business." The Chicago, Milwaukee & St. Paul; Chicago & North Western; Chicago, Rock Island & Pacific; Kansas City Southern; and especially the Union Pacific expressed this interest, which at times was keen. When stories of the Union Pacific's courtship

reached Wall Street late in 1904, Great Western common soared from $6 to $24 a share. But Stickney and fellow owners refused all offers. They fervently believed that their property's value would increase steadily as its earning power rose. As the CGW was the only major "independent" in the Midwest, stockholders could sell at any time and probably at a good price.[28]

By 1907, however, several indicators dashed expectations for a profitable or even a comfortable future for the road. Although the Maple Leaf enjoyed its largest year's traffic in history, its overall financial condition grew steadily weaker. The June 30, 1906, balance sheet revealed cash on hand of $1,340,920; a year later the cash item totaled a mere $224,000. On the same date, bills payable surpassed accounts receivable by $337,000, and current liabilities exceeded current assets by $612,000. Most important, the company faced a staggering

$8,491,848 worth of short-term notes, $3,342,545 of which came due in 1908 and $4,069,061 in 1909. Although Stickney and his associates had sought to make their road "insolvency-proof," these obligations proved to be its undoing.[29]

Near the end of 1907, the Maple Leaf reached a crisis point. The impact of that year's bank panic not only damaged the economy of the road's service territory, lowering freight and passenger revenues, but it ruined all efforts for refinancing. To make matters worse, operating expenses increased and then labor relations momentarily soured when machinists and boilermakers struck at Oelwein, disrupting operations considerably. When the Finance Committee of the Board of Directors found it impossible to arrange for an extension of the notes in either Britain or America, relief was sought through the courts. On February 10, 1908, the CGW entered receivership.[30]

Ironically, the "insolvency-proof" Chicago Great Western Railway Company, survivor of the nation's greatest economic disaster to date—the 1890s depression—fell victim to a less calamitous downswing. This unhappy turn of events meant that an era was about to end.

CHAPTER FOUR
YEARS OF GROWTH, 1895-1904

EXPANSIVE MOOD

BEFORE financial disaster struck in 1907, the Chicago Great Western succeeded in becoming more than just a Twin Cities–Chicago–Kansas City route with a few minor appendages. At the time the CGW emerged in 1892, its mileage stood at 913; and when receivership came in 1908, the total was 1,467. During this time the company absorbed several Minnesota and Iowa short lines and pushed into the strategic Omaha gateway. And many unfulfilled construction plans circulated; in fact, the railroad had some grand dreams, perhaps entry into the Rocky Mountain West and even beyond.

The general mood of railroad owners between the business collapse of the mid-1890s and the Panic of 1907 was one of unbridled optimism. This bullishness paralleled closely that euphoria that had permeated the industry throughout much of the 1880s. Not only were carrier consolidations popular during both periods, but in the trans-Mississippi West, especially, thousands of new lines opened for service. And unexecuted building schemes multiplied as well. In 1897, the final year of depression, the nation's railroad mileage totaled 188,844; a decade later it reached 236,949 miles.[1]

The newly created Chicago Great Western Railway

Company could not expect to grow immediately. The economic troubles of the mid-1890s essentially precluded acquisition of existing mileage or major line expansion. Yet the Stickney road still managed to enlarge its own system, albeit in a limited fashion; and it did so with considerable imagination.

DEKALB & GREAT WESTERN

DURING the depths of depression the Chicago Great Western concocted a successful plan to gain entrance into DeKalb, Illinois. This community of 2,579 could be easily reached by extending a six-mile branch south of Sycamore. DeKalb residents were hardly transportation starved; they benefited from the Chicago & North Western's (C&NW) Chicago to Omaha and Caledonia to Spring Valley lines, with the latter, in fact, passing through Sycamore. Yet, like so many others, the people of DeKalb wanted to break a railroad monopoly. This was of particular importance to the local wire industry which firmly believed that increased rail competition would yield lower rates. Furthermore, a Great Western connection would allow convenient access to the Twin Cities and the Northwest.[2]

An anemic company treasury forced the Great

Western to try to shift most of the initial financial burden to the DeKalb citizens. On March 13, 1895, town sponsors filed with the Illinois Secretary of State the required papers of incorporation for the DeKalb & Great Western Railway Company (D&GW). Raymond DuPay, a Stickney associate, formally joined the backers of the D&GW, and the CGW acquired a portion of the company's $100,000 of capital stock. A St. Paul contractor, Foley Brothers, quickly graded the right-of-way and laid the track. By October the creative synergy of the Chicago Great Western and the DeKalb interests resulted in multiple freight and passenger trains running daily between DeKalb and Sycamore. Soon the Chicago Great Western operated, albeit briefly, full-fledged suburban service between DeKalb, Sycamore, St. Charles, and Chicago. These were CGW movements; and so in December 1911, the firm at last officially absorbed the D&GW. The Maple Leaf's income of one third of the DeKalb station's earnings had by this time generated the financial means to purchase the remaining D&GW stock.[3]

Prior to the DeKalb & Great Western's corporate disappearance, the Stickney regime had toyed with the idea of vastly lengthening it. During the boom years of the new century, the D&GW's charter was amended so as to allow for a 120-mile extension to Peoria. At that time, rumor also hinted at the line's eventual entry into St. Louis. From various points it would send out spurs to tap mines in the rich central Illinois coal fields. But, in the end, other projects, seemingly more promising, blocked the D&GW from being more than just a puny appendage.[4]

MANTORVILLE RAILWAY & TRANSFER

ANOTHER undertaking that resembled the De-Kalb & Great Western was the Mantorville Railway & Transfer Company (MRy&T), launched seven months after the Illinois carrier. In 1889, the Chicago, St. Paul & Kansas City had opened a four-mile branch from Eden to Wasioja, Minnesota. De-signed largely to serve the rock industry, the line greatly stimulated local quarrying. Then, during the mid-1890s, the Mantorville Stone Company asked Stickney to provide service to its nearby namesake town. Mantorville itself eagerly joined the quest. This seat of Dodge County, founded in 1854, had never developed much beyond a sleepy village. Its 460 citizens longed to end their isolation and hoped that arrival of steam cars would trigger a boom. Just as the residents of DeKalb had faced the Great Western's request for a hefty financial commitment to a short line company, so did Mantorville's population. Notwithstanding the difficult times, the publisher of the *Mantorville Express* proclaimed in his issue of April 10, 1896, "Simply, the road will be built."[5]

In a classic illustration of community self-help, the people of Mantorville literally created the MRy&T themselves. Aided by an illegal appropriation of village funds, parties of able-bodied men shaped the 3.5 miles of roadbed on donated right-of-way east of Wasioja, constructed bridges and culverts, and erected the depot, earning stock in the firm for their efforts. And scores of citizens, probably those unable to do manual work, liberally subscribed to stock; these funds paid for rails, ties, and fastenings. By September the dirt grade awaited the steel; two months later, the road was finished. The delay in the arrival of a turntable, however, postponed the grand opening until Christmas.[6]

Although the MRy&T was originally home owned, residents agreed to surrender their assets to the Chicago Great Western, at the latter's insistence, in September 1896. Perhaps management feared that the Chicago & North Western might enter Mantorville and devour its friendly feeder. (The C&NW did, in fact, shortly send a spur into the Dodge County seat from Kasson.) The Mantorville line then became just a CGW branch. Rather than reaping possible dividends from the line, local backers simply acquired access to a railroad. "If any one has seen occasion to regret the investment so made," editorialized the *Mantorville Express,* "they have thus far failed to express it."[7]

Soon after the Great Western took formal possession of the Mantorville Railway & Transfer Company, talk of further expansion spread. The area press reported, indeed encouraged, tales that the parent company was about to push the line to Rochester, fourteen miles to the southeast, or even to Winona, a distance of fifty-three miles. These rumors continued until another event did much to squelch them. On June 1, 1899, the Great Western assumed operation of the Wisconsin, Minnesota & Pacific Railroad Company (WM&P), a firm that soon found its way into the system; and by 1901, this road served both Rochester and Winona, thus making any extension of the Mantorville branch a low priority at best.[8]

MINNESOTA CONQUESTS: THE WM&P

THE 276-mile Wisconsin, Minnesota & Pacific had an inordinately complicated past. By the time the Chicago Great Western formally leased the property early in the 1900s, it consisted of three distinct units: the so-called Cannon Valley Division; the Duluth, Red Wing & Southern Railroad Company; and the Winona & Western Railway Company. The Great Western physically connected these sections when it opened a twenty-six-mile line between Rochester and Zumbrota, Minnesota, on January 18, 1903.[9]

CANNON VALLEY DIVISION

THE Cannon Valley Division of the future Wisconsin, Minnesota & Pacific traced its beginnings to territorial days. On May 23, 1857, Minnesota's pioneer lawmakers passed "An Act to Incorporate the Minnesota Central Rail Road Company," yet the firm remained dormant until 1878. That year the Minnesota Central's home state owners acquired the Cannon River Improvement Company, another moribund corporation, that was chartered in 1865.

It held the rights to construction of a slackwater navigation network from the Mississippi River near Red Wing via the Cannon and Le Sueur rivers and intervening lakes to the Minnesota River at Mankato. In 1883, the legislature, recognizing that the iron horse would surely eclipse the steamboat as the principal means of transportation for freight and passengers, agreed to the wishes of stockholders and residents and allowed the Cannon River Improvement Company to enter the railroad business. Significantly, this change included the company's original rights to a land grant of 300,000 acres of "swamp land." The Minnesota Central had thus acquired a potentially valuable asset.[10]

Money and franchise troubles, however, hampered the start of construction. Survey crews finally located a line through the often rugged terrain between Red Wing and Mankato during the spring of 1882, and grading soon commenced. By August, 1,000 men and 200 teams of horses and mules were shaping the sixty-six miles of right-of-way southwestward from Red Wing through Cannon Falls, Northfield, and Faribault to a connection with the Minneapolis & St. Louis (M&StL) at Waterville. Crews speedily laid the rails, and service began by the year's end.[11]

Why the infant Minnesota Central ended twenty-eight miles shy of its announced destination of Mankato is unclear. When the property came under the control of the Chicago, Rock Island & Pacific (CRI&P) on January 1, 1883, the new steward conceivably caused the temporary halt. Its affiliate and the actual operator of the feeder, the Minneapolis & St. Louis, gained a useful main line connection. Waterville, then, marked an appropriate stopping point. Yet, Mankato, a bustling community of 4,440, offered much more. Not only did the Blue Earth County seat hold attractive traffic possibilities, especially as a producer of stone and brick, but its political clout in St. Paul had prompted the state to withhold 40,000 acres of the Cannon River Improvement Company's land grant until the project was finished.[12]

When the Minnesota Central, the soon-to-be

"Cannon Valley Division," at last reached Mankato in May 1887, it possessed another name, the Wisconsin, Minnesota & Pacific, for on August 14, 1883, a reorganization, instigated by the Rock Island, fused the Minnesota Central with the nearly completed "wheat line" or "Pacific Division" that spanned the 122 miles between Morton, Minnesota, and Watertown in Dakota Territory (now South Dakota). Yet fifty miles separated the two units of the newly created WM&P, and they never met, although the owners planned such a linkage. As with the Red Wing–Waterville–Mankato segment, the Rock Island turned the Pacific Division over to the M&StL to run. "The road was a separate entity on the statute books although Rock Island was emblazoned on some of the day coaches and M&StL employees took up tickets and operated the trains."[13]

The Cannon Valley Division failed as a moneymaker. In 1891, William H. Truesdale, the M&StL receiver, lamented that the line had never earned its operating costs. Only one daily (except Sunday) local passenger train and a poky peddler freight traveled between the Mankato and Red Wing terminals. And rail rivalries were keen. The Milwaukee (CM&StP) in particular sapped potential traffic; its thirty-six-mile Red Wing–Northfield branch competed directly with the Cannon Valley's eastern end. It was the Panic of 1893, however, that inflicted the knock-out punch. The mortgage holder, the Metropolitan Trust Company of New York, foreclosed; and on November 16, 1893, the Wisconsin, Minnesota & Pacific, including both the Cannon Valley and the Pacific divisions, was sold. It thereby came into the hands of President Ramson R. Cable of the Rock Island and his two colleagues, Truesdale and Albert E. Clarke, five months later. For the first time, the CRI&P owned, rather than controlled, the WM&P.[14]

The reign of the Rock Island over the reconstituted Wisconsin, Minnesota & Pacific lasted five years. Low earnings cooled the interest of the parent road. So, in 1899, the Minneapolis & St. Louis, now "liberated" from the CRI&P, purchased the Pacific Division; and soon the Chicago Great Western leased the Cannon Valley Division. The latter was not unexpected by those who closely watched the Minnesota railroad scene. Not only had A. B. Stickney, the one-time M&StL vice-president, supervised construction of the Minnesota Central, but he had bid on the Cannon Valley Division at the 1893 foreclosure sale. In the intervening years, Stickney and fellow CGW officials had kept a close eye on this trackage.[15]

Why the Great Western head sought the WM&P's eastern unit is relatively obvious. He believed that when fully developed these ninety-four wobbly, weed-covered miles could generate sizable volumes of feeder traffic. In particular, substantial carloadings of stone, lime, and cement from Mankato and clay products from Red Wing were anticipated. And the line might be further extended, perhaps into northern Iowa or western Minnesota, or even on to Montana. Stickney surmised that if the Maple Leaf Route upgraded the existing property, on-line boosters would surely embrace the company, routing business over his rails. Indeed, the local press universally applauded his endeavor. "Mr. Stickney is one of the ablest, clearest-headed railroad men in the west," ran the reaction, "and he recognized the advantages of the road and will see that they are utilized."[16]

Within two years, the Great Western would alter drastically its financial relationship with the WM&P. Rather than merely operating the road for the Rock Island shareholders, the company actually acquired the entire capital stock; however, it continued to run the WM&P as a separate entity.[17]

DULUTH, RED WING & SOUTHERN

INCLUDED in the 1901 restructuring process of the Wisconsin, Minnesota & Pacific was a small, one-time independent carrier, the Duluth, Red Wing & Southern (DRW&S). Typical of Midwestern short lines of the late nineteenth century, the "Duluth Route" once held grand expectations, which it achieved only in an extremely limited fashion.

Incorporated on October 26, 1886, by a group of Duluth and Red Wing investors, the DRW&S planned to serve the territory of its corporate name. Specifically, the "Most Important Projected Line in the Northwest" would depart Duluth in a southerly direction, passing through the Wisconsin communities of St. Croix Falls, New Richmond, and River Falls, crossing the Mississippi River at Red Wing, Minnesota, and continuing south through Zumbrota to Rochester. Between the latter two Minnesota towns the road would veer southeasterly to Owatonna and then turn south again through Geneva to Albert Lea. If constructed to this format, the Duluth Route would operate about 260 miles. An 1887 prospectus suggested that the road would ultimately tie Tower, in the far-reaches of northern Minnesota, to central Iowa, "terminating at or near either Tama or Des Moines." When finally completed, the DRW&S, according to its enthusiastic backers, "will connect the richest and most highly cultivated agricultural regions of Minnesota and Iowa, and the coalfields of the latter state with the Great Lakes affording a more direct and cheaper route to the Eastern markets and thus insuring a profitable business to the road."[18]

Duluth Route proponents longed for more than a thriving enterprise. Consisting mostly of small shippers from towns and farms along the anticipated route, these men of good hope viewed their "paper" company as a potentially lethal weapon in the ongoing war against the railroad "trust." To their way of thinking:

• • •

this road practically solves the question of competition in freight rates for the entire region in Iowa, and of Minnesota south and east of the Minnesota River, except for a short distance, it does not parallel any other road, but it cuts directly across every road between Chicago and Milwaukee and St. Paul and Minneapolis. . . . It was demonstrated long ago that the country could hope for no relief from exorbitant freight rates through parallel lines having the same general terminus. Self-preservation and common interest will always result in the pooling of rates over such lines. It is a fact of common conver-

Although carrying CGW markings and numbers, this small 4-4-0-type engine once served the Duluth, Red Wing & Southern as its #2. It is pictured here in the Red Wing yards shortly after the purchase. (William Armstrong Collection)

sation that as parallel lines of road multiply the relative rates increase.[19]

• • •

While potentially a money maker and a device to insure equitable transportation charges, the Duluth, Red Wing & Southern began to take shape very slowly. Survey teams entered the field and located an acceptable route between Duluth and Albert Lea by September 1887. And months before any construction bids were taken, the trade press reported that the company was considering a major change in its line projection. Instead of terminating in central Iowa, Sioux City, strategically situated on the Missouri River in the northwestern section of the Hawkeye State, would be the end point: "the consolidation of this project with the [paper] Sioux City & Northeastern has been practically agreed upon." Then, in August 1888, the Duluth Route let the contract for the 25.5-mile stretch between Red Wing and Zumbrota and soon announced that it expected to award another one for the Zumbrota to Albert Lea segment; Duluth and Sioux City would be reached later.[20]

Actual construction, however, began quickly. The contractor, Keating & Company of Pittsburgh, Pennsylvania, hurried to shape the grade before a January 1, 1889, deadline. By Thanksgiving the roadbed awaited rails; tracklaying then proceeded without delay. By mid-December, twenty miles had been installed south from Red Wing, but there the work stopped. A dispute between the DRW&S and the Keating Company led to the annulment of the latter's contract. The railroad immediately formed its own building affiliate, simply named The Construction Company, and the remaining 5.4 miles into Zumbrota were finished.[21]

The tiny Duluth, Red Wing & Southern dispatched its first train on May 7, 1889. Crammed with officials, dignitaries and supporters, this excursion special caused excitement and delight along the route. Six days later the carrier inaugurated regular revenue service. The maiden timetable listed two daily (except Sunday) mixed trains; running speed averaged a leisurely sixteen miles per hour. Within months the road drastically revamped its operations. It arranged two connecting through passenger trains for the Twin Cities via the CM&StP at Red Wing and for Rochester via the C&NW at Zumbrota.[22]

The beginning of the Duluth Route coincided with a deepening agricultural slump, which by 1890 had inflicted enormous financial losses on Minnesota farmers. Although the company extended a three-mile branch to "Clay Banks," which tapped rich deposits of sewer pipe and pottery clay, business—primarily agricultural traffic—lagged. Yet the DRW&S avoided receivership, largely by cutting operating costs to the bone. By 1891 the road's limited service so annoyed the editor of the *Stillwater Democrat* that he publicly blasted it as the "worst managed, worst equipped and unreliable bob-tail, one-horse, Jim-Crow railroad on the face of the North American continent."[23]

Irrespective of public relations problems, Duluth, Red Wing & Southern backers still wanted to expand. However, difficulites with Duluth citizens over right-of-way matters and, most of all, a $100,000 cash subsidy promised earlier led to the formation of a parallel company, the Superior, Red Wing & Southern. Dubbed the "Red Wing Road," its supporters—namely, parties interested in the DRW&S joined by a group of French investors—intended to make Duluth's next-door neighbor, Superior, Wisconsin, the northern terminus. The objec-

tive was to link the Wisconsin lake port with Red Wing. The road lacked plans to push on into Iowa, for that would be the prerogative of the DRW&S.[24]

The Superior, Red Wing & Southern venture seemed to hold considerable promise. With bonus money from Superiorites, the company awarded a contract in August 1891 to build six miles from West Superior to a connection with the Eastern Minnesota Railway, a Great Northern affiliate. The Red Wing Road would then lease trackage rights over that carrier to Kerrick, Minnesota, thirty-seven miles southwest of West Superior, and eventually construct its own route south through Stillwater and River Falls, Wisconsin, to Red Wing.[25]

While the Superior, Red Wing & Southern succeeded in completing the first segment of the grade, the economic paralysis caused by the Panic of 1893 halted further construction. In fact, the owners proceeded to liquidate their meager assets. Still, the Red Wing Road's sister enterprise (the DRW&S) limped along; a property ripe for corporate takeover. Why neither the North Western nor the Milwaukee absorbed the tiny line is unknown. But as soon as the Great Western could, it arranged for its acquisition, not in the Stickney company's name, but under the banner of the WM&P. The twenty-eight-mile Duluth, Red Wing & Southern officially entered the Maple Leaf system on July 5, 1901, for a price of several hundred thousand dollars.[26]

WINONA AND WESTERN

THE final component of the Wisconsin, Minnesota & Pacific was the Winona & Western Railway Company. Resembling in particular the Cannon Valley Division, this road too had a long and complex past. Technically it was born on February 26, 1856, when Minnesota's territorial lawmakers chartered the Winona & La Crosse Railroad Company (W&LC) to build from the booming Mississippi River village of Winona to a point opposite La Crosse, Wisconsin, a distance of approximately fifteen miles. The devastation wrought by the Panic of

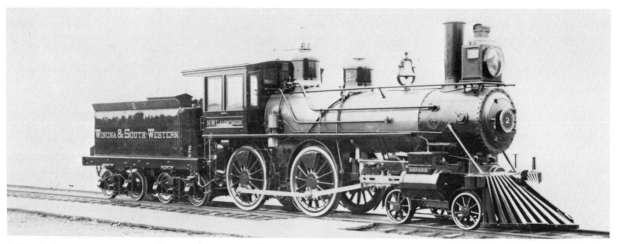

A Brooks locomotive company photographer caught this newly built 4-4-0 destined for service on the Winona & Southwestern. As was common in the late nineteenth century, this iron horse sported both a number and a name. It honored H. W. Lamberton, an organizer and stockholder of the W&SW. (Alco Historic Photos)

1857, however, prevented the W&LC from becoming anything more than a paper proposition for several decades.[27]

Just as A. B. Stickney would later breathe life into the charter of the Minnesota & Northwestern, a group of Winona businessmen early in the seventies energized the dormant Winona & La Crosse document. These budding railroaders, led by merchants H. W. Lamberton, M. G. Norton, and Thomas Simpson, sought to enhance their community's trading position by improving transportation connections with the surrounding hinterlands, specifically through a rail outlet to the southwest. They won legislative approval for two charter revisions, a name change (after February 29, 1872, the company was known as the Winona & Southwestern Railway [W&SW]), and, more importantly, the right to build southwesterly to the Iowa line.[28]

The reconstituted Winona & La Crosse got off to an auspicious start. Winona residents overwhelmingly approved a $150,000 bond issue at an April 9, 1872, special election. Other Winona County communities likewise voted construction subsidies. The Winona & Southwestern's good luck lasted only briefly, however. With the hard times that followed

the Panic of 1873, the project stalled, before even the first shovelful of earth could be turned.[29]

Since "going-it-alone" seemed hopeless during much of the 1870s, the Winona & Southwestern leadership toyed with a proposition presented to them by nearby railroad promoters. These small-town entrepreneurs wanted to construct a twenty-five mile narrow-gauge pike from the village of Hesper, Winneshiek County, Iowa, near the Minnesota boundary, to Houston, a hamlet in Houston County, twenty miles south of Winona. The Winona & Southwestern would run its line—presumably of slim width—to a Houston junction. Although construction costs for a narrow-gauge road would be relatively low, the Winona sponsors in time rejected this "hot-air" scheme, and thereby avoided a potentially disastrous situation. Not only would the Hesper-Houston route face difficulties in generating adequate traffic, but eventually it would have to convert to standard width. Midwest narrow-gauge operations rarely survived as such beyond the turn of the century.[30]

The next burst of activity came in 1887. The economy started showing signs of "permanent" strength, and Winonans continued to long for that

This winter view of a Winona & Western engine on a steel trestle near Rollingstone, Minnesota, fourteen miles west of Winona, dates from the late 1890s and shows the road's costly construction and maintenance problems. (Minnesota Historical Society)

"southwestern artery." Soon voters approved more funds; and a favorable bond market, coupled to a successful stock subscription drive, insured sufficient capital to launch construction. On August 11, 1888, the Winona Board of Trade held a traditional groundbreaking ceremony, even though crews had already tackled the arduous terrain. The first phase of building ran for twenty miles in a westerly arc through Minnesota City and Rollingstone to Bear Creek. Before spiking down the rails, workers installed twenty-six bridges, two of which measured an impressive 700 feet each in length and towered seventy to seventy-five feet above the valley floors. On November 23, 1888, three weeks before the company began service, management hosted a gala over-the-road excursion. This second celebration enjoyed widespread press attention. "The locomotive Winona No. 1 was decked with flags," reported the *Fort Dodge* (Iowa) *Messenger*. "There were 312

guests on board by actual count from Winona, and a few more were added at Rollingstone."[31]

The reason for the Iowa newspaper's interest in the physical development of the Winona & Southwestern relates directly to the current railroad speculation. For months, stories had circulated that the Winona-based firm was likely to evolve into something more than a plug-line operation. As early as May 1888, the *Chicago Times* had indicated that the aggressive leadership of the Delaware, Lackawanna & Western (DL&W) entertained the grand notion of becoming a transcontinental or, at least, a semi-transcontinental system. This seemed to be happening. Primarily a New York to Buffalo trunk carrier, the DL&W controlled the 200-mile Flint & Pere Marquette and had recently purchased the 250-mile Green Bay, Winona & St. Paul. According to the *Times*, the DL&W also held (it should have said sought) an interest in the James J. Hill—

controlled Mason City & Fort Dodge, a road that spanned the seventy-two miles between its namesake towns. If pushed the 140 miles between Winona and Mason City, the W&SW could serve as the vital connecting piece. And if the Mason City & Fort Dodge closed the 130-mile gap between Fort Dodge and Omaha, the DL&W would possess a monumental network, missing the Pacific Ocean by 1,700 miles, however, and relying on Great Lakes steamers for links between the home property and the affiliated roads.[32]

Gossip likewise spread that the Winona & Southwestern might jointly work with, even acquire, the Mason City & Fort Dodge, irrespective of the Delaware, Lackawanna & Western's intentions. And there was more. Thomas Simpson, the W&SW secretary, announced in a letter to the *Fort Dodge Messenger* his company's hope "to build also to Sioux City." Added Simpson, "We think our road will pay to reach the Missouri River at both points [Omaha and Sioux City]."[33]

For reasons that are unknown, the Delaware, Lackawanna & Western's relationship with the Winona & Southwestern dissolved by the early 1890s. Yet the Winona company did extend beyond Bear Creek, the 1888 stopping point. During the 1889 building season crews added eleven miles in a southerly direction through Altura and Bethany to Utica, site of an interchange with the Chicago & North Western's Winona to St. Peter main line.[34]

It appears that the enormous cost of crossing the hills and dales of southeastern Minnesota was deleterious to the W&SW's financial health. Rather than the anticipated $20,000 to $25,000 per mile price-tag, the bill averaged $35,000 per mile. The principal contractor, Foley Brothers, then of St. Cloud, Minnesota, withdrew in a dispute over payments; and backers launched the Winona & Southwestern Improvement Company to continue construction.[35]

Also, as commonly occurred, Winona & Southwestern directors in 1890 faced a tough decision about routing plans. The question centered not on the ultimate terminus but on which of two workable options immediately west of Utica should be se-

lected. A southern route included the prosperous Minnesota communities of Saratoga, Chatfield, and Spring Valley, while the northern one reached a thriving St. Charles but also the less dynamic Dover, Eyota, Marion, and High Forest. A spirited bidding war between the two sets of contenders ensued; the latter group, however, voted more bond and bonus money. Still, the extension was not permanently fixed. Rochester, the Olmsted County seat of 5,321, entered the contest. Naturally, it favored the northern route, being within ten miles of that projected line, for as a local paper noted, "if they decide to build through ... Chatfield and Spring Valley, it would be impossible to come here." By June 1890, Rochester lost its bid, probably for two reasons. Winona interests intensely disliked the threat that Olmsted County capital posed to the area's trade patterns. They wanted to keep the "back-country" exclusively their own preserve. Winona already boasted a population of 18,208, and its growth seemed unlimited. Moreover, the *original* northern path would mean lower construction costs. Noted a somewhat reconciled Rochester newspaperman, "The road will run from Dover Center southwest onto the high prairie, passing southwest of Marion Village ... thence to Stewartville and Spring Valley. The route is a very feasible one and the company find[s] an easy grade."[36]

The summer and fall months of 1890 saw laborers and teams shaping the right-of-way for the sixty-eight miles from Utica to McIntire, Iowa, and a connection with the Chicago, St. Paul & Kansas City. On Saturday, December 20, the tracklaying gang of about 100 strong reached Spring Valley, in western Fillmore County. The town gave the workers a regal welcome: "The mayor and city council of that place met the construction train as it entered the city limits at six o'clock, and escorted them into the city where a supper was given them." By the year's end, regularly scheduled freight and passenger trains journeyed the eighty miles from Winona to Spring Valley. Even though the countryside was already heavily settled, the coming of the rails spawned what would almost immediately be-

The Winona & Southwestern crossed the Chicago Great Western at McIntire, Iowa, and this busy location thus required a larger than average depot. In the 1890s the Great Western built this attractive structure that features a decorative tower. A hand-powered turntable is in the foreground, and a handsome 4-4-0-type engine stands to the left. (James L. Rueber Collection)

come an important grain shipping point, Simpson (named in honor of the company secretary), twenty-one miles from the end-of-track at that time.[37]

As soon as weather conditions allowed, the Winona & Southwestern Improvement Company's contractors prepared the Spring Valley to McIntire segment. Simultaneously, work progressed on the sixteen miles between McIntire and Osage. The latter community, seat of Mitchell County, voted a generous $25,000 bonus and offered both right-of-way through town and twenty acres of land near the business section for a station and yards. But the state's Attorney General indicated that Iowa law invalidated the balloting. Since the Winona & Southwestern possessed a "foreign" or non-Iowa charter, it was ineligible to receive subsidies unless it acquired incorporation papers from the Hawkeye State. Wanting the money, the directors had no choice but to send a representative to Des Moines to file for creation of a new firm, the Winona, Osage &

Southwestern Railway Company (WO&SW). The Iowa Secretary of State granted the request on May 22, 1891. In June, Osage citizens returned to the polls, and this time legally approved the funding.[38]

On a hot Thursday, August 6, 1891, the first Winona & Southwestern passenger train steamed along the 114-mile course from Winona to Osage. But, no rolling stock bearing the Winona, Osage & Southwestern herald ever entered the new southern terminus. That corporation conveyed its assets to the Minnesota company on October 20, 1891. Still, the WO&SW was more than a paper entity. During the year, it graded and railed a puny 1.37 miles of the Iowa Division west from Osage, ending on the deserted banks of the Red Cedar River. Although never operated, and removed a few years later, this trackage was headed toward Mason City, twenty-five miles to the southwest.[39]

Appearance of the tiny portion of the Winona, Osage & Southwestern materially indicated that Os-

The Winona & Southwestern built the Little Cedar, Iowa, depot in the early 1890s. Apparently, the community lacked adequate housing, so the company selected a design that included an up-stairs living area. Station stock pens, so common before the advent of motor trucks, are seen in the right background. (James L. Rueber Collection)

age was not intended to be the permanent stopping point. Surveyors had, in fact, journeyed throughout much of north central and western Iowa attempting to fix a suitable route (indeed routes) to the Missouri River. Shelby County's *Harlan Republican* revealed in early 1891 that a local minister had seen the W&SW's survey map and happily announced that the road's course from Fort Dodge (the Mason City & Fort Dodge's end-of-track) "is southwest through the counties of Green [*sic*], Carroll, Audubon, and Shelby towards Omaha." Later the same year the press reported that W&SW personnel traveled west from Mason City through Forest City and Esterville, toward a possible Sioux Falls, South Dakota, destination. While these two projections may be classified as preliminary, crews completed a final survey from the Red Cedar to Mason City. In fact, much of that right-of-way was purchased.[40]

The real estate work came to naught. Negotiations between the Winona owners and James Hill's Mason City & Fort Dodge collapsed, and once more

a sluggish economy, which turned even worse after the May 1893 panic, ruined chances for an expanded W&SW. With the coming of a full-fledged depression, the road entered receivership on November 21, 1893; it appeared on the auction block ten months later. The successful bidder was the old owner, H. W. Lamberton, and several of his colleagues. Within a month, these men officially reorganized the property as the Winona & Western Railway Company (W&W).[41]

For the next several years, the Winona & Western management conducted a holding action. Little work was done either to upgrade the physical plant or to acquire better equipment, and no new line construction occurred. With return of more prosperous times toward the end of the century, the balance sheet once more permitted the sending of surveyors into the field. No longer did they seek a way to Omaha or any other point on the Missouri River but instead merely examined the relatively level terrain north of Simpson to Rochester. On August 28,

Between 1899 and 1900 the Winona & Western pushed a seven-mile branch from its Winona-Osage main line into Rochester, Minnesota. This view shows work in an Olmsted County farm field. (Minnesota Historical Society)

1899, after the reports and maps arrived in Winona, the board unanimously agreed to build the 7.5-mile "air-line" extension. When it opened a year later, Rochester residents seemed pleased in finally gaining the Winona road. As the *Olmsted County Democrat* commented that October, "The railway yards are being macadamized with crushed stone hauled by the train-load from Winona and thus the place made better in all respects. With the Stevenson elevator, the Gates elevator, the Reiter potato house and the warehouse and depot all the result of the Winona & Western's coming to Rochester, this end of the city is made better looking and more business-like than could have been imagined." Concluded the paper, "Surely we have no reason to regret the building of this line from Simpson."[42]

But as with many other lines at this time, the Winona & Western officially lost its independence on September 10, 1901. The company entered the Stickney system as part of the Wisconsin, Minnesota & Pacific, as had the Duluth, Red Wing & Southern just two months before. On September 26, the W&W's operating personnel began to function under a merged command; train dispatching, for example, took place in Oelwein rather than Winona. Within a year, virtually all of the former W&W equipment bore the new owner's markings.[43]

A. B. Stickney had revealed his interest in the Winona railroad more than a decade before its acquisition. The *Minneapolis Tribune* argued in the fall of 1890 that the Maple Leaf Route leader saw value in the Winona & Southwestern as a possible tap to the "Iowa Coal fields," for the road "will at once continue operations southwest from Osage." While Stickney may have initially coveted the property for a dimension never achieved, its 121 miles did give him additional trackage conveniently tied to the Great Western's northern main stem. For access to the rich soft coal lands of the Hawkeye State, he turned to the Mason City & Fort Dodge, the Hill property so many saw to be the logical continuation of the W&SW.[44]

Construction workers enjoy a break from their labors in a camp along the Winona & Western's seven-mile line between Simpson and Rochester. This roadbed was easily shaped, and the extension opened in 1900. (Minnesota Historical Society)

MASON CITY AND FORT DODGE

ALTHOUGH the Mason City and Fort Dodge Rail Road was not incorporated until June 10, 1881, the idea of a seventy-two-mile rail link between the two north Iowa county seats of the company's title had existed for a decade. In fact, Mason City interests organized the Mason City and Fort Dodge Rail*way* Company on September 4, 1871, to provide "direct communication with the best coal field of Iowa and the large scope of country southwest." Predictably, hope for the firm's future initially ran high. "The enterprise is in the hands of reliable, go-ahead men who will leave nothing undone to insure the success of the project." While the infant firm made plans to build the thirty-three miles between Mason City and Belmond in order to connect with the developing Iowa Pacific—the Mississippi to Missouri via Fort Dodge project—and concurrently sold some stock, the Panic of 1873 stymied the venture.[45]

Then, in 1881, in the midst of a nationwide railroad construction boom, the "Mason City Road" scheme revived. New incorporation papers were drawn (this time for the Mason City & Fort Dodge Rail *Road*), stock subscribed, and several tax levies voted along the projected route. As with the previous attempt, local backers dominated the enterprise. Still, the dream of a Mason City to Fort Dodge trafficway went unfulfilled at this time, principally because of inadequate funding.[46]

Aid eventually came, however. James J. Hill, the aggressive founder-head of the St. Paul, Minneapolis & Manitoba, core of the future Great Northern system, turned his attention to the Hawkeye State. Since he owned coal properties in north central Iowa, a railroad that would help to tie them directly with the Twin Cities understandably attracted him. At that time, Iowa's largest producing mines, those near

What Cheer in Keokuk County, were quite far from the Minnesota marketplace and hence made coal a relatively expensive commodity. Thus Hill hoped to turn his holdings into a major, dependable source of cheap locomotive fuel. His financial presence, together with extensive community and township bonuses, provided sufficient capital for construction.[47]

Crews entered the field in late March 1886, with the advent of warm weather, and their tasks were not particularly arduous. The general terrain, since it was rolling prairie, could be quickly shaped; and only the narrow Iowa and Boone rivers required substantial bridges. Indeed, a sizable portion of the right-of-way already existed, having been built by the ill-fated Iowa Pacific in 1872. Acquired for the modest price of $20,000, this so-called Duncombe grade stretched for nearly forty weed-choked miles from Belmond southwesterly through Clarion and Eagle Grove to Fort Dodge. The principal contractor, Henry & Balch of Minneapolis, started in Fort Dodge and worked at repairing the eighteen miles of grade northeastward to Eagle Grove; the firm also began carving out a fifteen-mile branch southeast from Fort Dodge to Lehigh, nestled beside the Des Moines River in the coal lands of Webster County.[48]

Soon other laborers turned their attention to the northeastern portion of the main line. In April, Belmond became the base of operations. "The location [of the line] from Belmond to Mason City is about complete," wrote Hamilton Browne, a Hill associate and adviser in Iowa railroad and coal matters. "Grading will commence on the 19th from Belmond east and from Mason City west by 28th inst. We have a satisfactory line. Maximum grade 0.8 and curve 4° with amount of earth work inside my estimate." Repairs were swiftly made on the old Iowa Pacific grade southwestward toward Eagle Grove, and the new right-of-way was pushed toward Mason City.[49]

Construction progressed rapidly. By early summer the track work was done on the Fort Dodge to Eagle Grove segment. On July 1, limited revenue service began, and the Fort Dodge Messenger could claim that the initial portion of the Mason City & Fort

Dodge was "first class in all respects." Such a conclusion likely was merited. "The result of using the old grade is very apparent to one in riding over the line," explained the paper, "for it is so settled and smooth that it rides like an old ballasted thoroughfare." Throughout the remaining summer months and into the fall, work continued at a brisk pace. In mid-October the contractor finished the Clarion to Mason City section, and only a seven-mile gap awaited steel. Then, on Sunday, October 24 at 10:30 in the morning "out between Eagle Grove and Clarion," the Mason City road became an "accomplished fact." The first through passenger train made its way between Fort Dodge and Mason City eight days later. The fifteen-mile Lehigh branch and a nearby eight-mile spur from Carbon Junction to Coalville, however, did not open officially until early 1887.[50]

James J. Hill's involvement with the Iowa railroad was missed at first by the regional press. Journalists repeatedly talked about Des Moines capitalist Hamilton Browne as the "Napoleon for the enterprise." Admittedly, Browne held stock in the Mason City road, but he owned only slightly more than seven percent. Hill, on the other hand, possessed forty percent, and the remaining shares were in the hands of his non-Iowa friends. After Hill, the largest single investor was his close business partner John S. Kennedy of New York City who controlled about thirty-five percent of the firm. Yet, a Fort Dodge newspaper duly reported in November 1886 that the local road had received the first of its new engines from the shops of the Manitoba road, a positive public indication of the Hill connection.[51]

Whether the public knew or cared about Hill's relationship with the newly opened Mason City & Fort Dodge is not recorded. Residents in the general service territory, however, surely thought that the pike held great promise, that it would likely emerge as something more than a ninety-two-mile short line. Even before the Mason City & Fort Dodge finished its main stem, residents of Dayton, eight miles southwest of Lehigh, talked about extending the road to their thriving village, one that had just re-

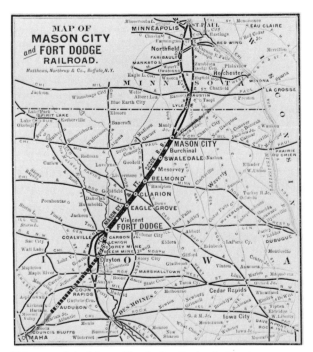

This map of the Mason City & Fort Dodge Railroad, a property controlled by James J. Hill, dates from the late 1880s and reveals printed and pencil projections to Winona on the northeast and to Omaha on the southwest. (James J. Hill Papers)

cently welcomed the arrival of the Minneapolis & St. Louis from Fort Dodge. Similarly, agitation for the carrier developed in Calhoun County, immediately west of Fort Dodge. But more voices were heard for connection of the Mason City & Fort Dodge with the Missouri River, Council Bluffs and Omaha, or perhaps Sioux City, and after the Winona & Southwestern took shape, with that route. Apparently the Mason City road did explore suitable paths. The *Gowrie Register* in March 1887 revealed that a surveying party had arrived in the community and confidently told its readership that the railroad "is to be extended from Lehigh to Council Bluffs, via Gowrie, Jefferson, and Templeton, providing the necessary aid is given, i.e., either a 5 percent tax or by private subscription."[52]

While route speculation continued, the Mason City & Fort Dodge merely turned toward exploiting on-

line resources. Perhaps its most important work dealt with spawning several settlements. Directly engaged in the townsite business, the company boomed four communities between Mason City and Belmond: Burchinal, Swaledale, Thornton, and Meservey (originally named Mt. Vernon, Pleasant Valley, Grimes, and Elm Lake, respectively). It also promoted Vincent, initially called Newark, eight miles southwest of Eagle Grove. Fortunately, the company's entry into the town development business proved moderately successful. While Burchinal failed to evolve much beyond the sleepy hamlet stage, the other settlements grew into bustling villages, good sources of passenger and freight traffic. This largely occurred not because these places attracted "live-wires" but because the "region . . . was practically unsettled before the road was built."[53]

James J. Hill's control of the Mason City & Fort Dodge continued for nearly two decades. Perhaps he erred in retaining the property for that long. Iowa coal failed to meet the Great Northern's enormous needs, and the short line showed a general inability to turn much of a profit. It was no great surprise then that Hill and his partners sold out in March 1901. The Chicago Great Western purchased the outstanding stock and bonds of the Mason City road and the assets of the principal mining operation, the Webster County Coal Company near Fort Dodge, for $1,500,000.[54]

Some railroad observers had expected another buyer. Reports had circulated widely that the Chicago, Milwaukee & St. Paul keenly desired Hill's possession, for that company contemplated a St. Paul to Des Moines line. The Milwaukee already operated the 140 miles from the Twin Cities to Mason City and the forty-one miles from Des Moines to Boone. By acquiring the Mason City road it would merely have to span the intervening twenty-five miles from Lehigh to Boone. The CM&StP could benefit, too, from a better route from the Twin Cities to Omaha, for the Boone branch crossed its Chicago to Omaha main line at Madrid. The company failed not so much because the Mason City & Fort Dodge "has been held at so high a figure by J. J. Hill" but due to the closeness between the heads of the Great Northern and Great Western.[55]

James J. Hill and A. B. Stickney were not only neighbors on St. Paul's exclusive Summit Avenue, but they shared an "affinity" for one another. Hill had admired the spunky Stickney since their days together fashioning the Canadian Pacific, and the "Empire Builder" had found Stickney reasonable as leader of the Maple Leaf, whose road provided the Great Northern useful access into Chicago and Kansas City. Stickney, too, liked and respected Hill and knew, of course, that friendship paid handsome dividends in the business world.[56]

Acquisition of the Mason City & Fort Dodge by the Chicago Great Western made sense. The Hill property could be incorporated conveniently into the Great Western by spanning territory at two points: the nine miles between Manly Junction and Mason City and the twenty-seven miles from Hampton to Clarion. Entry into Fort Dodge, moreover, made it easier to reach the Missouri River country. As early as 1893, the *Chicago Tribune* reported that Hill and Stickney met in the Windy City to discuss a route into the Omaha gateway. "The plan is to use the line of the Mason City & Fort Dodge . . . and to construct a new line from Fort Dodge to Council Bluffs. This will . . . give a direct route to Omaha from St. Paul and Chicago, a matter that has been much sought by the management of the Great Western company." While the depression in the 1890s curtailed any major construction, the prosperity of the new century made access to Nebraska a likely, indeed, a prompt reality.[57]

THE OMAHA EXTENSION

A WESTERN extension marked the Chicago Great Western's last major construction. Even before the company pocketed the Mason City road, it carefully scouted the Iowa countryside for suitable routes to both Sioux City and Omaha. Sioux City, with a population of 33,111, thrived as a point of considerable grain and cattle trade and as a developing meat-packing center, while the latter metropolis of 102,555 enjoyed being one of the nation's premier rail centers. When the economy rebounded at the end of the century, Stickney ordered numerous surveys. Considerable work occurred west of Hampton, the end-of-track in the vicinity and a logical starting point. In 1898 and 1899, routes were drawn from there to Sioux City. While the first one totaled approximately 170 miles and ran through Webster City and then west, a second went through Clarion, Humboldt, and Storm Lake, about a dozen fewer miles. A preliminary line was also run from Hampton to Omaha, via Webster City, a 170-mile survey known commonly as the Northern Route. At the same time, a crew selected a proposed path from East Peru, thirty miles southwest of Des Moines, west for 120 miles to the Nebraska gateway. This so-called Southern Route held an edge over the northern one: it was fifty miles shorter, passed through territory "little occupied by lines," and would not conflict with the Illinois Central's 131-mile extension from Tara (Fort Dodge) to Council Bluffs, opened in 1899. But all the survey work soon needed to be reexamined in light of the Mason City & Fort Dodge acquisition. Fort Dodge now emerged as the obvious beginning spot. While the Southern Route had some undeniable advantages, the Mason City road offered a less expensive and more convenient way to enter *both* Sioux City and Omaha. In no way could the East Peru path logically be made to reach Sioux City, although a line from Fort Dodge to Omaha, while slightly longer, could tap areas not directly served extensively either by the Illinois Central or by other carriers.[58]

With Fort Dodge fixed as the jumping-off point, events moved rapidly. For one thing, A. B. Stickney arranged for construction of a 9.13-mile connection between the company's end-of-tracks at Manly Junction and Mason City. Trains started to move over this vital segment on November 1, 1901. Simultaneously, he ordered surveyors to locate the best avenue to Omaha; a line would be mapped to Sioux City later. Immediately, shouts of "rod up!"

could be heard on the prairies of southwestern Iowa, and surely the echoes of that frequent call must have reverberated through the hills and valleys directly east of Council Bluffs. The Maple Leaf chief demanded that no routing errors be made. Never financially robust, the road could ill afford mistakes. The desire to make the company competitive with the five other carriers that already linked Chicago with Omaha seemed the guiding factor.[59]

Two routes got foremost consideration. The longer one would run south and southwest from Fort Dodge, passing through Gowrie, Jefferson, Coon Rapids, Audubon, and Harlan before reaching Council Bluffs and Omaha. The other would follow a nearly perfect southwesterly diagonal between the two terminals. Only the county seats of Carroll and Harlan would be served, together with a handful of sleepy villages spawned by the Chicago & North Western when it completed its thirty-five-mile Carroll to Kirkman branch in 1881, extended to Harlan eighteen years later.[60]

Shortly, Stickney and the board of directors agreed to follow the "air-line" proposal. The Great Western would have the second longest span between Chicago and Omaha, but its length would be only twenty miles more than the North Western and the Milwaukee, the most direct roads. As for the Minneapolis to Omaha path, the projection would become the shortest line, fifteen miles less than the Omaha Road's (Chicago & North Western). The rejection of the "settled" or "county seat" route likely occurred, however, for reasons other than its somewhat longer distance. As the officials knew, choosing existing communities often increased construction costs dramatically, a factor that partially explained the avoidance of most established towns when a Des Moines to St. Joseph line was surveyed in the 1880s. While local subsidies might be forthcoming, the expense of having to acquire homes and businesses escalated construction charges. (When the Omaha Extension passed through Carroll and Council Bluffs, the large volume of structures that had to be purchased and then either razed or moved proved burdensome in terms of price and time.)

Since the CGW's chosen route would slice through several areas of limited settlement, opportunities actually developed for townsite promotion. And Stickney also had his eyes set on Sioux City, for a line that left Fort Dodge in a more westerly rather than southerly direction provided a more convenient, less expensive way to that destination. The Des Moines River Valley near Fort Dodge required construction of a massive bridge, so if one were built that could accommodate both projects, substantial savings would accrue.[61]

The new trackage would be built by the Omaha & Sioux City Extension Syndicate. This association held considerable potential for lucrative dealings with the Chicago Great Western. Not surprisingly, Stickney and his financial associates, including the long-time English investors, made up the group. The Maple Leaf head and his backers also decided to retain the Mason City & Fort Dodge corporation. This firm would issue construction bonds and pay the coupons from gross earnings. Any surplus, however, would belong to the parent Great Western. The CGW would also operate the Mason City road, for it had become a wholly owned subsidiary; the Great Western had accepted the stock of the MC&FD on a share-for-share exchange. Soon this proprietary organization, the so-called West End, would consist of 375 miles of track that linked Hayfield, Minnesota, with Omaha, Clarion with Oelwein, and Fort Dodge with Lehigh and nearby mines. But before the CGW finished juggling the ownership of these properties, it incorporated the Mason City & Fort Dodge *Railway* Company on June 13, 1902. Designed to hold temporarily the Great Western's Hayfield to Mason City and Hampton to Waverly lines, this firm supervised construction of the 29.3-mile "Waverly Cut-off" between Waverly and Oelwein that opened on October 17, 1903. Then, on April 13, 1905, the 118 miles owned by the MC&FD *Railway* Company were transferred to the MC&FD *Railroad* Company, which had undergone a name change from the Mason City & Fort Dodge *Rail Road* Company to the Mason City & Fort Dodge *Railroad* on May 2, 1904.[62]

Construction began on the 133-mile link between Fort Dodge and Omaha in August 1901. Three contractors secured the principal assignments. The old Stickney favorite, Winston Brothers of Minneapolis, won the 40.3-mile segment from Carroll to Harlan and subsequently the 43.5-mile span from Harlan to Council Bluffs. McArthur Brothers, the well-known Chicago-based railroad builder, received the right to shape thirty-four miles of the Fort Dodge to Carroll line; and the H. Shugart Company got the remaining fourteen-mile section. Bates & Rogers Construction Company of Chicago signed the contract for bridges and culverts.[63]

The contractors and their various subcontractors faced a formidable task. The terrain was at times extremely rough, despite the fact that it was mostly prairie country. The bluffs presented the greatest challenge. These imposing loess hills, several miles east of the Missouri River, gave magnificent testimony to the work of ancient winds that had deposited countless tons of clay, sand, and silt. The line, also, was to be built to high standards. "There will be some . . . heavy work, owing to the fact that the road will often disregard hills and streams in its efforts to get short cuts."[64]

Fortunately, the technology of the dawning century made such labor less challenging than in times past. The press gave extensive coverage to the machinery employed; for example, the *Daily Nonpareil* reported:

• • •

Along a section five miles long and extending from Council Bluffs around the bluffs to the east and northeast 150 men are busy bringing the railroad. That the 150 men are there instead of 100 times that number is one of the wonders of the present. Twenty years ago 150 men put on a five mile section of heavy railroad grading would hardly have made a scratch in the right of way at the end of a year's time. Yet today the 150 men are making the dirt fly in a yellow stream, and before the first of November [1902] a broad and level highway will extend along the entire length of this section.

This is because muscle has been superseded by machinery and ingenuity in the railroad making

"On to Omaha!" This oft-repeated cry symbolized the Great Western's thrust to the Missouri River that occurred between 1901–1903. Pictured is the tracklaying crew of McArthur Brothers near Lohrville in Calhoun County. (Kathryne McDonald Collection)

business. Where a hundred men toiled with shovels two decades ago, two men pull levers on a steam shovel today. Miniature railways take the place of teams where the work is heavy. Even the scrapers, though they are still in use, are not the old hand scrapers of the past, but wheeled affairs, which are operated without exertion on the part of the man in attendance save for the profanity necessary to keep the mules in good running order. It is safe to say that the building of the Great Western extension will be accomplished almost entirely without severe manual labor, at least in the grading. The man with the shovel is a rarity in a grading camp nowadays.[65]

• • •

Just as modern equipment shaped the right-of-way of the Omaha Extension, sophisticated machinery installed the rail. A complex tracklaying device finished about two and one-half miles a day, and by mid-November 1902, seventy-five-pound steel connected Carroll with Fort Dodge. As the track equipment moved steadily toward the Missouri River, ballasting and fence gangs followed.[66]

Regular passenger service over the newly laid sections awaited completion of the 2,582-foot Des Moines River Valley viaduct at Fort Dodge, one of the longest spans in the Midwest. Surveys had begun in July 1901, with the sub-structure erection occur-

Several employees of Winston Brothers, the principal contractor for the Carroll–Council Bluffs portion of the Omaha Extension, proudly display a tusk that probably belonged to an ancient woolly mammoth. The photograph, taken at Harlan in 1902, shows the "modern" earthmoving machinery that drew widespread attention as the line moved through the undulating countryside. (James L. Rueber Collection)

ring during the following summer. The superstructure work started in October and was sufficiently completed to allow a ceremonial first train to cross on March 14, 1903. While the cost was considerable, approximately $450,000, there was no loss of life so common to such projects, and the most serious accident was the severing of a workman's finger.[67]

With the bridge open, the Mason City & Fort Dodge started operations from Fort Dodge to Carroll. The initial movement, a mixed train, made its run on May 2, 1903. By July, the road extended this "accommodation" service to Harlan. Soon thereafter the first passenger consist traveled the entire length to Council Bluffs. It was not revenue varnish but Stickney's private car attached to a high-stepping American standard locomotive. This run took place on July 15 and covered the 133 miles in slightly over five hours, "exceptionally good time to make on a new road." Scheduled passenger service between Fort Dodge and Council Bluffs commenced on September 1. Then, after the Maple Leaf hammered out a bridge- and trackage-rights agreement with a reluctant Union Pacific and made arrangements for rental space in Omaha's Union Station, trains finally terminated west of the Missouri River beginning November 7, 1903.[68]

When the first passenger train rolled over the Omaha Extension, it crossed a high-quality piece of trackage. The regional press agreed with the company that the "roadbed has been built with a view toward securing safety and speed." The *Council Bluffs Daily Nonpareil*, in particular, adored the freshly completed transportation artery: "The Great Western, built with its wide roadbed, roomy cuts, easy grades and slight curves, . . . impresses the most casual observer that its builders planned a railroad in the fullest sense, without regard to expense."[69]

To make the Omaha Extension run efficiently and to maximize earnings, the Chicago Great Western embarked on a variety of projects. In September 1903, it let a contract for a twenty-four stall round-house on donated land at Clarion, much to the anger of Fort Dodge residents. Their leaders quickly reminded Stickney that under terms of the franchise granted Hill's MC&FD "no shop could be erected within a distance of 65 miles." Although the round-house was not a shop, Great Western officials wanted "to avoid giving offense to all concerned by increasing their already extensive plant at Oelwein," demonstrating that the Clarion facility was not to do much more than make minor repairs. If there continued to be rankled feelings, Fort Dodgers felt much better when they learned in 1905 that the railroad planned a splendid $60,000 depot for their community. And the CGW also turned to land im-provement. In the same month that it awarded the Clarion job, the road consummated a major real estate deal near the commercial heart of Omaha. These five blocks in a "thickly populated" area cost $250,000 and gave the company a strategic site for freight yards and terminal facilities. By far the most important step in developing the Omaha Extension, however, was its formation of the Iowa Townsite Company (ITC).[70]

IOWA TOWNSITE COMPANY

IN areas devoid of settlement, the Chicago Great Western's new townsite affiliate splendidly met the task of creating needed communities. Established on July 10, 1901 (under the laws of Minnesota) with a modest $10,000 of capital stock, the Iowa Townsite Company consisted of five organizers, all loyal Stickney lieutenants. Later, the railroad itself ac-quired the securities. According to the company's charter, "its business shall be the buying, owning, improving, selling and dealing in lands . . . , and laying out town sites, subdividing lands into town lots, streets and alleys, and improving the same, and selling such lots," functions typical of similiar firms of this period.[71]

Townsite personnel scoured the countryside for choice locations for development as soon as the route from Fort Dodge to Omaha was fixed. Noth-ing was to be left to chance. "The old system of letting settlements spring up here and there wherever [there] happened to be an oasis on the desert has been side tracked forever for a more scientific method." Specifically, the Iowa Townsite Company considered several matters in its so-called scientific approach to community-making. An acceptable site needed to abut a prosperous farming area; it must not be too close to established towns; and it should be at the "right frequency" along the route, for stations needed to be at least five miles apart.[72]

The first of the Maple Leaf's new communities along the Omaha Extension was Lanesboro in northeastern Carroll County. This place seemed es-pecially promising, for it was the sole point in Iowa that lacked urban competition within a dozen miles. Early in March 1902, the Iowa Townsite Company purchased 280 acres from farmer George Lane, and for the next several months workers readied the site. By fall, the town of Lanesboro began to take shape. On October 4, 1902, the company filed the town plat, and three days later it held a gala sale. Hun-dreds flocked to the event, undoubtedly convinced that "it will be one of the best new townsites ever offered to the public as a business or residence loca-tion." Unlike at subsequent auctions, buyers had to come by buggy and farm wagon; the rail line was still under construction, and the Fort Dodge viaduct awaited completion. The sale itself was typical, however, for the art of townlot disposal had been developed fully. After a hearty, free lunch served in a designated, but as yet undeveloped public park, participants crowded around a large chalkboard that showed lot numbers and locations. Bidding was brisk for the best commercial properties and also active for the choice residential ones. The day's events were encouraging: about ninety lots sold at

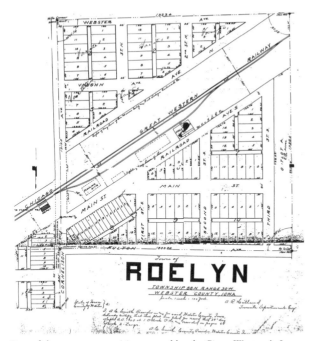

One of the new communities created by the Great Western's Iowa Townsite Company was Roelyn in Webster County near Fort Dodge. The official plat indicates how the railroad dominated the town. (H. Roger Grant Collection)

Two crewmen stand by their steel steed in the Clarion, Iowa, yards early in the century. The 4-4-0 style of motive power was particularly effective on light, fast "varnish" runs. (Rex C. Beach Collection)

prices that ranged from $155 to $340 for businesses and about half that for homes, depending in both cases upon location. And the company peddled additional parcels, mostly residential, during the following months. Soon this "beautiful new town site [that] sits like a queen on the magnificent prairie" saw a platoon of carpenters, masons, and painters start work. By March 1903 the *Oelwein Register,* the unofficial voice of the CGW's activities in the Hawkeye State, reported that "we are in receipt of volume 1, number 1 of the Lanesboro Journal . . . showing the development of Lanesboro from last October when the site was a prairie without a house till the present when it has a newspaper, bank, grain elevators, lumber yards, stores, saloons, schoolhouse, and about 500 population." Concluded the *Register,* "Another town made by the Chicago Great Western Railway."[73]

Lanesboro became the pride of the Maple Leaf,

but the Iowa Townsite Company continued its organizing efforts. Soon the company announced that it planned to launch eight additional places. These "scientifically selected" localities included Roelyn (Webster County), Rinard and Wightman (Calhoun County), Lidderdale (Carroll County), Tennant (Shelby County), and Bentley, McClelland, and Gilliat (Pottawattamie County). Between July 21, 1903 (for Lidderdale) and June 21, 1904 (for Rinard), the customary real estate auctions occurred, and the infant towns immediately took shape. The firm, too, developed two sites along the Clarion to Oelwein line, Coulter (Franklin County) and Readlyn (Bremer County).[74]

From the evidence available, the overall financial operations of the Iowa Townsite Company appear to have been profitable. Indeed, the cost of acquiring, surveying, and grading sites was reasonable, and the firm employed only a small staff. But more important, "Iowa's new communities" generated considerable freight and passenger traffic. In an age when the flanged wheel and not the rubber tire symbolized intercity travel, these towns served as vital trade centers, tapping prosperous and well-populated hinterlands. And it follows that some Great Western personnel reaped personal benefits from the labors of this captive corporation, for they shared directly in the proceeds of these town lot sales.

In order to serve both the Omaha Extension and other portions of the Mason City & Fort Dodge (Western Division), the Stickney regime constructed a roundhouse and other support facilities in Clarion, Iowa. Workers maneuver engine #15 on a hand-powered turntable in 1909. (W. L. Heitter Collection)

Big profits, however, would never come from the Iowa Townsite Company. But there was a lucrative firm. The syndicate that built the Omaha Extension, the Manly Junction to Mason City and Hampton to Clarion connections, and the Waverly cutoff sold these lines to the Mason City road corporation for an immense sum. The syndicate's bill totaled $11,575,416; and, in return for this cash outlay, it received $8,366,917 of four percent first mortgage bonds from the MC&FD and a whopping $30,089,034 of Chicago Great Western securities, specifically, preferred "B" and common stock. While the railroad omitted the details in its annual reports, the trade and financial press discussed them at length. The *Railroad Gazette* concluded that "this seems a most extravagant method of financing . . . and can only be explained on the English theory of turning over all profits at once to security holders while providing for all new expenditures by issues of additional capital." This evalua-

tion was correct, and soon the road's owners realized the errors of their ways.[75]

SEEKING SIOUX CITY

EVEN though the early years of the twentieth century marked the last major burst of steam railroad construction in the Midwest, the Chicago Great Western dreamed up wonderful additions to what had become a 1,500-mile network. While the Fort Dodge to Omaha trackage was actually the last substantial addition to the Maple Leaf system, the road *nearly* succeeded in also building the Sioux City Extension. In 1901, the Stickney people announced their commitment to the project, a plan they had discussed seriously since the early 1890s. Although surveyors' stakes marked several different paths, the company finally made its selection. The route would veer west from the future Omaha line at Somers, a village in eastern Calhoun County, sixteen miles southwest of Fort Dodge, thence through Rockwell City, Sac City, and Ida County to Anthon, where it would follow the survey of the stillborn St. Louis, Iowa & Pacific into the Woodbury County terminus. Running for 115 miles, this extension would provide the CGW the shortest distance between Sioux City and Chicago — 488 miles. The three other direct competitors all faced significantly larger mileages: the Illinois Central's route measured 510 miles, while the C&NW and the CM&StP each traveled 517 miles.[76]

During the next several years, there were positive indications that the Sioux City Extension would become a reality. In July 1902 the Great Western not only added the proposed line to its published map, but it also secretly bought the Sioux City Traction Company. Subsequently, the CGW acquired gravel-pit sites at several points along the projected span and eighty acres of real estate in Sioux City itself. However, after 1904, only rumors of the extension's intended construction were heard. Two years later the official statement of intentions was made by Stickney: "We have given up building the projected Sioux City line, though it was dropped with much reluctance. . . . The reason was the big expense of construction. It would have been one of the most costly pieces of road in Iowa or the middle west, more expensive than the Omaha line."[77]

The fact that the Maple Leaf delayed announcing its decision to abandon efforts to reach Sioux City is curious, and the explanations for this decision are unclear. There is reason to believe that the carrier had its eyes on the Newton & Northwestern Railroad (N&NW), a 103-mile short line, which opened in 1904, connecting Newton, east of Des Moines, with Rockwell City. The owners of this road planned to build to Sioux City and even talked of pushing southeast from Newton to St. Louis. Because the N&NW had been developed by Hamilton Browne, James J. Hill's former partner in the Mason City & Fort Dodge, Stickney may have thought that a buy-out could be easily arranged and that Browne

expected this eventuality. After all, the N&NW would fit into the Great Western's system; it crossed the Omaha Extension at Rinard, four miles southwest of Somers, and intersected the Kansas City line at Mingo. But no arrangement was made between the CGW and the N&NW except that the N&NW became a friendly feeder when by 1910 it had evolved into the Fort Dodge, Des Moines & Southern Railroad, an electric interurban.[78]

Another possible explanation for postponing the Sioux City project was the need to consider another routing possibility. Rumors circulated in 1905 that the Great Western wanted to shift the line to a more southeasterly direction. Carroll, not Somers, would then be the meeting point on the Omaha Extension. And construction could continue on through the county seat communities of Guthrie Center, Greenfield, and Creston to a Kansas City connection at Arispe in southern Union County. The reasoning behind this possibility seemed sound: the road could tap an area with "very poor" rail facilities, and the company could secure the through haul on much of the large volume of grain and livestock from the northwest by diverting it to Kansas City instead of permitting it to flow to Chicago and "allow other lines to get the benefit of the business."[79]

OTHER GREAT EXPECTATIONS

MAPLE Leaf personnel busied themselves with thoughts of other construction. Apparently the old dedication to "stem" rather than "branch" was going to be partially abandoned. The desire for more on-line generated traffic had increased. Stories appeared in 1901 that the system would extend the Mason City & Fort Dodge's Lehigh appendage south to Des Moines. The same year the public read of the possibilities of a New Hampton to La Crosse, Wisconsin, link, and later of completion of the once-started Osage to Mason City segment. In 1903, the CGW ordered surveyors to locate a cut-off between Reinbeck and Dubuque. By building through southern Black Hawk, Buchanan, and Delaware counties, the CGW could reduce its distance between Chicago and Des Moines and Kansas City by about twenty-five miles. And such construction would attract additional local business.[80]

Stickney entertained two more ideas for rail expansion in Iowa. One was another cut-off, the other a feeder. In 1903, the company attempted to close a deal for the purchase of the Des Moines, Iowa Falls & Northern Railway, a 70-mile pike that had opened that same year between Des Moines and Iowa Falls. By merely extending track for about thirty miles northeasterly through Hampton and then northwesterly to Thornton on the Mason City–Omaha line, the Great Western could reduce its Twin Cities to Kansas City run by close to sixty miles, or nearly two hours. But this locally owned project soon fell into the hands of the powerful Chicago, Rock Island & Pacific, which quickly fused it into that company's successful Twin Cities to Kansas City short line.[81]

Coinciding with his interest in the Des Moines, Iowa Falls & Northern, Stickney did acquire the franchise and real estate of the Des Moines & Southern Railroad Company, a "paper" line which connected Lida, sixteen miles southwest of Des Moines (and a station on the CGW) with the county seats of Winterset and Greenfield to the west. Perhaps the Great Western envisioned this property as a useful supplier of local traffic or maybe even another avenue to the Omaha gateway. Although one trade publication reported that "the contracts made between the Callahan Brothers and Katz Company of Omaha and the Des Moines & Southern for building the line have been taken over by . . . Stickney and grading will begin soon," nothing tangible happened. The expense of carving out a right-of-way through this rough "pot and kettle" countryside probably helped to stifle the project; and the Burlington and the Rock Island, which considered this territory their own, threatened to retaliate, if tracks appeared.[82]

These new line proposals and company takeovers seemed plausible, but an overambitious goal was

One of the several small independent short lines that fed the Stickney road was the Hanover Railway in northwestern Illinois. The road ran from a connection with the CGW at North Hanover, 2.5 miles south, to its namesake community. The company's tiny gasoline railbus is seen in this photograph taken about 1912. (C. W. Finch Collection)

also discussed. Railroads in America's mid-section all fantasized about a Pacific extension, and the Chicago Great Western was no exception. While the Chicago, Milwaukee & St. Paul actually reached the coast in 1909, and several carriers belonged to larger systems that owned trackage to the sea, those roads that actually embarked on such a course stalled far short of this objective. The Chicago & North Western, for example, quit at Lander, Wyoming, at the foot of the Rocky Mountains. The CGW's dreams for ". . . & Pacific" occurred as early as 1900, when Stickney told company officials in St. Paul: "Gentlemen, I expect to see the Great Western a transcontinental railroad." But more serious talks occurred during 1905 and 1906. The idea was to build from Omaha to Denver or perhaps lease the C&NW's Hastings, Nebraska, branch and then extend it to the Colorado capital. Once in the "Queen City of the West," the Great Western would not seek to move to the coast on its own; rather, it would join forces with two promising ventures, the Denver, Northwestern & Pacific (DNW&P) and the San Pedro, Los Angeles & Salt Lake (SPLA&SL).[83]

Shortly after the century began, David H. Moffat, a Colorado mining tycoon, launched a partially successful drive to build a direct standard-gauge route from Denver to Salt Lake City. There his DNW&P would meet the soon-to-be-completed SPLA&SL, the handiwork of William A. Clark, the Montana copper king and former United States senator, and gain direct access to the port of Los Angeles. But financial difficulties quickly crippled the emerging Moffat road, and the CGW's own growing money troubles ruined any serious efforts at accomplishing Stickney's monumental scheme.[84]

THE SHORT LINE CONNECTION

THE fostering of independent, friendly short lines offered a feasible means of attracting business through additional trackage. While not unique to it, the Chicago Great Western skillfully employed this clever, inexpensive technique. The development of the Manchester & Oneida (M&O) Railroad is the primary example.

The Chicago Great Western long coveted the sizable traffic generated by Manchester, the prosperous seat of Delaware County, Iowa. Residents, too, wished for better service and rates, for these 2,887 inhabitants had always experienced a railroad monopoly: the Illinois Central operated its east-west Iowa main line through the town and a branch from there south to Cedar Rapids. The Maple Leaf's Twin Cities to Chicago artery lay only eight miles to the northeast, and a connection could be easily and quickly installed.[85]

The people of Manchester asked Stickney to build a branch into their community, but he refused to do so. He told them instead to construct the line themselves; and, if they did, he would treat their labors with "kindness." At this suggestion, then, townsfolk, led by attorney E. M. Carr, organized the Manchester & Oneida Railroad Company. While supposedly a "secret" strategy, the Great Western's involvement was immediately detected. As the *Oelwein Register* straightforwardly reported, "[this]

is . . . a move on the part of the Chicago Great Western to enter Manchester." No doubt the officials of the august Illinois Central also recognized the Maple Leaf's role. But the CGW head was discreet. By telling the local citizens to construct their own carrier, he could conceivably lessen the IC's irritation and, equally important, save money. As the M&O's godfather, Stickney provided the necessary materials, including 800 tons of relaying rails at a bargain price, and sent them to Oneida, the future interchange point. By 1901, the short line's 4-4-0 locomotive began shuttling freight and passenger cars over the little line, and the Great Western officially listed Manchester in its public timetables, maps, and other publications.[86]

Before Stickney left the Great Western in 1908, the company had begun to work closely with other interurban and steam short line promoters. The CGW had extended aid to the ten-mile Mason City & Clear Lake Traction Company; the eight-mile Waterloo & Cedar Falls Rapid Transit Company (subsequently the more extensive Waterloo, Cedar Falls & Northern Railway); the six-mile Iowa Northern Railroad (later Colfax Northern Railway); and the 2.5-mile Hanover Railway Company. Like the M&O, these carriers provided healthy dosages of "hogs and humans."[87]

With absorption of the Wisconsin, Minnesota & Pacific and the Mason City & Fort Dodge and completion of the Omaha Extension, the Chicago Great Western might have thought of further expansion, but in reality it sought other means to strengthen itself. For example, the road's closeness to electric and steam short lines reveals just one innovative and inexpensive method it employed to bolster traffic. What the CGW did not do as long as A. B. Stickney handled the throttle was to sell out to another carrier or syndicate. But when he relinquished control, the company that he had nurtured for more than two decades lost its identity as a maverick property. For during this great age of business consolidation, the CGW entered the orbit of the House of Morgan and soon experienced the skills of an immensely talented Morgan man, Samuel M. Felton.

CHAPTER FIVE
REORGANIZATION, REHABILITATION,
AND RECUPERATION: THE FELTON
YEARS, 1908–1929

FELTON ASSUMES CONTROL

"I BUILT the Chicago Great Western Railway. I superintended the expenditure of every dollar it cost in first construction, and every dollar which has been expended on it for improvements and for rolling stock," said a proud, self-assured A. B. Stickney to the Minnesota Railroad and Warehouse Commission in 1906. But the relationship of the Maple Leaf head with the company that he sired and reared was about to change dramatically. When the road entered receivership in the winter of 1908, Stickney faced sharing power with the federal court and co-receiver, retired St. Paul businessman Charles H. F. Smith.[1]

Great Western officials believed that the period of court protection would be brief. "The receivership will be temporary," observed Frank B. Kellogg, special counsel for the receivers, "and I expect to see it abandoned within a few months." His reasoning appeared sound. "The Chicago Great Western Railway never issued bonds to raise funds for current expenses, and as a result when a number of short-time notes came due during the money stringency [of 1907], the road was unable to pay them. We must have some ready cash and all interests, after prolonged consideration, decided that the

appointment of a receiver was necessary to give the time for the reorganization and financing of the company." Added Kellogg, "The liabilities do not exceed $10,000,000, while its property is worth from $60,000,000 to $75,000,000."[2]

Attorney Kellogg was considering more than strictly financial matters; he also handled a potentially disastrous labor situation. Shortly after receivership began, Stickney and Smith proposed a sizable wage reduction for all operating personnel. Employees' tempers flared. Consumer prices were climbing steadily, and workers felt that they should not bear so heavily the owners' money woes. The four brotherhoods directly involved seemed determined to resist cuts at any cost. National industry, labor, and political leaders, including President Theodore Roosevelt, paid close attention to this volatile situation, because a general strike against the Great Western might precipitate a walkout that could shut down the country.

Roosevelt, who knew and trusted Kellogg, asked him to mediate the dispute. Kellogg agreed. Remarkably skilled at negotiation, the future Secretary of State in the Coolidge administration and the future architect of the famed Kellogg-Briand pact that outlawed war as an instrument of national policy discussed Roosevelt's concerns with the receivers and the brotherhoods. Both parties showed a genuine

CGW sectionmen, many of whom were Italian immigrants who returned home in 1915 to fight the Central powers, construct the

East Stockton, Illinois, train terminal in 1909. (C. W. Finch Collection)

willingness to cooperate and compromise. Thus, on April 10, 1908, Kellogg was able to wire the President that "receivers will today publish notice withdrawing schedule of rules and compensation proposed to engine, train and switchmen of Great Western, and among other things saying that in withdrawing notice the kindly feelings which the committee evinced during the discussion at the conferences leads the receivers to believe that all of the engine, train and switchmen will endeavor to aid the management in reducing terminal overtime, constructive mileage, and consumption of coal, to a minimum, so as to reduce expenses." He closed with remarks that Roosevelt surely loved to read: "It is the high regard which the Receivers have for you and the policies of your administration which has led them to take this step."[3]

While Frank B. Kellogg knew how to respond speedily to a labor dispute, his forecast of a quick reorganization proved inaccurate. Receivership lasted twenty months, because the Stickney interests could not arrange satisfactory refinancing. The

banking community provided little cooperation or encouragement because the railroad industry generally faced hard times. The Panic of 1907 severely pinched many of the oldest and strongest firms; and fifty-two weaker ones, operating approximately 42,000 miles of line, went to the wall. On August 21, 1909, Albert R. Moore, who represented the United States District Court for Minnesota, stood at the Great Western's sprawling freight house in St. Paul and auctioned off the road. Only one bid came, a $12,000,000 offer from a syndicate formed by the financial titan J. Pierpont Morgan, Sr.[4]

Entry of the House of Morgan surprised many; yet it was understandable. A combination of motives guided these financiers. For one thing, they wanted to end forever the disruptive antics of the Maple Leaf. After all, as the *Railway World* noted in January 1908, "The Great Western has been the thorn in the flesh of all conservative managers. . . . [T]here will be few tears shed if it passes into the control of some strong and respectable corporation." In addition, while the property needed considerable improvements, it was hardly a transportation "slum." The Morgan interests knew this. Recommendations made by consulting engineer Samuel M. Felton in his "Report on the Chicago Great Western Ry., March-1909," undoubtedly encouraged them: "Spend $15,000,000.00, save $1,000,000.00 per annum and have a property one-third better than the Chicago Great Western Railway of to-day and capable of operating, on present rates, at 65%." (The best operating ratio [relation of expenses to revenues] the company achieved occurred in 1916 at 69.74 percent; the worst came in 1920 with 110.07 percent.) Finally, a reorganization provided opportunities to reap considerable profits for Morgan's syndicate. If the words of United States Senator Smith W. Brookhart, the Iowa progressive, are to be believed, the Morgan people did nicely. "I learned that Morgan & Co. received a fee of $500,000 for assistance given in reorganizing the company, and in addition got $6,000,000 as commission for floating $18,000,000 of bonds."[5]

A. B. Stickney seemingly accepted the coming of the Morgan interests with good grace. Obviously the Great Western's financial troubles hurt him deeply, but he recognized the realities. The fact that the reorganization involved his long-time friend, James J. Hill, offered some consolation. Stickney, moreover, had apparently lost his zeal for battle; at sixty-eight he may have wanted an excuse to retire to his Summit Avenue mansion. In fact, he resigned as co-receiver on December 21, 1908, and lived out his remaining seven years in relative seclusion. The court immediately named a Morgan adviser, Horace G. Burt, as his successor. Burt was an experienced railroad manager whose career had included stints with the Chicago & North Western, Union Pacific, and Kansas City Southern.[6]

Nor was the response by the English investors particularly negative to the new arrangement. While they knew that they should have sold early in the century when several competing roads seemed willing to pay top dollar, they had not: "Instead of being tempted by such offers, [they] were the more convinced that they held the whip hand which

Soon-to-be-junked or sold locomotives fill "rip" tracks near the Oelwein Shops early in the Felton era. These mostly 4-4-0-type engines were both old and small by the standards of the 1910s. (H. Roger Grant Collection)

would yield much more money." Fortunately, J. P. Morgan & Company made a reasonable offer. Under the reorganization plan, holders of debenture stock received 110 percent in new preferred certificates, and preferred A owners got 120 percent in common. Preferred B and common stockholders faced a fifteen dollar per share assessment but received 15 percent each in new preferred stock and 60 percent and 40 percent, respectively, in common stocks.[7]

To meet its financial obligations, the reconstituted firm, named the Chicago Great Western *Railroad* Company and officially incorporated on August 19, 1909, under Illinois law, issued considerable amounts of securities. Preferred stock totaled $41,021,402 and common, $45,245,613. It also executed a mortgage for $75,000,000; bonds, secured by this lien, amounted to $18,500,000. When the reorganized Great Western started on September 1, 1909, it had the financial wherewithal to start afresh. The assessment of stockholders of the old company together with the bond sales produced a tidy $24,892,274 in cash. About $10,000,000 went for rehabilitation.[8]

The administration of the "new" railroad was given to the man who had recently analyzed the property, Samuel M. Felton. Morgan's choice made sense: Felton was smart, energetic, and thoroughly knowledgeable about the industry; in fact, he had become known among his colleagues as "the doctor of sick railroads." Differing from his predecessor, the builder, Felton was the manager, well trained and professional.[9]

Samuel Morse Felton, like Stickney, came from old stock. His ancestors had settled in Massachusetts Bay in 1633, part of the "Great Migration" of Puritan dissenters. Felton was born in Philadelphia, Pennsylvania, on February 3, 1853. His father, Samuel, was a railroader, who served as president of the Philadelphia, Wilmington & Baltimore, a Pennsylvania affiliate, during the Civil War era. Since the Felton family was prosperous, the future Chicago Great Western chief received a superb education, one of the finest a lad of that day could expect. He attended private Quaker schools in Philadelphia, then the nearby Pennsylvania Military Academy, and finally the Massachusetts Institute of Technology. He graduated from MIT in 1873 with a degree in civil engineering.[10]

Felton began his railroad career prior to entering college. Starting in 1868, he worked temporarily as a rodman for the Chester Creek Railroad, a company associated with his father's Philadelphia, Wilmington & Baltimore. After leaving MIT he spent one year as the chief engineer for the Chester & Delaware River Railroad (subsequently part of the Reading). Then, in 1874, the Pittsburgh, Cincinnati & St. Louis Railway named him general superintendent. Felton stayed with this Pennsylvania-controlled company until 1881, when he moved to the New York & New England (New Haven) as general manager. Between 1884 and 1889, he took a series of assignments in his steadily advancing career: assistant to the president, New York, Lake Erie & Western (Erie); general manager, New York, Pennsylvania & Ohio (Erie); vice-president of the New York, Lake Erie & Western in charge of traffic and operation; president, East Tennessee, Virginia & Georgia (Southern); receiver and president of the Cincinnati, New Orleans & Texas Pacific Railway

and the Alabama Great Southern Railroad (Queen & Crescent); and receiver of the Kentucky & Indiana Bridge Company and the Columbus, Sandusky & Hocking Railroad (Hocking Valley). When Edward H. Harriman acquired the Chicago & Alton in 1899, he asked Felton, the prodigious worker, to take the throttle. Felton agreed and stayed with this carrier for eight years. Two years before coming to the Great Western, he headed the Mexican Central and also served briefly as board chairman of the feeble Tennessee Central.[11]

Samuel Felton excelled as a railroader. His grandest triumph before joining the Great Western was with the Alton, for he turned a dismal property into an efficient and prosperous one. Between 1900 and 1908 the road boosted its tonnage per train mile from 231 to 406, and net earnings soared from $2,964,627 to $4,109,112. When Felton resigned to go to Mexico in 1907, Harriman wrote in glowing terms: "Your loyalty & faithfulness has been greatly appreciated & stands as one of the most gratifying results of the . . . Chicago & Alton enterprise."[12]

Although few, if any, could challenge Felton's skills as a manager of railroads, especially ill ones, his personality was a different matter. The editor of *The Maize,* the Great Western's in-house organ, offered a favorable assessment but still suggested the nature of Felton's character: "He is a strict disciplinarian but eminently just in his rulings; quick to observe merit and equally prompt in rewarding it."[13] While all agreed that Felton did not suffer fools gladly, the charge was also made that he customarily showed arrogance, even contempt toward subordinates. Compared to Stickney, he seemed gruff, humorless, and petty. The experiences of Walter P. Chrysler, the road's superintendent of motive power, support this viewpoint. Chrysler's initial impressions of the President were negative and, in his mind, soon confirmed. Within a year after Felton took office, he called the superintendent from Oelwein to Chicago to ask him about a hot box that had caused a three-minute delay on the *Great Western Limited.* When questioned about this minor problem, Chrysler replied:

Baldwin-built Mallet (2-6-6-2), #609, poses for an official portrait at Eddystone, Pennsylvania, in 1910. This "Snake" remained on the CGW for only six years. (H. L. Broadbelt Collection)

• • •

"Mr. Felton, I don't know."

"You don't know? You! The superintendent of motive power?"

"For a week I've been out over the divisions, inspecting the shops. I feel sure my chief clerk will have started an investigation on that delay. . . . As soon as I can get a little time in my office, I'll make a full report on the matter."

"You ought to know now. I shouldn't have to ask for a report."

• • •

That conversation proved too much for Chrysler. He quit on the spot, and the Great Western lost a capable and dedicated employee.[14]

THE FELTON REHABILITATION PROGRAM

REHABILITATION of the Chicago Great Western began immediately after Samuel Felton assumed control. Soon, much of the Twin Cities–Chicago main line had new eighty-five-pound steel rail, treated ties with screw spikes, and crushed rock ballast. The 240-mile stretch from Chicago to Oelwein, the system's busiest, received automatic electric block signals and thirty-three miles of double track. New train terminals were built at East Stockton, Illinois, on the Eastern Division and Concep-

tion, Missouri, on the Southern Division. These replaced obsolete ones in Dubuque and St. Joseph and met the company's mandated obligations to the 1907 Railway Hours Act that limited operating crews to no more than sixteen hours of continuous service. The road also constructed or rebuilt nearly a dozen water towers and coal chutes.[15]

The company's motive power and rolling stock required immediate attention. Much of it was described as being in "poor" condition. Eighty-eight locomotives, 4,269 freight cars, and ninety-three passenger coaches needed to be either repaired or rebuilt; and many others could only be sold or scrapped. The Felton administration also acquired heavier equipment, sometimes experimental. To increase freight train efficiency on the active and at times rugged Oelwein to Stockton segment (one percent grades), the road tried the Mallet-type locomotive. Named after French inventor Anatole Mallet, this design caught the fancy of several of the nation's longer railroads who sought to move huge quantities of freight but not especially fast. The Great Northern was the first to employ Mallets on a large scale; it ordered five from the Baldwin Locomotive Works in 1906 for use as "pushers" and a year later twenty-five more for general road service. Essentially two engines under a single boiler, the Mallet's rear high-pressure engine was attached rigidly to the frame, while the front low-pressure one

The massive size of the Mallet is evident in this circa 1912 photograph of #604 resting on the Oelwein turntable. Its 353,000 pounds played havoc with the roadbed. (Edward H. Meyers Collection)

pivoted so that it would swing independently of the rest of the locomotive on sharp curves. The Great Western purchased ten of these giant 505,000-pound 2-6-6-2's from Baldwin in 1910 and rebuilt three of its own Prairie types (2-6-2's) at the Oelwein shops into the novel design. Like most other railroads that tried Mallets ("Snakes," as Great Western employees called them), the experience proved generally unsatisfactory. While these monsters could pull a 4,000-ton train (the ordinary engine handled about 1,500 tons), they were exceedingly slow, prone to derail, hard on the track, and expensive to maintain. Within a few years the company wisely disposed of its fleet. In their place the railroad turned to highly reliable yet powerful Mikado-type (2-8-2) freight engines.[16]

The Great Western's use of internal combustion power proved more successful and even more innovative than its brief love affair with the mammoth Mallets. The CGW became one of the country's first major carriers to employ extensively this form of propulsion. In August 1910, it tried out four gasoline-fueled combination passenger-mail-express units. These vehicles, built by the McKeen Motor Car Company of Omaha, had six-cylinder, 200-horsepower engines, weighed 60,000 pounds, measured seventy feet in length, and seated eighty-three riders. Quickly these strange knife-nosed, tapered "wind splitters" replaced more expensive and less attractive steam-powered trains on local runs. Travelers on the Rochester-Osage, Waterloo–Des Moines, Mason City–Fort Dodge–Lehigh, and Parnell (later Blockton)–St. Joseph portions of the system enjoyed "interurban" service. Merchants in Des Moines seemed particularly delighted with the introduction of this equipment: McKeen cars meant a greater territory for them to attract customers. "Three-hour service [between Waterloo and Des Moines] will mean from six to eight trains a day each way and this service together with that af-

Employees of the East Stockton, Illinois, terminal surround Mallet #608 in 1910. Because of problems with the operations of this style of engine, the CGW soon sold its fleet to the Clinchfield Railroad. (C. W. Finch Collection)

forded by the regular through train service will draw Marshalltown and all intervening points much closer to Des Moines." When automobiles on better roads later siphoned off patrons, the company acquired more self-propelled cars. Frequently they pulled trailers to expand their revenue-producing capabilities.[17]

This interest by the Felton administration in the internal combustion engine led to one additional pioneering adoption. The road became a leader in the use of the small motor car for section crews. Trackmen no longer relied upon the slower, back-breaking hand-pump cars or tiny manual velocipedes to move from one work site to another. As with the McKeen equipment, the employment of these new units resulted in considerable savings; in this case, maintenance costs dropped noticeably. In 1914 the company reported that its fleet of 159 cars, which had cost $31,800 to procure, produced an annual savings of $39,000.[18]

While it would be nearly four decades before die-sel-electric locomotives would pull the road's principal passenger trains, rehabilitation produced two all-steel passenger equipment sets for use on the *Great Western Limited* between Chicago and the Twin Cities. "This is the only train west of Chicago of any of the different roads which is composed of steel cars," puffed a Dubuque journalist in April 1911, several months after the runs were inaugurated. "The floor of [each] . . . car is made of steel and laid in cement." Along with providing the traditional types of services, this rolling stock boasted one special feature — a women's parlor car. Luxuriously appointed, it offered massive plate-glass observation windows and the latest ladies' magazines.[19]

To symbolize the "new" Chicago Great Western, President Felton thought that the name change from Railway to Railroad was hardly sufficient. So, in June 1910, the company discarded the famed Maple Leaf decal and replaced it with the circular Corn Belt Route trademark. For the next forty years, the CGW employed the Corn Belt motto as its official

The crew and passengers of the Great Western's motorcar #1000, acquired from McKeen in 1910, pose at Gypsum, Iowa, on the Fort Dodge–Lehigh branch about 1915. (Harold K. Vollrath Collection)

nickname. Workers and others, however, continued to poke fun at the road by calling it the "Can't Get Worse," the "Gee Whiz," the "Chicago Late Western," "Cinders, Grass and Weeds," "Crab Grass and Weeds," the "Chicago Great Weedy," or simply the ever-popular "Great Weedy."[20]

Management hardly approved of the employees' negative designations or any like aspersions. General Manager Hiram J. Slifer, for one, blasted publicly the twitting made by a St. Paul minstrel troop, for he knew the comic routine had lost its truthfulness: "A negro porter was posting trains on the train bulletin board. They ran like this: Great Northern — forty minutes late — washout. Northwestern — two hours late — engine disabled. Great Western — on time — no excuse given." The need to joke about the Great Western lessened, obviously with the upgrading of the physical plant and equipment. Corn Belt officials surely took the following patron testimonial to the *Oelwein Register* in a much different light: " 'I was simply astonished at the wonderful improvement of the Great Western's southwest division,' said a citizen of St. Joseph who came up the line Thursday morning. 'You can now drink your breakfast coffee in the dining cars without having it splashed against the ceiling.' "[21]

Part of the Felton regime's desire to push forward with modernization included trackage changes. Soon

The pride of Samuel Felton's road was the *Great Western Limited*. This view of the clubcar interior (taken about 1911) reveals the train's elegance and why it was a joy to the traveler. (W. A. Vaughn Collection)

after the new management took over, the engineering department began to explore the possibility of relocating the main line in northwestern Illinois. The company faced two expensive problems. The Winston tunnel regularly caused trouble; maintenance seemed never-ending. And the Illinois Central extracted heavy tolls for the use of its Mississippi River bridge at Dubuque. The most likely solution to these problems was to build from a point west of Elizabeth, Illinois, directly to the river, span it at Bellevue, Iowa, and rejoin the main line near Du-

buque. For unknown reasons, the road was never relocated. Steep construction costs probably dampened management's enthusiasm, although studies for such a project continued intermittently until the Second World War.[22]

Another problem existed for the road in the St. Joseph–Kansas City area. The old route through Leavenworth necessitated expensive trackage-rights segments, and it was also too long. On November 27, 1909, Great Western trains started to move temporarily over Chicago, Burlington & Quincy track-

The *Great Western Limited*'s sixteen-section sleeping car offered this attractive and modern "Ladies' Toilet." In an era of smoke and cinders, passengers appreciated such accommodations. (W. A. Vaughn Collection)

age down the east side of the Missouri River between Beverly and Harlem, and across the CB&Q's bridge at Kansas City. This arrangement lasted until August 1, 1910. During the interim the Great Western not only negotiated more favorable rental rates but also altered the original path. The Missouri Pacific would replace the Kansas City, Wyandotte & Northwestern (Kansas City North-western) for much of the run. The advantages of the Missouri Pacific artery were twofold: the line was eight miles shorter and was much better engineered and constructed. The previous trackage had 1.4 percent grades, while the new one offered a maximum slope of only .4 percent. Once again, Great Western trains crossed the Missouri River at Leavenworth and served this busy Kansas metropolis.[23]

The lone addition to the Great Western system in this period occurred in 1910. The company ran a 6.43-mile branch in Goodhue and Wabasha Counties, Minnesota, from a point designated Belle Chester Junction, 1.8 miles south of Goodhue on the Rochester line, southeasterly to the village of Belle

Chester. Construction began on August 15 and ended in December. The reason for this tiny freight-only appendage is simple: the road sought to gain convenient access to rich clay deposits. Soon locals hauled the "mud" to nearby Red Wing for use in the manufacture of stoneware and sewer pipe.[24]

Rumors about other line extensions or acquisitions were infrequent during the early Felton years. In 1910 some talk about finishing that once-planned link between Osage and Mason City took place. Several years later a report circulated that the company would acquire the recently completed Iowa & Omaha Shortline (I&OSL) that connected Neoga (Council Bluffs) with Treynor, twelve miles to the east, and would perhaps extend it eastward to Des Moines. A portion of this route would consist of trackage owned by the farmer-built Atlantic Northern & Southern (AN&S), a railroad the CGW would also buy. This short line operated seventeen miles of track from Atlantic, the Cass County seat, north of Kimballton, which opened in 1908, and another thirty-seven miles south from Atlantic to Villisca and a connection with the CB&Q completed two years later. Rumors persisted, too, of the Great Western's tying the AN&S to the Omaha Extension at Manning, a scheme that would require about twenty miles of track to be laid north of Kimballton.[25]

Fortunately, neither the Osage nor the I&OSL–AN&S–Des Moines projects materialized. While both could have initially supplied useful quantities of traffic, they would have become exceedingly vulnerable to automobile and truck competition by World War I. Furthermore, the I&OSL and AN&S lines were cheaply designed and would have needed expensive rehabilitation. Problems would also have existed with access from Council Bluffs to Neoga and rivalry with the Rock Island between Atlantic and the Iowa capital.

In one instance, however, it made greater sense for the Great Western to lease its trackage to a short line. The Minneapolis, St. Paul, Rochester & Dubuque Electric Traction Company, better known as the "Dan Patch Line," assumed operations of all service over the CGW's Northfield-Mankato branch on July 1, 1914. While never electrified, this carrier used gasoline-electric passenger cars between Mankato and the Twin Cities; yet, it provided interurban-type service over its 108-mile system. The company moved carload shipments with a General Electric gasoline-electric freight locomotive, the first of its kind ever built.[26]

The Dan Patch arrangement worked nicely; it generated for the Great Western a modest annual income of $15,000 and most of the interchange freight and some passenger business. More importantly, the CGW rid itself of considerable unrest with branch line patrons over the scope of passenger service. "There is much complaint among the business men of Mankato, and the traveling public in general over the train service of the Great Western," reported the Mankato *Review* in 1913. "The accommodation is very poor and vexatious to travelers who wish to come here to spend the day." Thus, the people of Mankato and area residents understandably liked their five daily Dan Patch trains. They seemed pleased, too, that the short line had signed a fifty-year lease agreement. However, the little road's financial fortunes soured; and on February 1, 1916, the Great Western resumed control of the property, to the disappointment of many.[27]

The Chicago Great Western either established or continued to cultivate friendly contacts with other interurbans in its territory. Unlike most steam carriers, which at least initially viewed these "juice" roads as dangerous threats to their very being, the Felton management saw them (and correctly so) as sources of valuable interchange business. The Chicago, Aurora & DeKalb; Chicago, Aurora & Elgin; DeKalb–Sycamore & Interurban; Fort Dodge, Des Moines & Southern; Inter-Urban; Kansas City, Clay County & St. Joseph; Mason City & Clear Lake; St. Joseph & Savannah; and the Waterloo, Cedar Falls & Northern not only often found their lines shown in Corn Belt Route timetables and other literature but, significantly, received joint tariffs for less-than-carload freight and also for carload lots if they could handle the bigger, heavier equipment.[28]

The Chicago Great Western opened this massive freight house in Kansas City, Missouri, in 1901, one that covered nearly two city blocks. The enormous quantity of less-than-carload (l.c.l.) goods that once moved by rail is seen in this circa 1915 photograph. (W. A. Vaughn Collection)

The spirit of innovation, the wish to modernize, and the quest for maximum profits found expression in a variety of other Felton administration activities. Because of its vulnerable position, the road had always tried mightily to win traffic. Management made this a priority. For one thing, the Great Western led the industry in development of "off-lines" sales centers. Specially trained representatives operated widely throughout the country; their offices could be found from Boston to Seattle. Coinciding

with this pathbreaking effort, the company started the Chicago Great Western Station Agents' Association in 1911. It served several purposes: to educate its agents, to provide a sense of professionalism, and to gain business. Officials regularly issued pointers on how to get and retain patronage. General Manager Slifer, for example, told station personnel in 1912: "Do not get a reputation for being bluffers; not only give civil replies, but intelligent ones," and added, "A harsh answer turneth away cash."[29]

Station agent Bert Snodgrass, who "hired out" with the Great Western in 1902 and continued with the company until the 1960s, sits by his telegraph instruments in the Lamont, Iowa, depot office, about 1910. (C. W. Finch Collection)

Education of all employees likewise became important. In a time before the widespread presence of either public or private technical and business programs, the Great Western conducted its own. "It is the opinion of the officers that it is better for them to take a hand in the training of the men than to depend on recruits with no railway knowledge." Spearheaded by General Manager Slifer and influenced by the work of the New York Central and several other trunk lines, the CGW started lecture courses in 1910 on such topics as signaling, car service, and freight and passenger solicitation. In order to attract capable students, Slifer issued a circular to station agents that asked them "to get next

to promising young men in their several towns." The names of likely candidates were submitted to the division superintendent and then to Slifer's office, where they were selected. Agents were aided by the railroad's policy of not charging for tuition and even picking up the tab for board and room. The company established classroom facilities in Oelwein and selected supervisory personnel as staff. These workshops turned out a score or so of "graduates" annually at minimal cost. Since the program at Oelwein was too limited to teach fully the skills of telegraphy, the railroad opened a specialized school at Dubuque in 1912.[30]

While the Slifer schemes covered railroad training,

In a typical railroad scene of the early twentieth century, a CGW passenger train glides into Fredericksburg, Iowa, three stations north of Oelwein. As in most places, the depot served as the gateway to the community. (James L. Rueber Collection)

the Great Western also needed large numbers of well-prepared stenographers and other office personnel. The firm therefore arranged with the newly launched Corn Belt Business College in Oelwein for these trainees. Beginning in August 1910, the road advertised the school's offerings and agreed to hire qualified graduates; the college would staff the classes and pay all instructional charges, an arrangement that worked out nicely for the CGW.[31]

During this time the Chicago Great Western took the lead in another dimension of education: safety work. While not unique in the industry, the road joined a select group of carriers—the Baltimore & Ohio; Chicago & North Western; Delaware, Lack-awanna & Western; and the Frisco—when it established its own safety bureau. In late 1911 several individuals started to travel a predetermined lecture circuit, their key message being how to prevent accidents to employees and customers alike.[32]

Always mindful of how technology might improve operations, the Corn Belt Route also conducted an experiment that would gain it more recognition as an innovator. In the spring of 1914 the road began to use dictaphone equipment to convey information of train movements to dispatchers from places where operators were off duty. The plan, which functioned rather well, was ingenious: an agent merely connected the dictaphone apparatus to an open telephone line before he left his office. During the first test, "the dispatcher, fifty-seven miles away, heard the ringing of the engine bell, the exhaust of the engine and roar of a train passing the station." He also recorded the arrival and departure of a passenger train, "identifying it by the noise of loading milk cans." The company would use these devices in this capacity for the next two decades.[33]

Samuel Felton's creative no-nonsense approach to railroading produced positive results. Between receivership and federalization the leadership and investors especially could feel the golden rays of a steadily stronger company. For the fiscal year ending June 30, 1916, the Great Western's gross earnings reached $15,067,344, a twenty-four percent increase over the figure for the twelve months that closed mid-year 1910. Total net income amounted to $3,787,048 for 1916, up a healthy forty-five percent over 1910. The surplus reached $1,403,458 as compared to $360,536; this marked a spectacular 289 percent increase. Equally gratifying to the owners and managers was the steady decline in the transportation ratio, i.e., the percentage of gross earnings required to pay for actual operations of trains. In 1910 this figure stood at the rather high level of 41.8 percent, while seven years later it amounted to only 34.1 percent. This compared favorably with two larger neighbors: the Chicago, Milwaukee & St. Paul in 1916 claimed 35.7 percent and the Chicago & North Western boasted 34 percent.[34]

The gains made by the Great Western occurred in a relatively inauspicious environment, however. During this period the industry as a whole confronted consumer-sensitive regulatory bodies and lawmakers. These parties, at times hostile, often damaged the profit picture. Although the Great Western operated in states where political progressives dominated, it seemed rather more adversely affected by the activities of the federal government. In particular, the Interstate Commerce Commission, its powers strengthened markedly by the Hepburn Act of 1906 and the Mann-Elkins Act four years later, flexed its muscles. What hurt most was the ICC's refusal to grant general rate increases in 1911

and again in 1914 and 1915. And the railroad enterprise, including the CGW, disliked the passage of the Adamson Act in 1916, which supported demands made by railway brotherhoods for an eight-hour day, instead of the nearly universal ten-hour day, without any reduction of pay.[35]

These government actions did please railroad patrons. After all, the public had long felt the sting of acts of corporate arrogance. But the regulators were perhaps too hard on the regulated. There is little doubt that these controls did nothing to strengthen the transportation economy as a whole.

THE ERA OF WORLD WAR I

Entry of the United States into the war in Europe on April 6, 1917, led to monumental changes for American railroads. The volume of rail traffic rose dramatically. In fact, the increase caused chaos in Atlantic coast terminals where tremendous quantities of freight, destined for shipment to the fighting zones on the continent, could not be unloaded quickly enough. While loaded cars jammed these centers, other sections craved empties. The Railroads' War Board, a voluntary organization of railroad executives that represented 693 carriers, sought valiantly to unsnarl the growing congestion. But old competitive rivalries and the enormous scope of the task led the Woodrow Wilson administration, using the authority of the Army Appropriation Act of 1916, to federalize most of the industry under the banner of the United States Railroad Administration (USRA). This fateful event for the Great Western took place on December 29, 1917.

Although the Director General of the Railroads, William Gibbs McAdoo, and his successor, Walker D. Hines, tried to operate the country's hundreds of carriers as a single consolidated system, their efforts met with mixed results. While men and materials eventually reached their domestic destinations, they encountered lengthy delays. It took time for the USRA to iron out the kinks. Initially, the govern-

Great Westerners turned soldiers are seen in August 1917 near Paris, France. "Our Boys" belonged to Company C of the Thirteenth Railway Engineers, and they did much to keep the French railroads running. (H. Roger Grant Collection)

ment's plans for standardization (locomotives, boxcars, and the like) had little impact, although truly unified operations required such an approach. Yet, the USRA performed better than the former voluntary Railroads' War Board.

The Wilson administration did not actually nationalize the carriers. Companies kept their own identity and operating personnel. The USRA did force roads to dispatch movements in the most efficient fashion, regardless of established traffic patterns. As for compensation, the federal government was generous. Firms received a yearly payment equal to their average annual operating income for the three-year period that ended June 30, 1917. Uncle Sam assumed expenses but kept railroad-generated revenues.[36]

When the Great War came, Great Western employees, from top executives to lowly engine wipers, nearly without exception devotedly backed the cause. President Felton and many others actually joined the colors. Secretary of War Newton D. Baker appointed the Corn Belt head as Director General of Railways on July 17, 1917, a post subsequently called Director General of Military Railways so as not to be confused with McAdoo's title. Felton quickly established himself as a capable administrator; he got considerable acclaim for successfully shipping fully assembled locomotives to France, something experts thought impossible. Hundreds of CGW workers entered military service. As early as 1915 the company lost scores of Italian laborers who returned to their homeland to join in the fight against the Central Powers. With America's entry into the war, the draft began to take employees but more volunteered; the road even fielded Company C of the Thirteenth Railway Engineers. "Our Boys" traveled to France in the summer of 1917 to "Railroad the Kaiser."[37]

War itself produced a variety of responses on the homefront. The Great Western, like most other trunk lines, turned to female labor because of the shortage of qualified males. Although women had been employed on the CGW since the days of A. B. Stickney, their numbers increased appreciably between 1917 and 1919. Most of these "Corn Belt Belles" became office workers, some became agents and operators, and a few became coach cleaners; none, however, entered train or maintenance-of-way service.[38]

Workers, whether male or female, bought war bonds with enthusiasm. The *Oelwein Register* proudly announced in October 1918 that "the CGW shop employees have decided that they will be 100% Fourth Liberty Loan," and the *Sheridan Advance* revealed in the same happy spirit that "every employee of the Southern Division has reason to feel proud of the fact that this Division was first to go 'Over the Top' on subscribing to the Fourth Liberty Loan, and that his money helped to make it 100%."[39]

The war spirit also found expression in another act of loyalty—the renaming of towns. The company suggested that German Valley, a community between Byron and Stockton, be called "Stephenson," "New Era," or "Liberty Valley," because the old name "smacks too much of Kaiserism." But local residents, largely German-Americans, refused. The railroad heartily accepted the name change endorsed by citizens of Berlin, in Tama County, Iowa, on the Oelwein to Des Moines line. The town thereafter became "Lincoln," and the CGW immediately installed the corrected depot signs. This way of thinking was not uncommon; to the ultrapatriotic, German measles became "liberty measles," dachshunds, "liberty pups," and sauerkraut, "liberty cabbage."[40]

Residents served by the Great Western started to make transportation sacrifices, just as they did for the wheatless Mondays, porkless Thursdays, and gasless Sundays. Largely because of fuel shortages, the CGW annulled various trains, especially local

This unknown Illinois National Guardsman protects the strategic Winston tunnel during World War I. He and fellow troopers must have found this assignment extremely tedious. (Mrs. Donald Richardson Collection)

passenger ones, during the harsh winter of 1917–1918. And because competitors often operated the better routes between gateways, the USRA diverted some freight runs away from the Corn Belt rails.[41]

Federal operation of the railroads sparked widespread discussion about their ultimate fate. This war-time experiment cost taxpayers dearly; the government lost approximately $1 billion dollars during the twenty-six-month existence of the United States Railroad Administration. Yet most Americans believed that Uncle Sam's foray into railroading had been wise. The conflict, of course, demanded that a public interest take precedence over any other. The experience, furthermore, convinced many that consolidation made sense. Whether the goal was greater efficiency or lower charges, elimination of wasteful duplication offered bright prospects.[42]

Political progressives, led by Republican Senator Robert M. La Follette of Wisconsin, sparked the crusade to prevent the lines from reverting back to private management and thereby reestablishing the status quo. They showed keen interest in the railway brotherhoods' scheme, drafted by attorney Glenn Plumb, that proposed national ownership of most carriers under which the government would purchase the roads and operate them through a tripartite board that represented the public, management, and labor. The so-called Plumb Plan advocated that half of the net earnings of this unified system be set aside for payment of the bonds issued to finance the take-over; the other half would go to executives and workers as dividends on wages.[43]

Congress, however, ignored the Plumb Plan but not the desire for a better, more rational rail network. Indeed, this attitude typified the actions of the industrialized countries toward railroads at this time: Canada created its 23,000-mile Canadian National combine at war's end; Great Britain, under the British Railway Act of 1921, amalgamated numerous carriers into four regional units; France reacted similarly with its Comité de Direction and Conseil Supérieur des Chemins de Fer; and Germany acquired the railroads heretofore owned by the separate states. After considerable debate and political maneuvering, lawmakers in Washington approved and President Wilson signed what became known as the Esch-Cummins Act or Transportation Act of 1920. This monumental piece of legislation did more than end federal operation on March 1, 1920; it produced major changes in the relationship between government and industry. Generally speaking, the measure allowed the Interstate Commerce Commission to exert much greater authority over carriers, whether it be in the field of security sales or rate-making. And it called for creation of a nine-member Railroad Labor Board to hear employee-management disputes.[44]

Perhaps the most significant features of the Act dealt with creating an equitable rate structure within the framework of an enterprise that contained firms with mixed financial strengths. Unlike truly monopolistic utilities where regulators could easily set fair charges, railroads presented a more complicated problem. Since they competed at various points, different rates for different roads meant that those who charged the most would surely lose customers. Yet the weaker companies needed to charge higher rates in order to survive. As Senator A. B. Cummins of Iowa recognized, owners of the Chicago Great Western earned only a modest return on their investment while owners of competitor Chicago & North Western realized a handsome one. Therefore, a level of rates adequate for the mighty North Western would be insufficient for the Great Western, and those suitable for the latter would yield outrageous profits for the former.

The Transportation Act of 1920 attempted to handle this problem by directing the Interstate Commerce Commission to fix rates "so that carriers as a whole will, under honest, efficient, and economical management, . . . earn an aggregate annual net railway operating income equal, as nearly as may be, to a fair return upon the aggregate value of the railway property." This idea was fully consistent with the ICC's progressive orientation since it was at that time in the process of appraising the individual roads under the terms of the Valuation Act of 1913. The new 1920 measure contained several specific features designed to insure justice for consumer and investor alike and to recognize the presence of the robust and the sickly. One was the "recapture of excess earnings" clause. If carriers generated more than a certain percent yearly on the value of their property (initially 5.5 percent for a two-year period), they could keep half, with the remainder going into a revolving fund from which the ICC could make loans to those that were less fortunate. Lawmakers further directed the Interstate Commerce Commission to give special consideration to

Peru, Iowa, thirty-five miles south of Des Moines, enjoyed its status as an important station on the Southern Division. A long freight waits near the depot, about 1920. (Paul J. Tilp Collection)

the weaker roads when it determined how rates on joint hauls should be divided. Also, the government actually encouraged combination. The ICC obtained the power to permit traffic pools if costs would be lower and the service better and even to sanction one railroad's acquisition of another as long as it was to the public's benefit. The law actually instructed the ICC to prepare a consolidation plan that would ultimately create a limited number of competitive systems of approximately equal strength, thus eliminating the problems associated with having carriers of mixed economic resources.[45]

The overall intent of the Transportation Act of 1920 differed rather dramatically from the reality that followed. In the spring of 1920 the newly launched Railroad Labor Board gave a substantial retroactive wage increase to the nation's railroad employees, and the ICC boosted rates effective August 26, 1920, "sufficient to meet the increased la-

bor and other operating costs." But these advanced charges had barely become operative before consumer pressures and competitive conditions produced their gradual reduction. In the case of the Great Western, the average rate per ton per mile received during the final four months of 1920 (which reflected the Commission's increases) totaled 1.117 cents. It subsequently dropped to 1.025 cents in 1922 and to less than one cent (9.58 mils) by 1925. Most carriers then, including the CGW, failed to make the prescribed returns on their investments that the act allowed. Furthermore, the government plan to capture excess earnings worked badly. Although the Supreme Court in the case of *Dayton–Goose Creek Railway Company* vs. *United States* did uphold the concept, the weaker roads got virtually no financial assistance. The stronger carriers effectively curtailed profits that were subject to recapture by simply increasing expenditures.[46]

The engineer of a handsome Pacific, or 4-6-2-type engine, awaits the "highball" before leaving Minneapolis with a passenger train in 1922. (J. Foster Adams Collection, State Historical Society of Wisconsin)

Finally, efforts to produce railroad consolidation failed as well. On August 31, 1921, the ICC published a tentative plan that contained eighteen systems largely shaped by Professor William Z. Ripley of Harvard University. The Chicago Great Western found itself included in System 14: "Burlington-Northern," along with the Chicago, Burlington & Quincy; Northern Pacific; Minneapolis & St. Louis; and Spokane, Portland and Seattle. The CGW's principal value to this arrangement was to span the gap between Omaha and the Twin Cities. Eight years later the Commission issued its final pairings. This time the Corn Belt Route entered System 17 of a twenty-one-part network. Placed in the "Santa Fé" grouping, the CGW joined the Atchison, Topeka & Santa Fé; Kansas City, Mexico & Orient; and a number of short lines. As in the earlier proposal, the Great Western fit beautifully; it connected with the AT&SF at St. Joseph, Kansas City and Chicago and offered the larger road entry into the Omaha and Twin Cities gateways and a second route to the Windy City.

Essentially none of the ICC's proposals materialized. The Chicago Great Western never united with any of the "Burlington-Northern" or "Santa Fé" roads. The guidelines failed for several reasons. Stronger roads naturally objected to assuming the burdens of the weaker ones, although they eagerly sought to absorb the best properties; those marriages that the powerful desired usually conflicted with the master plan. The Commission, moreover, lacked jurisdiction over holding companies, and some unsanctioned consolidations occurred through this then-popular device. Finally, the Crash of 1929 devastated the industry. Virtually no company was anxious to consider takeovers when its own financial life was at stake.[47]

INNOVATION AND CHANGE IN THE 1920s

THE tenure of the United States Railroad Administration had not been kind to the Chicago Great

Western. No one challenged an angry Samuel Felton when he asserted that "the property was used as a convenience by the Government and not for the best interests of the company." The Great Western suffered in various ways. Traffic it had spent years to develop was diverted to other lines. When a shortage of rails, ties, or other materials occurred, the bigger, favored roads got first consideration. And the government failed to maintain adequately the CGW's equipment. Freight cars, especially, were wretchedly out of repair.[48]

But the Great Western had known adversity before, and once more it responded to the challenges of the times. Immediately after USRA rule ended, the company recovered $1,600,000 in damages, since the government failed "to return the property in as good condition and repair as when taken over by the United States." Washington in fact had made such a commitment in 1917. Soon, too, management began heavy spending in order to improve the physical plant. It also increased traffic solicitation activities, upgraded freight schedules, and streamlined the work force from 8,854 in 1920 to 7,555 in 1926. Retrenchment was most apparent among station agents, for the company began the slow and continual process of closing poorly patronized depots.[49]

The Chicago Great Western's most touted efforts at self-help dealt with its passenger operations. The response took varied forms: inexpensive excursion fares, convenient schedules, quality service, and modern equipment. In this case, World War I had little negative impact on the company's business; rather, increased use of automobiles and the advent of buses (the "cancers" in the belly of the rail industry) steadily eroded patronage and income. The Great Western was particularly vulnerable to "rubber-tire" competition since local and short-haul traffic generated roughly 70 percent of its passenger revenues.

At this time also the Great Western management once again embraced the internal-combustion motor train, a form of equipment for which it had been a pioneer. The choice made sense since the regulatory authorities objected to service cutbacks, and most

WHITING CORPORATION, Harvey, Ill. (Chicago Suburb)

Whiting Motor Car Turntable in Service
Chicago Great Western Railroad, Waterloo, Iowa

Whiting Motor Car Turntable

This table was especially designed for use in turning gasoline motor-driven cars and has proven very satisfactory in actual service.

It requires no pit; may be installed at any convenient point at small expense. It is also readily moved should terminal location be changed. The distance from track rail to foundation rail is only 21⅛ inches.

Capacity: 15 to 20 tons; 35 to 40 ft. in diameter.

This table is of the center bearing type. The outer wheels are equipped with roller bearings.

The Consolidated Purchasing Agency of the American Short Line Railroad Association, Mr. J. W. Cain, Manager of Purchases, has favored us with Contract C. P. A. No. 57. We hope you will apply your orders for Turntables against this contract.

For complete specifications and prices, write to

WHITING CORPORATION
(Formerly Whiting Foundry Equipment Company)
Harvey, Ill. (Chicago Suburb)

Pictured in this 1924 advertisement for the Whiting Motor Car Turntable is #M-205, which Russell built for local service on the Des Moines–Waterloo route. This thirty-passenger vehicle faithfully served the road for a decade. (Don L. Hofsommer Collection)

runs attracted healthy quantities of "head-end" mail and express traffic. The motor train could comply fully with the government dictates and easily accommodate the revenue business. Too, this rolling stock proved economical to operate, because of reduced labor and fuel costs. Felton liked the prospects: "My theory is that with the low overhead on the gasoline-driven train, we can afford to stop at every crossing, farmhouse or small station, if necessary." And he added, "We expect to give the kind of service which will be appreciated by the Iowa farmers and build up a good interurban traffic."[50]

So Great Western patrons began to see a new

"M-300," the first Electro-Motive Company-designed car, is seen in this 1924 builder's photograph. With a passenger capacity of fifty-four and powered by a 175-horsepower General Electric engine, "M-300" served the Great Western until 1930, when the entire train burned. (H. Roger Grant Collection)

motor train service during the latter part of 1922. On September 17, a Russell-built vehicle began operating on the Des Moines to Marshalltown line (and later was extended to Waterloo). A year later the railroad bought two Sykes gasoline rail buses to serve the communities between Fort Dodge and Council Bluffs and Fort Dodge and Oelwein. Soon, other motor sets traveled between St. Joseph, Missouri, and Blockton, Iowa, and between McIntire and Waterloo, Iowa. In 1924, the CGW even exchanged steam for internal combustion on trains 3 and 4 that operated daily over the 509 miles between Chicago and Omaha, making it one of the longest such motorized runs in the country. (The "M-300" unit that traveled this route had the distinction of being the first Electro-Motive Company gas-electric car ever built.) Some of the old McKeen equipment also continued in service, although it operated almost exclusively on branch lines.[51]

By far the CGW's most famous piece of nontraditional equipment was the *Blue Bird,* which the company duly billed as "America's Premier Deluxe Motor Train." The Oelwein shops creatively used the underframes of several McKeen cars to build a plush three-car train: "the first, a combined motor, baggage and mail car; the second, a comfortable day coach; and the third, a combination parlor-club-cafe-lounge car." Powered by a heavy-duty Electro-Motive gasoline engine, the consist, which replaced a steam one, catered to the traveler visiting the world-renowned Mayo Clinic in Rochester. The *Blue Bird* even offered a four-berth Pullman section in the third car for those who required rest. Inaugurated on January 13, 1929, this "smokeless, sootless, cinderless" name-train that operated via Red Wing departed Minneapolis at 5:30 P.M. for the 112-mile run to Rochester and a 9:15 P.M. arrival time; it left Rochester on its return trip at 7:25 A.M. for an 11:15 A.M. entry into Minneapolis.[52]

While the Chicago Great Western enthusiastically endorsed internal combustion, it did not ignore steam. Its five handsome yet powerful Pacific-type locomotives (4-6-2's) received from Baldwin in December 1913 and January 1914 proved "most satisfactory" in pulling as many as fifteen to twenty cars and provided the backbone of the CGW's passenger

A Chicago Great Western company photographer took this "official" view of the *Blue Bird* near the Oelwein shops in January 1929. Workers had just completed the rehabilitation of several old McKeen motorcars into this unique "streamlined" train. (Tom Ryan Collection)

power on the principal runs. The road made every effort to furnish quality, standard trains, hoping of course to capture a greater share of the long-haul intercity business. Schedules were carefully prepared, equipment meticulously maintained, and crews "imbued with the spirit of Great Western courtesy." Management gave the dining-car operation special attention. As with other carriers, this aspect of people moving never paid for itself, yet often the image of the company rested upon the quality of its meals.[53]

Although travelers did not select the Chicago Great Western solely for its food, those who rode it did experience one of the great eating pleasures of the golden age of rail travel. If they picked train 1 or 2 between the Twin Cities and Chicago, they met genial R. C. "Mac" McCullough, described by the *Rochester Daily Post and Record* as "one of the most courteous stewards on any diner in the United States." It seems Mac took "great delight in seeing that your plate is well filled and that you are doing justice to your food." Patrons rarely, if ever, complained about the food on any Corn Belt Route diner. Quite the contrary, they often raved about the cuisine. For example, a consulting engineer, who rode the rails frequently, wrote the passenger department in 1924 to marvel about the baked apples, the best he had ever eaten.[54]

The name-trains of the Great Western during the 1920s provided quality service. Travelers knew and especially appreciated the *Tri-State Limited* and *Mill Cities Limited* between the Twin Cities and Kansas

City; the *Rochester Express* and *Bob-O-Link* that tied Rochester with Chicago; the *Omaha Express* and *Nebraska Limited* and the *Twin City Limited* and the *Twin City Express* that linked Omaha with Minneapolis and St. Paul; and Des Moines's own overnight train for the Windy City, the *Chicago Special.* And there was the *Red Bird,* the company's first Twin Cities to Rochester luxury varnish that made its debut on July 15, 1923. Pulled by a streamlined Pacific, this flashy, "Venetian-red" four-car train did not operate exclusively over Corn Belt rails; rather it steamed from Minneapolis–St. Paul to Dodge Center, where, without stopping, it switched over to the Chicago & North Western for the final leg into Rochester.[55]

Trains 1 and 2 between Chicago, Rochester and the Twin Cities, however, emerged as the favorites of employees and patrons alike. Indeed, they symbolized the "Great Trains of the Great Western." In 1924 the company re-equipped what had heretofore been called the *Great Western Limited.* Like the *Red Bird,* a handsome Pacific-type locomotive—the standard fast passenger power of the day—handled the consist. This English-style engine sported a streamlined look; a shimmering outer casing concealed all the piping. The rest of the train equaled the sporty 4-6-2. As the CGW described it: "The equipment— open-section sleepers, observation lounge car, club, dining car and coaches."

This overnight train also offered a convenient schedule; it proved a good competitor with similar runs on the North Western, Milwaukee, and Bur-

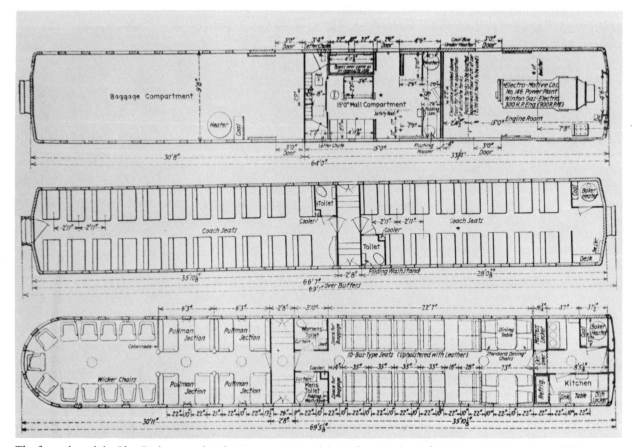

The floor plan of the *Blue Bird* appeared in the May 1929 issue of the *Railway Mechanical Engineer*. (H. Roger Grant Collection)

lington. Leaving Chicago at 6:30 P.M., the Rochester cars were set out at McIntire, Iowa, for a 6:50 A.M. arrival; the remainder glided into St. Paul at 7:30 A.M., and Minneapolis forty minutes later. The southbound Number 2 departed Minneapolis at 7:40 P.M., St. Paul at 8:15 P.M., Rochester at 9:30 P.M., and entered Chicago's Grand Central Station at 8:30 A.M., in time for the business day.

Mostly to publicize the new equipment, the passenger department sponsored a nationwide train-naming contest. In the tradition of A. B. Stickney's quest for an appropriate nickname, the road offered cash prizes, albeit modest ones: $50 for the top nomination and $5 for each of the ten next best. Hundreds of suggestions poured into the Chicago office of the General Passenger Agent by the July 31, 1924, deadline. Since four individuals submitted the same winning entry, *The Legionnaire*, the company awarded a $50 check to each. The other prize-earning names included the *Cornfield Flyer, Flour State Express, The Golden Bantam Limited, The Interlaken, Maize Limited, The Maizeland Special, The Overstates, Parkland Limited*, and *The Prairian*. None of these names, however, ever graced a Great Western train, and when the company in the 1930s decided to drop *The Legionnaire* banner, it selected *The Minnesotan* instead. Trains 1 and 2 would be formally christened *The Legionnaire* on January 16, 1925, because the railroad desired to "honor the millions of men who brought glorious victory to our

CHICAGO GREEN WESTERN RAILROAD

Travel on this beautiful train · · on your next trip to or from Rochester

The **Blue Bird** *Premier*

DE LUXE MOTOR TRAIN

between

ST. PAUL—MINNEAPOLIS

and

RED WING — ROCHESTER

THE BLUE BIRD	
Lv. Minneapolis .	4:50 p.m.
Lv. St. Paul	5:25 p.m.
Ar. Red Wing. .	7:20 p.m.
Ar. Rochester . . .	9:20 p m.

NORTHBOUND

Lv. Rochester . . .	7:25 a.m.
Lv. Red Wing. .	9:11 a.m.
Ar. St. Paul	11:15 a.m.
Ar. Minneapolis .	11:50 a.m.

THE RED BIRD
Non Stop Companion Train

Lv. Minneapolis .	9:15 a. m.
Lv. St. Paul	9:45 a. m.
Ar. Rochester . . .	12:05 p. m.

NORTHBOUND

Lv. Rochester . . .	4:00 p. m.
Ar. St. Paul	6:20 p. m.
Ar. Minneapolis .	6:50 p. m.

The CGW vigorously promoted the *Blue Bird*. This widely distributed ink blotter shows an artist's view of the train and concontains its schedule. The timetable for the companion *Red Bird* is also included. (H. Roger Grant Collection)

colors in the late World War." Perhaps, too, the road sought to court the newly formed and rapidly growing veterans' organization, the American Legion.[56]

In still another effort to tap the passenger market, the plucky Chicago Great Western arranged for through sleeping cars from Minneapolis and St. Paul to Los Angeles, in conjunction with the Atchison, Topeka & Santa Fé at Kansas City. Throughout most of the twenties the schedule called for tri-weekly service except for daily trips during the winter months when wealthy, weather-weary Midwesterners sought a more hospitable climate. Beginning in 1925, the company offered daily Pullmans from the Twin Cities to Dallas–Fort Worth, San Antonio, and Houston through Kansas City via the Missouri-Kansas-Texas (Katy).[57]

For the well-heeled and adventurous traveler, General Passenger Agent R. A. Bishop devised a train-plane arrangement. He imaginatively sought to utilize the newly established commercial aviation routes. Passengers would take *The Legionnaire* or *Chicago Special* for the Windy City, where a chartered bus would then provide the short transfer between Grand Central Station and Municipal Airport. Next, they would board a Universal Air Lines ten-passenger tri-motor to either St. Louis or Cleveland. The early morning arrival of the trains allowed for an easy connection with the 9:45 A.M. St. Louis flight, which landed in the Missouri metropolis at 1:00 P.M. The Cleveland plane, however, did not take off until 4:00 P.M. for its four hour and forty-five minute trip. But the Great Western viewed this favorably: "A time saving schedule providing for a business day in Chicago, dinner in Cleveland, with plenty of time to make connections with faster trains for New York and other seaboard cities."

The inaugural St. Louis and Cleveland coordinated service began on February 25, 1929. "Leading

UPON leaving St. Joseph, you are invited to use our dining service which features a most tempting selection of ready to serve dishes, excellently cooked, moderately priced — enabling one to procure a complete meal for less than a dollar. :: :: ::

There's a hint of "Old Virginy" in the Cooking and Service

CHICAGO GREAT WESTERN RAILROAD

If a railroad seriously sought travelers during the 1920s, the golden years of intercity service, it needed to provide good dining car service. Here the CGW excelled. This enlargement of a small card that passengers on northbound name-trains out of St. Joseph received urges them to partake of the moderately priced quality meals. (H. Roger Grant Collection)

as Usual" boasted the Great Western. The road, indeed, was in the vanguard, although it was not alone. That same year Transcontinental Air Transport, Inc. (TAT), and the Pennsylvania and Santa Fé railroads presented a forty-eight-hour, cross-country air-rail package. Patrons traveled from New York City to Columbus, Ohio, by Pullman on the Pennsy's evening *Airway Limited.* At the Port Columbus airport they boarded a TAT tri-motor for a daytime flight to Waynoka, Oklahoma. There they entered a set-out Pullman for a night connection with the Santa Fé's *Missionary* to Clovis, New Mexico, and from there a final plane connection to Los Angeles. Better aircraft and guidance systems would soon eliminate the need for overnight rail trips. However, it was the disastrous impact of the October 1929 Great Crash that actually killed the Corn Belt Route's infant land-air enterprise.[58]

The passenger operations of the Great Western revealed the personal touch. The firm continued to

provide trains for charter; specials carried hundreds of teachers, veterans, and lodge members to conventions and National Guard troops and Boy Scouts to camp. The most unusual illustration of tailoring service to fit patron need occurred in the summer of 1925 when the road offered what may have been the nation's first air-conditioned equipment. A sick milk company executive from Kansas City, Kansas, required a cool environment for his journey to Minnesota. His physician contacted the CGW's Assistant General Passenger Agent, George W. Bristow, for help. He responded positively and quickly offered a common, although specially modified, refrigerator car. Recalled one CGW employee, "Accordingly a refrigerator car was iced and sent to mail dock at Kansas City Union Station early the following morning, a bed, chairs, storage battery and lights installed. Mr. Chapman [the patient] accompanied by two nurses was immediately placed in the car." Soon the "reefer" was switched onto the afternoon

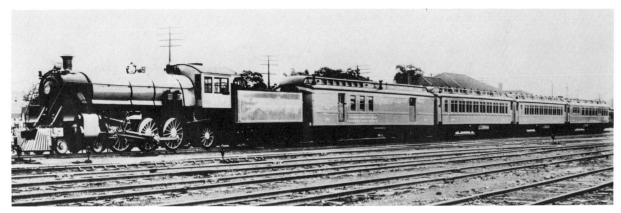

The *Red Bird*, the Great Western's initial luxury train between the Twin Cities and Rochester, stands in the Oelwein yards, about 1925. The company used this photograph in various pieces of advertising. (Otto H. Skubina Collection)

Mill Cities Limited. When the locomotive took water at Lorimor, Iowa, the dining car crew delivered dinner. "As there was no tariff to cover this move, we billed Mr. Chapman on basis of special move on a Pullman car, i.e., 25 one way fares and 12 lower berths."[59]

The Felton administration valiantly tried to bolster passenger traffic. The "what is left must be held and built up by reason of superior service, speed and comfort" credo failed to stem the downward trend. Ridership declined steadily throughout the twenties, from 2,498,822 in 1920 to 730,730 in 1929. A year later it plummeted to a meager 427,686. Revenues, however, were not as bad proportionately. The company succeeded in attracting substantial numbers of long-distance travelers with its name-trains and interline Pullman service. Still, the situation worsened; passenger income stood at $4,884,562 in 1921 and totaled only $2,813,744 at decade's end.[60]

Management did not restrict its imaginative responses solely to the passenger sector. Since freight generated the lion's share of income, the road understandably sought to maximize profits from these activities.

Throughout most of the 1920s, the Great Western relied on its existing fleet of motive power. The Mikado, or 2-8-2-type engine, served as the stan-dard through freight locomotive, just as it did for many railroads. The CGW's stable of "Mikes" was relatively new. The Baldwin Locomotive Works had delivered ten in 1912, ten more in 1916, and another ten in 1920. The Great Western also owned ten "USRA" 2-8-2's, which Baldwin built for the government in 1918. The Mikados provided dependable service at a reasonable cost. At times, though, trains had to be "doubled" on the grades, especially out of the Mississippi River valley.[61]

As the decade closed, the Great Western decided to try a more powerful locomotive, the Texas or 2-10-4. (The type got its name from the seventy engines of this design that the Lima Locomotive Works built for the Texas & Pacific in 1925.) These fuel-efficient giants were earmarked by the CGW for service in areas with the heaviest grades—St. Paul to Chicago and Oelwein to Kirmeyer, Missouri (Missouri River)—thus eliminating the need to use expensive and time-wasting doubleheaders. An order for fifteen 2-10-4's went to Lima in December 1929; the engines arrived on the property the next year. A second order of six more went to that builder in October 1930; another fifteen came from Baldwin that same year. Except for the slightly more powerful H-Class 4-8-4's operated by the Chicago & North Western, the CGW possessed the Midwest's largest locomotives. In succeeding years, however,

The elegant Pacific-type engine, #916, that powered the short-lived *Red Bird* between Minneapolis and Rochester sports English styling. Its sparkling appearance suggests that it has just left the paint shop. (Otto H. Skubina Collection)

both the CGW and C&NW monsters would be eclipsed by even bigger ones used by the CB&Q, the Santa Fé, and the Pennsylvania.[62]

All freight power received regular, careful maintenance as well as upgrading. The Oelwein shops frequently made significant improvements: superheaters, Nicholson syphons, larger air-pumps, and bigger fireboxes. With the introduction of the Texas-types, the trusty 2-8-2's then replaced lighter, less economical equipment, especially the Consolidations or 2-8-0's, on other parts of the system. In fact, the company in 1927 began to rebuild many of these 2-8-0's for assignment to transfer and heavy switching service.[63]

The quest for economy in freight operation manifested itself in additional ways. For example, the road bought one of the nation's first gasoline freight locomotives, a twenty-five ton switcher acquired from Baldwin in 1925. Most powerful in low speeds, it easily shunted cars and operated with only minimal attention. While the purchase price was a hefty $18,249, "Motor 1" easily earned its keep, for it faithfully ran on the Cedar Falls branch until the early 1950s. While gasoline found only limited use initially in the scheme of Great Western freight operations, the company strove to get the best possible returns from coal. In 1928 it began what proved to be a successful experiment to reduce fuel expenditures. By this time the CGW no longer served mines of any consequence; therefore, since the road bought on the open market, it decided to try a top-grade variety. And the better quality fuel worked well: the average pounds consumed per 1,000 gross ton miles dropped from 157.8 to 135.1. The resulting savings more than offset the higher costs.[64]

One means of stimulating freight business centered on boosting area agricultural output. Obviously, the Corn Belt Route served America's breadbasket. The farmers, who had long sparred with the company (but less so than with most carriers) over matters of rates and services, needed to be courted, even educated, not simply for their political support but also, as Knowlton, Iowa, agent J. B. Forsythe noted, "because [they] are the sinew and backbone of our transportation revenues."[65]

Throughout the 1920s the Great Western had bucked a downward trend nationally in the shipment of agricultural commodities by rail. The combination of a deepening farm recession that began early in the decade and increased motor truck competition largely explained the slump. For the CGW, the tonnage figures for goods labeled "Agriculture" generally reflect this trend. For example, in 1922, the road carried 1,759,429 tons; 1,588,289 tons in 1925; 1,470,714 tons in 1927; and 1,609,998 tons in 1929. On the other hand, carloadings of "Prod-

The CGW bolstered its passenger revenues in the 1920s by offering through sleeping cars from the Twin Cities to California via the Atchison, Topeka & Santa Fé. (H. Roger Grant Collection)

The Great Western's brief experiment with integrated air service is revealed in this 1929 advertising copy designed for its Waterloo, Iowa, area patrons. (H. Roger Grant Collection)

ucts of Animals" (livestock, fresh meats, poultry, hides, and the like) actually increased during this period: 526,270 tons in 1922; 543,367 tons in 1925; 587,929 tons in 1927; and 650,146 tons in 1929. As for the percentage of overall traffic carried, "Agriculture" dropped from 30.1 percent in 1922 to 21.2 percent in 1929; "Products of Animals" slipped slightly, 9.0 percent in 1922 to 8.6 percent in 1929.[66]

The Corn Belt Route's desire to promote the agricultural sector was neither new for the company nor unique to the industry. During the depression of the 1890s, A. B. Stickney had asked Iowa plowmen to embark upon commercial potato production. Such a crop, he believed, offered them an opportunity to diversify, thus providing some measure of protection from downswings in the corn and livestock economy. And Stickney hired a prominent Iowa creamery man to build up milk and cheese cooperatives

A monster Texas-type engine stands outside the Baldwin Loco-motive Works' main plant at Eddystone, Pennsylvania, in 1930.

This locomotive superbly glorified in steel an independent spirit. (H. L. Broadbelt Collection)

and to promote raising of dairy herds. These activities, of course, promised to augment the Great Western's tonnage. Early in the twentieth century, Granger roads, in particular, awoke farmers to the possibilities of the "New Agriculture" through exhibits and lectures. Railroad personnel frequently joined forces with the faculties of land-grant colleges who already had mastered farm demonstration techniques. Prior to World War I, the Soo Line, for example, remodeled a baggage car, filled it with educational displays that preached the gospel of "Better Seeds and Better Sires," staffed it with trained representatives, and sent it along its system in Wisconsin, Minnesota, and the Dakotas.[67]

The Chicago Great Western formally launched its own agrarian educational and publicity arm in December 1920. For the Midwest, this was a rather late date. Not only had most neighboring roads had such departments since the turn of the century, but, after 1914, the government extension service and county agent system provided an institutional means of contacting the rural population. During this early period the Great Western had relied upon industrial agents to promote agricultural activities, whether strawberry culture in Missouri or dairy herds in Minnesota. When the CGW finally started its own educational network, the company named Develop-

ment Agent T. A. Hoverstad, a Kenyon, Minnesota, native, to coordinate efforts; and he received assistance from two experienced plowmen, J. J. Sprenger, who farmed near Zumbrota, Minnesota, and Forrest Henry from rural Dover, Minnesota. They were busy folks. The men spent April through November contacting on-line farmers and from December through March conducting farmers' institutes in depots, schools, churches, halls, or, more commonly, in a refurbished 1888 passenger coach, specially lettered AGRICULTURAL DEVELOPMENT DEPARTMENT. In 1924, for example, the company hosted seventy-nine of these free gatherings, which attracted nearly 16,000 farmers, schoolchildren, and other interested people. They learned of better farming practices, discussed a variety of agricultural and transportation topics and received a miscellany of printed literature. The Great Western also worked closely with Iowa State College, a leading promoter of scientific agriculture. In 1929, the jointly sponsored, three-car "Lime, Legumes and Livestock" special toured the system and attracted thousands of on-line residents. What impact the CGW's farm education work had on its overall earnings is impossible to determine. Unmistakably, however, management correctly sensed the value of progressive agriculture.[68]

The Great Western naturally employed other

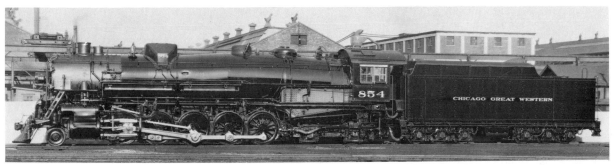

Texas engine #854, fresh from the shops, rests in front of the massive Lima Locomotive Works complex in Lima, Ohio, in 1930. Soon the Corn Belt Route herald replaced the name on the tender. (Allen County Historical Society)

means of increasing freight revenues. Off-line traffic solicitors continued to seek out customers. The company also hired a Chicago advertising agency in January 1922 to promote freight and passenger services. The message adopted was hardly original: the CGW offers "personal railroading." The road also brought out a successor to *The Maize* in February 1922. Called *The Great Western Magazine,* this attractive monthly publication served various audiences—employees, travelers, and shippers. Even President Felton personally entered the crusade; he regularly asked shareholders and employees to drum up business. The Corn Belt Route also received outside support. Several communities that depended heavily on the railroad's payroll sought to help bolster its freight income. The Clarion, Iowa, Chamber of Commerce, for instance, urged its membership in September 1928 to buy nothing from wholesale houses that moved by truck.[69]

Unfortunately, the thinking of the Felton regime toward motor competition lacked any major innovative flare. Unlike some railroads, the CGW never entered the bus business, although a few small, independent operators coordinated their schedules with the company's passenger movements. As for trucks, the Great Western apparently failed to recognize the future impact of this mode of transport. After all, the country lacked a massive network of all-weather roads during the 1920s, and equipment was small and not particularly dependable. But there were early warning signs that trouble lurked ahead. A

Missouri teamster, for example, ran this ad in the *Parnell Sentinel* in 1921: "SHIP BY TRUCK. I now have a Reo Speed Wagon, the fastest truck shipment on the road. Special attention given to stock shipments to St. Joseph and other points." By the decade's end, the *Oelwein Daily Register* observed: "It seems to us that inasmuch as this new method of transportation [motor vehicles] is bound to come sooner or later to all communities, the best thing that can be done is for the railroads to go into the bus and truck line to take care of the short hauls and make them an adjunct and a feeder for their rail line." And the paper gave the Great Western some practical advice: "It would seem to us that the sooner the CGW also gets into this line of transportation . . . the better it will be." The company did buy several truck and trailer units in 1929 to handle freight shipments between terminals in the Twin Cities.[70]

Notwithstanding recession and "rubber-tire" competition, the freight story for the 1920s generally held a positive theme. The company steadily improved volume and income, although fluctuations understandably occurred. The combined carload and less-than-carload tonnage totaled 5,853,531 in 1922; 6,601,962 in 1925; and 7,599,755 in 1929. The bright spots were the transportation of petroleum products and commodities handled in privately owned cars. Although the road operated in a notoriously poor territory for good divisions of through rates, freight revenues reached respectable levels:

The complexity of a Texas-type steam locomotive is revealed in this interior view of the cab. The boiler backhead is a maze of valves, pipes, gauges, and wires. (Allen County Historical Society)

$17,730,271 in 1922; $18,844,285 in 1925; $20,739,859 in 1929, with the latter being the best year. Volume became so great that in order to move the cars the operating department dispatched extra trains powered by ten locomotives rented from the Pennsylvania and followed by cabooses borrowed from the Great Northern. The CGW wisely emphasized throughout the period its value as a bridge route between major Midwestern gateways, "without complicated and involved terminal problems." Also, to its advantage, less than 25 percent of the company's trackage consisted of branches. By the twenties, such appendages were often highly vulnerable to truck competition. After 1928, another factor explained the increasing freight tonnage and hence greater income — the patronage brought by a group of traffic managers from prominent shippers whose controversial activities would receive considerable attention a decade later.[71]

The overall financial picture of the Great Western during the 1920s is largely reflected in the previous freight figures. The net income realized in 1922 was $432,769; $628,920 in 1925; and $1,235,879 in 1929. Admittedly, these published annual totals lack exactness. While a financial improvement unmistakably occurred, the company failed, following the 1909 reorganization, to accrue depreciation of its equipment on a reasonable basis. Had this amount

The Baldwin Locomotive Works produced this 25-ton, 175-horsepower gas switcher for the Great Western in 1925. It re-mained in service on the Cedar Falls, Iowa, branch until 1956. (James L. Rueber Collection)

been added to other operating expenses, in accordance with the regular accounting rules of the Interstate Commerce Commission, net income would have been reduced significantly. As early as 1917 the ICC complained about the situation, and in January 1926 a member of the Commission's Bureau of Accounts called the matter "one of the worst cases of procrastination and evasion that has come to my attention."[72]

LABOR RELATIONS

At the end of World War I, the American laboring classes expressed a new militance. They desperately sought to preserve wartime wage gains in the face of inflation, hard times, and a seemingly more reactionary business community. In 1919 nearly twenty-one percent of all workers struck their employers, five times more than in an average prewar year. And unrest continued during the first part of the 1920s, especially in coal mining and railroading, before calmer days finally returned.[73]

Reflecting the national picture, labor-management relations on the Chicago Great Western underwent noticeable change during the postwar years. Unhappiness in the blue-collar sector characterized the early twenties, while tranquility reigned by mid-decade. Innovation, that ubiquitous theme on the Great Western, played a role in the unfolding of events.

A principal feature of the Transportation Act of 1920 called for creation of the United States Railroad Labor Board. This body, together with individual railroad boards of labor adjustment, soon heard grievances over rules, working conditions, and wages. Generally, the Labor Board, which gave way to the Board of Mediation in 1926, took a pro-management stance. It gained widespread hostility from the unions' rank and file when it recommended substantial wage cuts in 1921 and 1922. A 13 percent reduction for the 400,000-strong American Federation of Labor shopmen's unions, announced on June 6, 1922, proved to be too much; they struck the carriers on July 1. About 90 percent effective, this walkout was not joined by other unions, although the maintenance-of-way, signalmen, and clerks brotherhoods did threaten to leave their posts.[74]

On the Chicago Great Western, members of the shop crafts cursed wage slashes, and they also harbored deep grudges against the Felton administration. In the summer of 1917, workers had walked out for fifteen days to protest their wage scales. They saw them as being too far below those that prevailed on other area roads. The shopmen's protests brought moderate concessions: they won increases that ranged from three to nine cents per hour. In the months before the national strike, Oelwein employees, in particular, were once again in a poor mood. The postwar recession of 1921 practically closed the complex for weeks. When the facility reopened, scores of men faced layoffs. Then, to worsen matters, management concocted what it surely must have viewed as a clever, even brilliant, change: it would lease branches of work, including shops activities, to a private contractor. So, in the spring of 1922, the Chicago-based A. S. Hecker Construction Company technically became the employer of hundreds of Great Western operatives. "The men maintain that the move is only a subterfuge to get them from under the jurisdiction of the federal railway wage board," correctly observed one newspaper editor, "and that though nominally working for A. Hecker & Co., they would actually be working for the railway."[75]

The shopmen's strike on the Great Western itself proved nasty. Workers, of course, felt bitter against both the Railroad Labor Board and the company. In this time before unemployment insurance and when so many already had experienced the sting of layoffs, the three-month dispute caused considerable suffering. An uneasy calm did prevail at most locations, including the giant Oelwein complex, but problems erupted in South Des Moines. On the evening of August 2, a mob of about seventy-five strikers and sympathizers, armed with clubs, brickbats, and stones, stormed the CGW roundhouse. Yelling "Scabs!" the angry men quickly routed the sixty workers from their jobs. Some found safety in "bunks, under engines and in box cars," but the dozen or so souls who were unable to escape were "surrounded and pleaded for mercy." The attackers dragged these men into the nearby weedy bottoms of the Raccoon River, where they were beaten. The next day, peace returned. Aided by a hastily erected search light atop a sixty-foot tower, local police and special railroad deputies patrolled the site and prevented further violence and vandalism.[76]

By fall, conditions nationally and on the Great Western reverted to more normal levels. Repeating management's victories over labor in virtually all of the postwar conflicts, railroad owners broke the national strike with the assistance of an injunction secured by "union-hating" Attorney General Harry M. Daugherty. A majority of workers reluctantly accepted the reduced wages and returned to their jobs in late September and early October. Some, however, stubbornly stayed out until the next summer. The shop crafts on the CGW resumed their posts on October 5, 1922. Earlier, the Railroad Labor Board had given some good news to Corn Belt Route employees. It denied the practice of farming out portions of the company's work to a private contractor. The railroad therefore terminated its contract with the Hecker firm on July 16, 1922.[77]

Unlike the labor relationship, the white-collar personnel and the company hierarchy remained on good terms. Even though the CGW usually paid its employees less than its competitors, it still attracted competent, dedicated people. Most hailed from the railroad's home territory; some, in fact, had known

The labor intensive, dirty work of railroading in the days of steam is revealed in the photograph of two employees repairing a locomotive in the St. Paul enginehouse about 1915. (W. A. Vaughn Collection)

the road since childhood, coming from Great Western towns and families. And, since the carrier's bureaucracy was not massive, its streamlined structure allowed individuals to know their co-workers.

While both white- and blue-collar employees frequently saw the Great Western as a "big family," the former seem to have developed the notion more fully. D. Keith Lawson, who joined the company in 1925 and spent his career in personnel work, remembers that "there was something about the way the officers got along and the way they treated you that made me think—there is something about these people that makes me want to be like them. Now what is it? Well, I didn't know at the time, but a few years later I discovered that they were all Masons. So in 1930 I became a Mason." Lawson recalls what is likely the key to explaining the esprit de corps that existed among the white-collar force, and perhaps among most Great Western employees: the Chicago Great Western was a Protestant road. In the twenties, angry groups and their hate literature eagerly promoted "100% Americanism." Not only were Jews and blacks singled out for alleged misdeeds, but Roman Catholics, too, felt bias. The powerful Ku Klux Klan, most of all, blasted Romanism, charging, for example, that the Knights of Columbus indulged in obscene rites and that the Pope wanted to take over the country. While the Klan certainly did not capture the Great Western management, the question of religious affiliation seemed especially important to many.[78]

Actually, the industry by this time had its "Protestant" and "Catholic" railroads: the Great Northern and the Southern Pacific belonged to the ranks of the former, while the Milwaukee and the Northern Pacific joined the latter. Obviously, there were Catholics who worked for the Chicago Great Western. Oelwein, the community with the largest concentration of Great Western employees, had sizable numbers of German and Italian Catholics. Yet no Catholics were counted among the railroad's top officials. Not only were these men Protestants, they were also Masons. And this same fact also held true for hundreds of blue-collar workers.

While this common fraternal order and religious affiliation served as a bond among Great Westerners, especially those at the highest levels, other factors contributed to a sense of closeness. Since the early years of the century, employees, particularly shopmen, had enjoyed participation in company-sponsored baseball teams. A systemwide bowling league, launched in 1924, also found enthusiastic support. And there was the "Great Western Glee Club" for the nonathletic. After 1920, workers could join a gun club and three years later, a "veterans' association." The latter was the brainchild of A. L. Wilhelm, a dispatcher at St. Paul, who designed it "to foster social feelings, to create and maintain mutual interest in the common welfare and to diffuse knowledge of railroad science and administration." The organization quickly grew; scores of employees enthusiastically signed membership applications. The entire railroad, but most of all the Western Division, took great pride in winning the highly coveted E. H. Harriman Memorial Medal in 1924 for the "Division of an American Steam Railroad which has been most successful in protecting the lives and health of its employees and the public." The labors of the safety department had paid off handsomely.[79]

TWILIGHT OF THE FELTON ERA

BY 1925 the benefits of Samuel M. Felton's leadership seemed clear: the Chicago Great Western had established itself as a progressive, innovative railroad. Felton and his staff, of course, knew that they really had little choice if their road was to survive the competitive environment of Midwestern railroading. The Great Western could also boast that its financial house was in reasonably good order. Largely to streamline bookkeeping chores, the parent company dismantled the corporate structure of the "captive" Wisconsin, Minnesota & Pacific in May 1920. Felton also labored mightily throughout his tenure to improve the market for company bonds, which had not done well since 1911. When possible, the road used surplus net profits to retire its obligations and those of the satellite Mason City & Fort Dodge and the WM&P. By 1925 the par value of these outstanding securities totaled $25,592 per mile, with the interest charges being $1,022 per mile. In this respect the CGW compared most favorably with its competitors. Since the 1909 reorganization the company had spent $32,909,872 on physical improvements, or $23,334 per mile, slightly more than 90 percent of its bonded indebtedness.[80]

At the Board of Directors meeting held at Great Western headquarters in the Peoples Gas Building in Chicago on November 2, 1925, Samuel Felton voluntarily stepped down from the presidency. He was seventy-two and in failing health. The Board, however, named Felton to be its chairman and endorsed his recommendation for president, the well-trained Nathaniel Lamson Howard.[81]

Less a "blue-nose" than Felton and possessing a much warmer nature, Howard was tall, slim, and only forty-one. At the time of his appointment, he won national attention for being the youngest president of a Class I railroad. Born in Fairfield, Iowa, on March 9, 1884, and raised in that southern Iowa community, Howard left home in 1903 to enter West Point; he graduated from the academy four years later. Rather than pursuing a military career, he opted instead for one in transportation, starting that September as a civil engineer for the Chicago, Burlington & Quincy. Soon the boyish railroader transferred to the road's operating department, serving as trainmaster at Centerville, Iowa, assistant superintendent at Galesburg, Illinois, and then superintendent at Burlington, Iowa. In 1916 he left the Hawkeye State to head the Hannibal Division in Missouri. Fittingly, Howard joined the Army during World War I and, in May 1917, became a Lieutenant Colonel (later Colonel) of the Thirteenth Railway Engineers, the unit that contained so many Great Western men. From August until the following spring he served under Samuel Felton in France, where they struck up a close friendship. Returning home in May 1919, Colonel Howard won appointment as assistant to the federal manager of the CB&Q in Chicago and later the same year became general manager of the Missouri District at St. Louis. Howard remained in the Gateway City until July 1923, when he assumed the superintendency of transportation for the CB&Q, with headquarters in Chicago. The future CGW president then went on to head the Chicago Union Station Company in August 1924.[82]

Colonel Howard's presidency of the Chicago Great Western would closely reflect the thinking and wishes of his predecessor. Howard had taken orders from Felton during the war, and he continued to do so on the Corn Belt Route. Not surprisingly, Howard's tenure as president ended when Felton stepped down. At the October 7, 1929, meeting of the Board of Directors, Felton requested that he be relieved of all active work, due most likely to a combination of increasingly poor health and the appearance of hostile new financial interests. Howard, too, submitted his resignation, which, according to the trade press, he did so that "he might recover from an illness from which he has been suffering for the past two months." In reality, the emerging force in the Great Western, the Bremo Corporation, headed by Patrick H. Joyce, a wealthy railroad car manufacturer, had its own candidate for the job, Peoria & Pekin Union Railway president Victor V. Boatner. In fact, the Board immediately named Boatner as Howard's replacement. The Colonel, however, did not join the ranks of the unemployed; he became chairman of the board and president of the Chicago-based North American Car Corporation.[83]

The end of the Samuel Morse Felton regime marked the close of a second phase in the history of the Chicago Great Western. The third would be the Patrick Joyce era, which would run for nearly two decades. These years would be eventful, for both scandal and bankruptcy descended upon the road.

CHAPTER SIX

SCANDAL, DEPRESSION, AND WAR,

1929–1948

JOYCE AND THE BREMO CORPORATION

A SKELETON dangles in the Great Western closet, and it belongs to the Bremo Corporation. This organization, which wrestled control away from the forces of Samuel M. Felton, seemed initially to promise its promoters spectacular personal gains. It was a hard-driving and flamboyant Irishman, Patrick H. ("Pat") Joyce, who spearheaded the clever but sordid activities of this investment clique.

Pat Joyce's background resembled A. B. Stickney's much more than it did Samuel Felton's. Like the Great Western's founder, Joyce had a rags-to-riches career. Born in Chicago on March 6, 1879, and raised in the city's "back of the yards" district, the future railroad executive received only a grammar school education, typical training for the time. Joyce entered the labor force not in an office but outdoors, when he became a switchman for the Chicago & Alton (about the time Felton headed this carrier). Joyce's stint with the Alton was temporary; he soon left railroading for manufacturing. First he worked for the Liberty Car and Equipment Company in Chicago Heights, and then in early 1909 he established what soon became a prosperous concern, the Hammond, Indiana–based Illinois Car & Manufacturing Company. On March 1,

1928, Joyce merged the firm with the Standard Steel Car Company, where he remained in an executive capacity. Two years later the Pullman Company acquired Standard and formed the giant Pullman-Standard complex.[1]

The future Great Western head enjoyed life. An associate recalls that he "cut a pretty wide swath as a young man." Once established financially, Joyce became known in his business and social circles as a "big spender" and a "sportsman." For example, he bought expensive race horses. One colt, *Dick O'Hara,* named after his Bremo Corporation partner, ran, albeit unsuccessfully, in the 1930 Kentucky Derby.[2]

Even though certain elements of the national economy boomed during the late 1920s, Pat Joyce felt that the railroad equipment-building business was slowing up and that he had the time, energy, and money to devote to some fresh enterprise. While the exact circumstances are unknown, it seems likely that Joyce, in talking with acquaintances at the Union League Club of Chicago, particularly Richard "Dick" O'Hara, laid the groundwork for the future Bremo Corporation. The Union League Club had a long-standing reputation as a "spa for railroad traffic men." Dick O'Hara was one such individual; he served as transportation manager for the meat-packing giant, Swift & Company.[3]

O'Hara apparently convinced Joyce that the railroad sector offered attractive investment opportunities. The Chicago Great Western specifically seemed to hold the best prospects for their inital attention. The company's securities were widely scattered among small investors; no individual or group held enough shares to repel a take-over bid effectively. The controlling interests, once established, could make ownership of the preferred stock extremely profitable. Since the 1909 reorganization, the Great Western had paid only modest, scattered dividends on its preferred certificates, yet these instruments bore cumulative dividends at the annual rate of $4.00 from July 1, 1914. By 1928, arrears amounted to approximately $50 per share. O'Hara thought (probably incorrectly) that new, more aggressive leadership could produce the necessary revenues to pay these accumulated preferred dividends. As he said, "The Great Western had very, very bad management [under Felton]. As manager of transportation for Swift over a period of years I knew what good railroad and bad railroad management was."[4]

But the whole idea was more than simply supplying the Great Western with proper guidance. What O'Hara and Joyce had in mind, most of all, was attracting to their investment ranks those people who had the power to route freight over CGW lines. If traffic directors, managers, and others in the field committed themselves financially to the enterprise, presumably both they and the carrier would prosper. These investors could reap substantial windfalls through dividends and security appreciation by merely diverting business to the company in which they held a personal stake. And a busy railroad would mean a variety of wondrous things—contented workers, better equipment, and, most of all, power within the industry and region.[5]

Obviously, Pat Joyce could not afford to buy control of a Class I railroad by himself. So in November 1928 the logical happened: about sixty persons raised $1,842,000 to start the purchase of Great Western stock. Most came from the ranks of the traffic world. For instance, there were O'Hara and several associates from Swift; George A. Blair, traf-

fic manager for Wilson & Company; Jasper W. Robb, traffic manager for Cudahy Packing Company; Edmund L. Dalton, traffic department of American Radiator Company; and Thomas A. Gantt, assistant traffic manager, Corn Products Refining Company. Joyce was the largest contributor; he invested $250,000. Under his direction, the syndicate, whose activities were kept secret, soon acquired a substantial chunk of CGW preferred and a small amount of common stock. Then, in December, the participants decided to incorporate their pool. A holding company, the Bremo Corporation, was formed; and on January 5, 1929, it took over all the securities and stock market activities. Instead of receipts for cash contributions, investors received Bremo stock certificates. Soon, others joined. By the end of 1929, more than a hundred hopeful souls collectively held 123,600 shares of Great Western preferred stock and 12,100 shares of its common. The cost totaled nearly $6,000,000, but most of the securities were bought on margin; Bremo backers borrowed heavily from the brokerage firm that transacted the purchases, Paine, Webber & Company, and from Midwestern banks. Although representing considerably less than a majority of CGW's outstanding securities, the syndicate possessed the largest block.[6]

Once the Bremo Corporation acquired its control of Chicago Great Western's assets it began to push for a change in the railroad's leadership. Dick O'Hara pressed hard for the immediate ouster of Samuel Felton. "Mr. Felton, through his management and unfriendliness toward the shipping public," argued the Swift & Company official, "drove more traffic off that railroad than the traffic organization could solicit for it." The first step toward this end occurred several weeks before the April 1929 annual stockholders meeting. John W. O'Leary, president of Chicago's National Bank of the Republic and a Bremo stockholder, conferred with Arthur Anderson of J. P. Morgan & Company about the future of the Corn Belt Route's management. Since the House of Morgan served as the Great Western's banker and controlled a large number of its proxies, Anderson held a more than passing interest in its operation. Moreover, one of the Morgan partners, Charles Steele, sat on the CGW's Board of Directors and Executive Committee. So, Anderson agreed to back the syndicate's plan to have board representation and to install fresh managerial blood.[7]

It would be Steele who would try to ease out Samuel Felton. In a letter to the Great Western's chief executive officer, he stated that "Mr. Anderson said that we [J. P. Morgan & Company] had no particular interest in the property except to see it prosper and that we saw no objection to his [O'Leary's] suggestion of having representation on the board, provided it all met with your approval." Added Steele, "Anderson understood from O'Leary that they [Bremo] had hoped you would be disposed to go along and help them and that they recognized the fact that you should occupy a dignified position and receive ample consideration." This letter angered Felton; he was not about to cooperate. "I have stood by the Great Western through thick and thin, and protected its interests to the best of my ability. I believe I would be severely criticized if I deserted my post at a time like this. . . . You [J. P. Morgan & Company] reorganized it, started it, and but for the war it would have been a success. I don't want to see it wind up in a receivership just because of the control being secured *by a lot of pirates* [italics added]."[8]

Samuel Felton and his backers were not fools. They realized that the Bremo people lacked command of a majority of the railroad's stock. The Felton forces would resist. However, in the proxy fight that began in March 1929, they would face a major, indeed, fatal handicap. While the Joyce group eagerly marshalled support, J. P. Morgan & Company only half-heartedly took to its task of soliciting proxies for the incumbent management.[9]

Thus, the Bremo Corporation steadily assumed power over the Great Western. At the April 2 annual meeting, the Joyce faction held proxies for about 390,000 shares, while Felton's side controlled only 290,000. And, at that time, Pat Joyce and John O'Leary won seats on the fifteen-member Board of Directors. In October 1929, Felton resigned as Chairman of the Board (he continued as Vice-Chairman of the five-member Executive Committee), and President Howard quit, to be replaced by Joyce's man, V. V. Boatner. Shortly before the next annual meeting, Felton died, and Joyce managed to arrange a favorable agreement with the remaining directors: they allowed him to designate five members of the Board and two members of the Executive Committee. Joyce himself not only gained a place on the Executive Committee but also became its chairman.[10]

The Corn Belt Route's fourth president hailed from the South. Born on May 6, 1881, in Bethlehem, Mississippi, Victor V. Boatner received more than a common-school education; he attended both Mississippi College in nearby Clinton and Kentucky's Bowling Green Business University. In 1901, Boatner started his lengthy railroad career with the Yazoo & Mississippi Valley Railroad, an Illinois Central affiliate; and there he rose from station helper to division superintendent in the next sixteen years. In August 1917, the parent firm named him superintendent of its important Memphis Division. Four years later, Boatner left the Illinois Central to head the Peoria & Pekin Union Railway, a major mid-Illinois switching company. "He modernized the road's equipment, laid new, heavy rails over all its lines, and put the road on a basis where it was earning substantial returns."[11]

When V. V. Boatner assumed the Great Western presidency in October 1929, he immediately pushed ahead the Joyce group's plan for cutting fat. Operations drew his attention. The arrival of the monster Texas-type locomotives that required less frequent servicing led Boatner to order the closing of the large engine terminals at East Stockton, Illinois, and Conception Junction, Missouri, and thus the dismissal of hundreds of employees. The appearance of the new motive power also helped to prompt consolidation of the four operating divisions (Eastern, Southern, Northern, and Western) into three. Under the arrangement that became effective on March 1, 1930, the Illinois Division would now cover the Chicago to Oelwein end; the Iowa Division would include the

When the Boatner administration closed the engine terminal at East Stockton, Illinois, it ordered the relocation of the dis-patchers' office in Stockton. A work train moves the structure to its new site on August 7, 1930. (C. W. Finch Collection)

Oelwein to Kansas City trackage; and the Minnesota Division would contain the remaining network. Clarion, Iowa, was especially hard hit, for it had been the headquarters for the Western Division. With the revised structure, dispatchers and other personnel either lost their jobs or were shifted elsewhere, mostly to St. Paul. The Iowa community was left with only a few officials: assistant superintendent, traveling engineer, and roadmaster. Other retrenchments likewise occurred during Boatner's tenure. Thus, hundreds of employees found themselves in the job market during the midst of a national depression. Support for the president, especially among blue-collar workers, declined markedly; he became known, not so affectionately, as "Vicious Vic."[12]

In July 1931, Boatner lost the respect of Pat Joyce as well. It was not Vicious Vic's conduct as president but rather his personal life that suddenly ended his career with the Great Western. As one official remembers, "Boatner was living in a swanky hotel in Highland Park, a suburb north of Chicago. . . . It [the hotel where he lived] had a circular staircase leading from the second to the first floor and a big dining room off of that. . . . On a Sunday morning after church . . . you would have the socialites gathering for brunch. On one such Sunday morning, lo and behold, V. V. Boatner comes walking down the staircase stark naked! When that got to Pat Joyce, he fired him right then and there." The public explanation for Boatner's departure, however, was simply: "He has resigned on account of poor health." Thus, on July 9, Joyce became the Great Western's acting president and four months later, its head.[13]

The passing of V. V. Boatner failed to alter the work of the Bremo Corporation. Both before and after his departure, Joyce and his associates managed to siphon off as much of the Great Western's cash as possible. Admittedly, Bremo backers diverted some traffic to Corn Belt rails, but the negative impact of the developing Great Depression and, more important, the CGW's accounting practices that failed to charge equipment depreciation as operating expenses meant that the railroad's net income in 1929 and 1930 was woefully inadequate to allow any dividend payments. Although the company claimed earnings of $1,309,000 for 1929 and $900,800 for 1930, a more accurate figure was $60,000 for 1929 and a huge $3,500,000 deficit the following year. Yet the Board of Directors authorized dispersal of $1.00 per share on preferred stock in early 1930, the first such payment since 1919. And, in 1931, the Board declared further dividends that aggregated $2.00 a share. The sum of these expenditures reached nearly $1,500,000.[14]

The Joyce regime sought to bolster its financial position in a way that smacked of sheer dishonesty. The stock market crash of October 1929 soon sent the value of Great Western shares tumbling to only a fraction of their previous value, threatening, of course, the Bremo Corporation's very existence. But, if trading in CGW certificates could be stimulated by a series of substantial purchases, quotations should rise. So, an ingenious plan was devised to institute a set of just such buys. The Great Western's Illinois charter prohibited acquisition of its own stock; therefore, officials merely turned to the Mason City & Fort Dodge, the wholly owned affiliate, instead. The MC&FD was chartered in Iowa, where no ban on such purchases existed. Joyce and his fellow board members directed the subsidiary to acquire about $250,000 of CGW stock in October and November 1930, with the money coming directly from the Great Western treasury. If the price of their stock should soar, the Joyce people apparently planned to buy these shares for themselves at the same rate charged the MC&FD. That did not happen, however, for the worsening economy caused the value of these securities to shrink markedly, and ultimately the CGW's quarter-million-dollar investment nearly evaporated.[15]

The wheeling and dealing of Pat Joyce and his cohorts extended beyond the pale of the Chicago Great Western. In fact, the group entered the realm of America's greatest railroad magnates, two brothers from Cleveland, Ohio, Oris Paxton and Mantis James Van Sweringen, commonly called the Vans. By 1929 these two financiers controlled a vast empire valued in excess of $3 billion that included five major steam roads, the Chesapeake & Ohio, the Erie, the Missouri Pacific, the Nickel Plate, and the Pere Marquette, and an enormous holding company, the Alleghany Corporation.[16]

As the Joyce-O'Hara syndicate was taking shape, the Vans realized the potential value of their financial backing. If the Bremo people could throw business to the Corn Belt Route, they might surely do the same for the Vans' own properties. But friendship could mean much more: these upstarts might become so dependent upon their aid that they could dominate the Great Western, even control it totally. In the meantime, it would do them no harm to have this strategic railroad in genial hands.[17]

The Van Sweringen organization liberally favored the Bremo cause. Various officials invested in it; John J. Bernet, president of the C&O, regularly advised Pat Joyce; and the Vans' stockbrokers, Paine, Webber, executed numerous chores for them. In fact, Kenneth D. Steere of that firm, who had once served as a special assistant to the brothers, acted as the first president and treasurer of the Bremo Corporation.[18]

The involvement of the Van Sweringen combine grew steadily. From the start, the Bremo syndicate relied heavily on Paine, Webber to finance its acquisition of Great Western stock. Since these purchases were made on margin, the Bremo debt to the brokerage house soared, and eventually totaled about $4,000,000. As collateral, Paine, Webber held all of Bremo's CGW shares. When the railroad's stock "fell out of bed" after the Crash, conditions reached critical levels for Joyce and his associates. Beginning in October 1929 and at various times in 1930, the Vans came to the rescue by extending cash and credit. Finally, in December, they assumed the full risk of Paine, Webber in Bremo's stock-market venture. The brothers loaned the failing holding company nearly $4 million through a C&O subsidiary, the Virginia Transportation Corporation. This debt was represented by a promissory note payable on demand. Thus, the Vans were in a position to foreclose at any time and to take over for themselves all of Bremo's assets in the Great Western.[19]

While continuing to skate along, Pat Joyce and his colleagues found themselves on dangerously thin ice. Bremo could not repay the Virginia Transportation Corporation debt; it even had difficulty meeting the interest charges. However, so long as the railroad could be made to yield dividends on its preferred stock, funds could be channelled to cover the mandatory installments. But as income dropped, Bremo backers faced a precarious situation: the heretofore friendly and indulgent Vans might be forced to destroy their enterprise.[20]

The Van Sweringens had no desire to crush the Joyce group. Rather, they sought a favor from them. The Vans, too, were experiencing serious money woes. Their giant holding company, the Alleghany Corporation, desperately needed an infusion of funds. They therefore sought to sell to the Great Western the Alleghany's 20 percent interest in the Kansas City Southern Railway Company (KCS) at an exorbitant price. The brothers had several other reasons for wanting to divest themselves of their KCS portfolio. For one thing, the Alleghany Corporation never had received the Missouri Public Service Commission's permission to acquire the Kansas City Southern stock. This railroad possessed a Missouri charter, and local law prohibited any party from acquiring more than ten percent of a carrier's stock without the Commission's approval. Problems likewise existed with federal authorities. The Interstate Commerce Commission's railroad consolidation plan of 1929 allocated the KCS to the Union Pacific and not to the Vans' Missouri Pacific. Since the KCS and Missouri Pacific competed in the Kansas City to Gulf territory, the brothers' control of these two rival roads probably violated the anti-trust code.[21]

So the Alleghany Corporation offered 104,500 shares of Kansas City Southern common stock to the Joyce road. The price tag was a staggering $30 a share, for a total of $3,135,000. This represented double the market price at which these securities were then being traded on the New York Stock Exchange. To protect themselves fully, the crafty Vans' arrangement required that in case the purchase should turn sour, the entire loss would fall on the hapless Great Western. But if a profit should occur within two years, the Alleghany Corporation could claim half of it. This agreement was expressed in the form of an option, exercisable by Alleghany or any of its subsidiaries, to buy back 52,250 shares for $30 each at any time within the next twenty-four months. On October 5, 1931, the Chicago Great Western entered into this most unfavorable contract.[22]

The Great Western had no business acquiring the Kansas City Southern stock. First of all, the CGW's overall financial condition was extremely poor. The road's cash resources, drained by the improvident declaration of dividends, had dried up to such an extent that it had to borrow $200,000 to cover its regular interest charges which came due on March 1, 1932. And soon the company got nearly $3,000,000 in loan money from the Reconstruction Finance Corporation and the Railroad Credit Corporation to cover taxes, interest, and other pressing obligations. (Somewhat surprisingly, John W. Barriger III, head of the RFC's railroad division, had called the CGW, "A mountain railroad in a prairie country serving a traffic vacuum.") To meet its commitment for the KCS securities, the CGW begged $300,000 from Chicago bankers and issued two-year bearer notes for $3,175,000.[23]

The investment agreement, of course, had other obvious flaws. While in better shape financially than the Great Western, the Kansas City Southern certainly was not robust. Two weeks before the Joyce deal, the KCS board decided to omit dividends on common stock. That was not all. Although Joyce told Great Western investors in the 1931 annual report that "it is believed that the two roads have a mutual interest as supplementing lines in caring for traffic augmenting on each line and carried over both," traffic managers, not railroads, generally determined the movement of tonnage. Joyce surely knew that unrouted cargoes were the exception; Dick O'Hara clued him in on that fact of railroad life when the two hatched the CGW take-over scheme. Moreover, the whole KCS deal smacked of questionable legality. The Great Western was buying shares from a concern that had never been sanctioned by Missouri authorities to own them. There was also an Illinois law to consider — the prohibition against any locally chartered railroad acquiring stock in a connecting carrier of another state unless it purchased at least two thirds of its securities. The CGW was an Illinois company, the KCS a Missouri one, and they interchanged at Kansas City.[24]

The Joyce management attempted to jump the two principal legal hurdles. It belatedly asked the Missouri Public Service Commission for a hearing on the acquisition of KCS stock, and it once again turned to the Mason City & Fort Dodge to dodge the Illinois prohibition. The MC&FD then bought the shares from Alleghany.[25]

By 1933, however, the entire plan was doomed. The Great Western moved steadily toward bankruptcy, and the legal problems seemed even messier. If the CGW fell into the hands of the court, the Vans had no way of knowing the fate of the 104,500 shares of KCS stock. To make matters worse, the Joyce road had never been able to acquire clear title to these securities, and it could resist payment on the multimillion-dollar notes.[26]

In July, the Great Western withdrew from the Alleghany deal with full approval of the Van Sweringens. The worried brothers together with the equally concerned brokers at Paine, Webber decided to tear up the notes in exchange for the KCS stock. However, they kept the $300,000 cash. While the CGW lost a considerable amount of desperately needed money, it freed itself from the expense of the agreement and possible future litigation. And, too, the Vans still expressed friendship toward Joyce and his partners. As it turned out, the brothers would no longer be involved in the affairs of the Corn Belt Route. Soon their once-mighty empire stood in shambles, and, shortly, both men died.[27]

In a sense, the Chicago Great Western died as

well. On February 28, 1935, the company sought court protection under section 77 of the Bankruptcy Act of 1898. But before the District Court for the Northern District of Illinois appointed a receiver, Congress amended the bankruptcy code to require that two trustees be named, one of whom could not have had any connection with management for at least a year.[28]

Although the antics of Pat Joyce did much to land the Great Western on the financial rocks, on October 14, 1935, the court, nevertheless, selected him to serve as one of the two trustees. It named Chicago attorney Luther M. Walter as the other. These men were not only to submit a plan for reorganization, but they were also to report "any facts pertaining to irregularities, fraud, misconduct, or mismanagement, as a consequence of which the debtor may have a cause of action arising therefrom against any person or corporation." Needless to say, Joyce was not about to disclose any shortcomings, nor was Walter. While lacking official ties to the Great Western, he was a close friend of its general counsel, Ralph M. Shaw; in fact, both Shaw and Joyce had suggested his appointment.[29]

Fortunately, the public interest found support from the Senate Committee on Interstate Commerce, chaired by the progressive Montana Democrat, Burton K. Wheeler. Between 1936 and 1938, Wheeler and an investigating subcommittee would explore a myriad of alleged railroad industry misconduct, including that of the Great Western in 1937. This probe would force the co-trustees to give the federal court their long-delayed report on "any facts pertaining to irregularities." Supposedly, it was the handiwork of Luther Walter, for "Mr. Joyce, in deference to the obvious conflict in his position, did not sign it." Irrespective of its authorship, the study would ignore most of the regime's weaknesses. It would skirt the involvement of the Bremo Corporation and while mentioning the disastrous purchase of Kansas City Southern stock, it would fail to explain the Van Sweringen connection. Wrote Luther, "I find no evidence that President Joyce acted in bad faith. He had invested a large portion of his funds in the capital stock of the Chicago Great Western Railroad Co., and he believed the acquisition of the Kansas City Southern Railway Co. stock would improve the position of the Chicago Great Western Railroad Co."[30]

Pat Joyce, his investment allies and Great Western associates would never face any prosecution for their acts. They either found loopholes (ones that the Wheeler Committee suggested that Congress plug), or they managed to avoid the already prescribed legal consequences. Their *only* penalty, although not insignificant, was the loss of the value of their Bremo Corporation securities and an enormous diminution in the value of their CGW portfolio.

Technically, the holding company, the Bremo Corporation, was legitimate. Yet, its activities unquestionably overstepped acceptable ethical bounds. The respected trade journal, *Traffic World,* superbly appraised the moral dimensions of the scheme shortly after its inception. "To us it would be surprising if anyone, . . . failed to see at once that what was proposed was unethical. . . . And yet the persons said to be involved either are consciously dishonest—which we hesitate to believe—or their moral sense is so blunted that they know not what they do."[31]

The Joyce group, however, disregarded the Elkins Act of 1903. This law made recipients of rebates, together with the railroads and their officers that offered them, liable for criminal action. What the Great Western management did was to grant unusually generous allowances to favored shippers when they filed claims for alleged mishandling and damaging of freight in transit. The leading case involved a Chicago wholesale fruit company, Joseph Brothers. The owners invested $20,000 in the Bremo Corporation and immediately diverted a considerable part of their traffic from the C&NW to the CGW. Soon, too, Joseph Brothers made extensive damage claims. Subsequently, the ICC's Bureau of Inquiry found that the railroad settled such cases "on a basis more favorable to the shipper than the facts warranted." In 1932 the Commission turned the matter over to the United States district attorney in Chicago. In an ensuing trial the judge concluded that insufficient evidence existed for a criminal conviction, but he personally believed that "there had been rebating and consequently violations of the Elkins Act by the defendent by means of the payment of excessive amounts on account of loss and damage claims."[32]

THE CGW IN THE 1930s

WHILE the Bremo Corporation and financial matters dominated the life of the Chicago Great Western during the 1930s, the company did continue to go about the business of operating a railroad. After the major personnel cutbacks at the beginning of the decade, employment levels remained generally stable. Indeed, if the road were to move freight and passengers, layoffs could not persist. When the volume of business increased during the late thirties, the company recalled or hired many workers. In Des Moines, for example, some furloughed Rock Island trainmen joined Great Western crews on Oelwein and Kansas City runs. But before that upturn, scores of regular operating employees faced either unemployment or underemployment. In 1967, engineer Milton Smith of Oelwein, who "hired out" in 1920, recalled that "the rough times came [for me] during 1932. . . . I can remember working only two trips that year, and extending my credit at the New Home and Majestic restaurants on the basis that my job-call status was just a little more secure than most others held by railroaders."[33]

During the thirties the Joyce regime had to cut substantially passenger service. Intercity travel lost much of the glamor of the twenties. A few name-trains survived, but the crack *Legionnaire,* the "Great Train of the Great Western," was downgraded and became the not-so-ritzy *Minnesotan.* The *Red Bird* and *Blue Bird* gave way to local motor runs, and varnish vanished entirely from the Randolph-Mankato, Winona-Rochester, McIntire-Osage, and Waverly-Sumner branches. Also, the company withdrew all of its through sleepers, substituted "cafe-lounge" cars for its traditional diners, and closed its city ticket offices.[34]

And other adjustments had to be made. Like most carriers, the Great Western slashed fares to boost ridership. A thirty-day round trip coach ticket cost as little as 1⅘ cents per mile. Yet revenues declined steadily, although a slight upturn took place in 1935 and 1936. The road collected $1,261,794 in 1931 but only $480,522 in 1939. To economize, the company tried replacing several steam-powered trains with gasoline rolling stock, new but not fancy. In 1932, four of these Pullman-built motor cars commenced operations between Oelwein and Kansas City and between the Twin Cities and Omaha.[35]

Just as passenger operations shrank, so did trackage. The harbinger of future abandonments took place in 1932. In that year the company got permission to pull up eleven miles of the Lehigh branch because of mine closings and also to run over the largely parallel and far superior Chicago & North Western route between Winona and Utica. Although the Iowa segment had to be retired, the Minnesota one generated enough traffic to warrant continuation of service in the area. But much of the CGW's Minnesota line was a nightmare to maintain and operate. The eight miles between Altura and Rollingstone were especially troublesome: sixteen bridges, twenty-one culverts, excessive curvature, and a monstrous westbound grade of 3.3 percent. Scrappers removed this section in 1934. Although the through trains now used C&NW rails, CGW locals continued to shuttle cars over the ten miles from Utica to Altura and the fourteen miles between Winona and Rollingstone. And the Joyce administration soon signed a trackage rights agreement to include an additional 17.4 miles. Beginning July 1, 1935, Great Western freights moved onto the North Western at Planks Junction, 8.5 miles east of Simpson, and traveled on to Utica and Winona. The CGW quickly ripped up the redundant mileage, except for station tracks at Dover, St. Charles, and Utica. Then the east end of the original Winona-Simpson line started to disappear. The 7.6 miles between Gilmore and Rollingstone were dismantled

in 1936; service ended on the three miles between Sugar Loaf and Gilmore three years later; and the remaining 1.6 miles came out in 1943.[36]

While few patrons complained officially about the elimination of service on either the Lehigh branch or portions of the Winona-Simpson line, a much different reaction occurred in November 1933 when the Great Western revealed its plan to retire the seven-mile Eden to Mantorville, Minnesota stub. This announcement shocked and angered Mantorville citizens. Two years previously they had lost their only other rail outlet when the North Western abandoned its Kasson branch, and they were not about to be left without trains. The *Mantorville Express* reported the Great Western's intentions with a banner headline, "KEEP THE RAILROAD!" and warned that economic disaster lurked ahead if service ended. "If allowed, property values will drop to half its [*sic*] present worth. It [abandonment] will force several local concerns out of business." Townspeople knew full well that times were tough, and they did not relish any further dislocations. And the paper fittingly announced that "it is our intention to fight the railroad's proposal to discontinue their meager service to Mantorville with every honorable weapon at our command."[37]

Throughout 1934 the folks in Mantorville battled hard to retain the Great Western. Shortly before the Interstate Commerce Commission hosted hearings in a local hotel on the abandonment petition, the *Express* editor imaginatively offered, "Three one year subscriptions for the three best answers to the following question: Why should the Interstate Commerce Commission deny the petition of the railroad company to abandon the branch from Eden to Mantorville?" What responses, if any, this public-spirited journalist got are unknown. At the meeting, conducted in early March, community representatives charged that the railroad failed to maintain the line and had bled it dry. Speaking for the company, Division Superintendent E. W. Fowler admitted that little had been spent on maintenance; but he argued cogently that business was very poor, and the property simply did not warrant any sizable expendi-

The Chicago Great Western gained national recognition for being an early user of welded rail. This photograph, taken in 1938, shows a section of recently welded rail east of Oneida, Iowa. (James L. Rueber Collection)

tures. A month later the ICC hearing examiner announced his decision: he agreed with Fowler that the branch was a financial burden and should be retired. Since it was in such bad condition, the line could close at once. Undaunted by this ruling, the town officials appealed to the federal courts, but to no avail. This merely delayed the inevitable. On November 14, 1934, the last train puffed into the village, picked up several empty cars, and returned to the main line at Eden. The next spring the *Express* reported the line's swan song: "Echoes of times long past wafted through the air as groups of men and women watched a railroad crew take away the remnants of railroad equipment that one time connected Mantorville with the outside world."[38]

At the same time that the Chicago Great Western was trimming its trackage, a sister granger railroad seemed destined to lose much of its mileage, even its very existence. The 1,400-mile Minneapolis & St. Louis, appropriately nicknamed "Misery & Short Life" and "Maimed & Still Limping," appeared ut-

terly doomed. By the mid-thirties the conventional wisdom held that it was "of little worth as a railroad but of considerable junk value." Even though the company was blessed with a dynamic and talented receiver, there emerged in 1935 a proposal for liquidation. A group of neighboring carriers, including the Great Western, acting through the specially created Associated Railways Company, planned to acquire portions of the "Louie" and to abandon the rest. As part of the consortium, the Great Western had its eyes on eighty-eight miles of the M&StL's Mason City to Marshalltown main line. This artery would shorten considerably the CGW's route between the Twin Cities and Kansas City. Enormous public opposition and a remarkably revived M&StL, however, prevented the scheme's implementation. Of course, the Great Western was hardly in a financial position to purchase any mileage. Moreover, some shippers along the CGW, who also used the Louie, pressured the Joyce administration to withdraw from the pool.[39]

Talk of M&StL dismemberment captured considerable national attention, certainly in industry and banking circles. The Chicago Great Western, too, gained notoriety at this time, not for its involvement with Associated Railways Company, but for an innovative experiment—hauling loaded truck trailers on flatcars, the so-called piggyback service. Although it had been ravaged by the Bremo Corporation, the Great Western continued to display its inventive flair. Once more the road demonstrated the validity of the notion that competitive innovation usually springs from the weaker carriers. Unquestionably, the piggyback trial proved enormously significant to both the CGW and to American transportation.

The idea of hauling trailers actually predates its implementation in the 1930s. For years, steam roads had hauled circus equipment and occasionally placed wagons, later trucks, on flatcars. North Dakota's tiny Midland Continental in 1918, for example, carried such a fully loaded commercial vehicle. It was the electric interurban industry, however, that pioneered the modern concept. In 1926 the

The most famous innovation in Great Western history was the road's introduction of "piggyback" service. Here a truck is pick- ing up a trailer in the Chicago yards in 1936. (William Lenoir Photograph)

Chicago, North Shore & Milwaukee, a Samuel Insull property, began to transport specially designed truck trailers on modified flat cars, initially to compensate for its inability to bring freight into downtown Chicago over the local elevated system. Soon, another Insull "juice" line adopted the idea. The Chicago, South Shore & South Bend proudly introduced its "ferry truck" service in 1927: "Trailers left at your door for loading, shipped overnight on special flat cars."[40]

In early 1935 the Great Western's traffic department called management's attention to this piggyback concept. The North Shore's success sparked the suggestion. Pat Joyce liked the idea and ordered his young and talented assistant, Samuel M. Golden, to work out the considerable details. One of the few Jews in a position of importance in American railroading at this time, Golden, a Wharton School of Commerce graduate, had been comptroller for the Illinois Car & Manufacturing Company and had then become Joyce's right-hand man at Standard Steel Car before joining the CGW in 1932. Soon

after arriving on the property, Golden revealed his creative bent by instigating, albeit rather unsuccessfully, what may have been the first attempt nationally at aerial weed spraying of rights-of-way. And he also tried not-too-serviceable hydraulically controlled highway traffic barriers on Euclid Avenue in Des Moines. Fortunately, another inspiration fared much better — the early adoption of continuous welded rail.[41]

Although several sources date the Great Western's inauguration of the modern trailer-on-flatcar service in 1936, the company actually tried it briefly during the previous year. In the summer of 1935 the road carried trailers (two per forty-foot flatcar) that belonged to the Chicago-Dubuque Motor Transportation Company between the Windy City and the Twin Cities. (Unlike the two Chicago-area interurbans, Golden's scheme allowed the use of regular semi-trailer equipment.) Although the trucking firm later returned to the highways, "so far as the railroad was concerned, the experiment was successful." The next year, the CGW was back transporting

Bitter cold and deep snows plagued the CGW during February 1936. The road, though, fought to keep trains running. Chilled workers stand near #882, a Texas-type engine, in Melbourne, Iowa. (D. Keith Lawson Collection)

loaded trailers; it established such service on a regular basis beginning July 7, 1936, between Chicago and St. Paul. The next month witnessed 870 vehicles being hauled and nine trucking firms participating, all members of the Illinois-Minnesota Motor Carriers Conference. The Great Western's "trailer trains" were extended to other parts of the system by the beginning of World War II. After the early fifties, intermodal traffic became increasingly important to most railroads and allowed them to regain revenues that they had lost previously to ever-growing truck competition.[42]

Events of the 1930s devastated the territory along the Corn Belt Route. While seemingly countless factories shut down and unemployment reached levels surpassed only by the 1890s depression, agriculture suffered most of all. The crippling effect of rock-bottom commodity prices early in the decade left farmers with no margin; ten-cents-a-bushel corn, twelve-cent oats, and hogs at less than one-half cent a pound destroyed their last savings and credit. The New Deal brought some relief, especially through the Agricultural Adjustment Administration, but good times did not return until World War II. To worsen matters considerably, in mid-decade Mother Nature went through one of her more brutal cycles. Hot summers brought drought, causing withered crops, thirsty livestock, and biblical-like plagues of insects. On July 26, 1936, an Iowa farmer wrote in his diary this vivid description of Carroll County, an area served by the Great Western: "The pasture fields are absolutely bare and black looking. All cattle and horses are fed hay. The corn plants were from a third to a half as tall as they should be and I cannot see how there can possibly be any corn to husk and I doubt if there will be any fodder. There seemed to be a hundred grasshoppers for every one we have here [Boone County]." Winters were equally miserable. The Mid-

A snow drift traps this Great Western locomotive near Melbourne, Iowa, in February 1936. (D. Keith Lawson Collection)

west faced heavy snows, high winds, and record-breaking low temperatures.[43]

The Great Western struggled through these years. The old adage "when there's no rain on the plains, there's no grain in the trains" had a ring of truth. Corn shipments, for example, dropped from 227,884 tons in 1934 to only 88,253 tons three years later. And the costs associated with coping with winter blizzards further ate away at income. February 1936 was by far the worst month. A nasty storm struck western Iowa on February 3; it took a large work party nine hours to release a stalled freight near Tennant. But the ugliest weather of that vicious season hit the Midwest on February 8. Awful things happened. A motor train with fifteen passengers got hopelessly stuck near Melbourne, south of Marshalltown, and 150 shovelers labored for two days to free it. The bitter cold that accompanied the snow "froze solidly" two carloads of hogs, some-

thing that no employee could ever recall happening. These unfortunate animals were aboard a side-tracked freight in Clarion. An especially graphic account of nature's wintry fury appeared in the Stockton, Illinois, *Herald-News:* "For the first time in the history of Stockton, train service was completely suspended for a period of nearly two days. On Saturday night [February 8], when snow banks became impassable, all trains were cancelled and efforts concentrated on getting those on the line into terminals." The paper noted also that the "shortage of coal added to the troubles of train crews, and it was necessary to confiscate coal from loads being hauled." Even a touch of drama existed in this bout with the elements. "The motor passenger train going [east] to Chicago on Saturday afternoon bucked snow so forcibly that huge chunks of frozen snow broke the front windows of the train, exposing the motorman to the frosty breezes. A stop was made at

A trim E7 class Ten-wheeler (4-6-0), built by Baldwin in 1910, pulls a passenger train through Eagle Grove, Iowa, during the Great Depression. (Joseph Sleger Photograph; W. S. Kuba Collection)

Byron to repair the windows, but they broke again before Chicago was reached."[44]

Despite the fact that Corn Belt Route crews did yeoman service keeping the flanged wheels rolling during the harsh times of the 1930s, few were inclined to quit; most counted their blessings since they had work when so many stood in unemployment lines. However, harmonious labor-management relations did not exist. While unrest the magnitude of 1922 did not recur, by 1936, signs pointed in that direction. This time the controversy involved about ninety switchmen in the Kansas City and South Des Moines yards, and the issues centered on starting hours, shift periods, and compensation.

Since the shopmen's strike, the overall structure of the federal government's role in railroad labor disputes had undergone significant change. In June 1934, President Franklin Roosevelt signed a measure that revised the Railway Labor Act of 1926, in part replacing the Board of Mediation with the National Railroad Adjustment Board. This act at last "put teeth" in the arbitration process; the board's decisions carried a finality that ones emanating from the Mediation Board lacked. Generally speaking, the government machinery prior to 1934 had taken a pro-business stance, but after that date, the balance turned in favor of the workers. In July 1936, the disgruntled switchmen got good news. The Adjustment Board had arbitrated in the matter and granted them $60,000 in overtime pay. However, while trustees Joyce and Walter changed the yard assignments, which had been the subject of the claims, they flatly refused to remunerate the employees. That action so infuriated the 1,800 members of the "Big Five" brotherhoods that on October 1 they began to take a strike vote. That same day the trustees filed a

Between May 2 and May 7, 1941, Irving Rusinow, a photographer for the Bureau of Agricultural Economics, visited Irwin, Iowa, and captured much of the town's life on film, including the Chicago Great Western. This view of Main Street shows how Great Western patrons enjoyed easy access to the commercial hub. The station (right) was not accidentally located. A. B. Stickney often ordered these structures strategically placed. As he said, "The depot should be built in as close to the business center of the city as possible. . . . That way, the public will remember you." (National Archives)

petition in federal court that assailed the labor board's ruling and asked that the award be overturned.[45]

Tensions heightened. Although no operating employees walked out in 1936, when the federal court instructed the trustees not to honor the Adjustment Board's pay decision they moved to strike in late January 1937. But before union members set up picket lines, President Roosevelt intervened. He issued a special proclamation that created a three-person emergency board to investigate the dispute. Convening in Chicago on February 15, the panel worked quickly and efficiently to find a solution. Several weeks later a financial settlement was reached between the unions, the company, and the court. Everyone breathed a sigh of relief: "one of the most encouraging pieces of news we have received in some time," claimed the *Oelwein Daily Register*.[46]

It's train time in Irwin, Iowa. Situated on the CGW's West End, this community was in decline by the early 1940s. The *Twin City* *Limited* pauses to discharge and gather mail and express and perhaps a passenger or two. (National Archives)

REORGANIZATION

BETWEEN 1935 and 1941, matters of financial reorganization dominated much of the attention of Pat Joyce and fellow trustee Luther Walter. Under bankruptcy laws, the court required a plan that would ideally place the company on an even keel, and the railroad worked hard at realizing this objective. Personally for Joyce, the defunct Bremo Corporation had hurt him in the pocketbook, and he was not about to lose further.

The process of extricating the Corn Belt Route from the legal morass of insolvency took many steps. The trustees filed the reorganization proposal with the court and the Interstate Commerce Commission on September 29, 1936. The Commission held the prescribed hearings during spring 1937 and then, on August 4, 1938, approved the basic blueprint for restructuring although some changes were subsequently made. Now it was the court's turn to act. On September 9, 1939, it accepted the ICC's slightly modified version and soon designated the classes of creditors and stockholders

The Irwin postmistress lugs mail to the Post Office, fifty yards away. The agent will be gathering the tire, hog cholera serum, and remaining express packages. The depot, with its open freight door, badly needs a coat of paint, but such maintenance was a low priority matter for a company just emerging from receivership. (National Archives)

to whom the document must be submitted for acceptance or rejection. On November 1, the Commission sent the agreement to the holders of the first mortgage bonds and preferred stock. Three months later the body certified the nearly unanimous endorsement by these investors. Next, the court officially confirmed the plan and appointed Joyce to head a reorganization committee to execute it. At last, on Valentine's Day in 1941, Judge Charles Woodward ordered that at 12:00 midnight, February 19, "all of the business, assets, and property constituting the Debtor's estate and all property in the possession of the Trustees be transferred to the Chicago Great Western Railway Company." Thus, the name for the new corporation was a re-

turn to the original one for the firm that existed from 1892 to 1909.[47]

There were many details covered by the reorganization. For one thing, several "captive corporations" disappeared. Assets of the Mason City & Fort Dodge Railroad Company, Leavenworth Terminal Railway & Bridge Company, Independent Elevator Company, and the St. Paul Bridge & Terminal Company (operated under lease since July 1, 1934) were conveyed to the new corporation. An important dimension centered on the significantly smaller capitalization. The old company held $131,000,000 worth of stocks, while the figure for the new one stood at $63,091,827. The desire was to reduce fixed charges so that earnings might easily

A company photographer caught this wartime oil train at South Des Moines, which typifies the heavy traffic moved during the conflict. Such tonnage added handsome sums to the road's treasury. (John Nash Collection)

meet these obligations. Under the structure adopted, the Great Western faced annual assessments of $829,000 rather than the former $1,600,000. Investors in the previous *Railroad* Company received securities that reflected this scale down. Owners of the first mortgage bonds took a package deal: on the basis of 25 percent of the principal amount of their holdings and accrued interest they got similar new securities; in exchange for another 15 percent of their bonds they acquired a comparable amount of new 4½ percent general mortgage bonds; and for their remaining 60 percent they took 45 percent in new preferred and 15 percent in new common stock. The holders of the $46,673,500 of preferred securities got $11,518,375 in common stock, while the former common stock owners found themselves stuck with worthless certificates.[48]

The revitalized Chicago Great Western faced the future with optimism. In a letter that Pat Joyce sent to the employees, this feeling was clear: "In entering upon its activities, the new company finds among its most valued assets the goodwill that has been developed through the years. To preserve and enhance this goodwill should be our constant and earnest endeavor. The railway possesses the plant, the equipment and the organization to perform promptly and efficiently all of the transportation service for which it may be called upon."[49]

WORLD WAR II

PRESIDENT Joyce had no way of knowing how future events would again tax the Chicago Great Western to the utmost. World War II was just around the corner for the United States. Fighting had been raging in Europe since September 1939, yet the United States remained officially free from the conflict. But with the Pearl Harbor attack of December 7, 1941, that soon changed, and immediately the populace, with few exceptions, pledged all-out support to the declaration of war. The American economy swiftly revved up to full-scale production to help insure total victory.

Not unexpectedly, the federal government entered the war-time transportation picture. The emergency meant that selfish, competitive objectives had to be subordinated to the national interest. While federalization had occurred during World War I, in World War II, the railroads remained in private hands, although supervised through the hastily created Office of Defense Transportation (ODT) headed by ICC Chairman Joseph B. Eastman. Soon the ODT produced a blizzard of bureaucratic paperwork, including scores of "Service Orders" that required the heavier loading of equipment, conservation of cars and motive power, and the like.[50]

The workhorse of the CGW freight fleet, the Texas-type 2-10-4 engine, carries an "extra" wartime freight through Gretna (later Carol Stream), Illinois, in 1945. (James L. Rueber Collection)

Volume of rail traffic quickly reached record levels. Booming factories, farms, and mines had goods to ship; the government had troops and military supplies to move; and "lost" patrons had reason to return to the rails. With severe rationing, especially of rubber products and gasoline, trucks, buses, and automobiles could no longer serve the nation as they had formerly. Once more the depot became a community's commercial gateway.[51]

The Great Western saw total freight tonnage soar from 6,069,807 in 1940 to a peak of 9,286,188 in 1943, and 8,882,972 in 1945. While the numbers of people carried are unavailable, passenger revenues reflect the enormous increase. Income zoomed from $489,129 on the eve of the war to $2,884,812 at the conflict's end.[52]

Although business was brisk, the Corn Belt Route faced serious problems. An inadequate work force quickly emerged as its foremost concern. Enlistments and the draft took large numbers of male

Engine #885 pulls a long string of cars near Marshalltown, Iowa, on August 1, 1943. (Joseph Sleger Photograph; W. S. Kuba Collection)

The *Mill Cities Limited* moves into St. Paul on May 31, 1947. (L. A. Stuckey Photograph; H. Roger Grant Collection)

employees. By 1943 more than 550 CGW men were in the war. And although few new skilled workers arrived to take their places, the Great Western tried to fill the void. This January 1944 ad in the *Oelwein Daily Register* is typical of numerous pleas for help: "CGW RY CO Wants Men to Work in Locomotive Department at Oelwein[,] Steady Work[,] Good Pay." The road also asked employees not to retire, because The Railroad Retirement Act of 1935 entitled workers to benefits that they heretofore had not enjoyed. "Every effort is made to encourage the men to continue their work in the interest of the war effort." And the company hired some women in jobs previously considered "masculine"; the CGW had its own "Rosie the Riveter."[53]

This labor shortage understandably caused disruptions. Life was sometimes hectic, even dangerous, for personnel. Recalls former Oelwein boilermaker Mac Hatch: "We just didn't have any help. We couldn't get any, so we worked day and night. Every engine that we had was junk. . . . War freights setting in the yards, telegrams coming in continually, 'Send that [locomotive] over! We've got to have it! The boys need it! The boys need it!' That was something! That's how I lost my hearing." With an acute

shortage of telegraphers, the railroad closed some wire offices. At times employees doubled up on jobs, and some facilities suspended service entirely. For example, the *Ravenwood Gazette* in October 1944 reported that "the depot was closed Friday for nearly a week because Agent Leo Fertig was working as relief operator on the third trick at Conception Junction."[54]

Still, the Great Western managed to function. Generally, freight and passenger movements passed over the road without too many long delays. Several regularly scheduled passenger trains ended their runs under orders from the Office of Defense Transportation, mostly to save fuel. And on July 15, 1945, ODT directed that all Pullman sleeping cars on trips of 450 miles or less be withdrawn from commercial service and assigned to carrying troops. (Pullmans returned to CGW rails in early 1946.) The company, too, was able to do some locomotive rehabilitation under the watchful guidance of Theodore (Ted) Olson, former master mechanic who became superintendent of motive power. When the three dozen Texas-type engines arrived a decade earlier, management mothballed some Mikados and Consolidations. Three of the former and four of the latter were rebuilt in 1941 and 1942. The company assigned the Mikes (now commonly called "MacArthurs" to honor the famous American general) to "fast freight service" between Oelwein and Council Bluffs, and the Consols found work doing heavy switching chores and short way-freight runs.[55]

World War II produced the same patriotic spirit that swept the Corn Belt Route during the First World War. There were, of course, those heavy enlistments, and management pushed the sales of war bonds. Within months after President Roosevelt spoke these solemn words, "Yesterday, December 7, 1941 — a date which will live in infamy — the United States of America was suddenly and deliberately attacked by naval and air forces of the Empire of Japan," the company converted a former seventy-foot passenger coach into a store department supply car that sported a solid red coat of paint with the slogan "BUY MORE WAR BONDS" stenciled on each side in two-foot high white letters. Employees took this message to heart. By the end of 1943, over 3,000 workers regularly purchased bonds on the payroll deduction plan, and many were also acquiring them on their own. The Great Western board, in a truly patriotic fashion, decided in 1944 to reward its fighting forces: "In recognition of the sacrifice of these employees and their service to the country, a Christmas check in the sum of $10 was mailed to each employee in the Armed Services and the Merchant Marine." At this time, the Chicago Great Western could afford to be generous. The company's net operating income reached handsome heights during the war years. The period 1942 through 1944 saw income levels in excess of $3,000,000, with the 1943 figure reaching $3,723,331. Not only did the value of the road's securities increase, but holders of preferred stock earned ten dollars per share between 1941 and 1945.[56]

Admittedly, however, the firm faced persistently rising material costs, taxes, and wages. The latter increased substantially when railroad labor nationally sensed both the shortage of good workers and the ability of carriers to assume higher rates of pay. In order to avoid a disastrous general strike, President Roosevelt issued an executive order for the War Department to take possession of the lines on December 27, 1943. But control by Washington lasted only briefly; the carriers were in private hands once more after January 22, 1944, for a settlement had been reached. Operating unions won a nine cent per hour increase, and nonoperating unions got a nine to eleven cent per hour hike; both pay raises were retroactive to April 1, 1943.[57]

THE BURTNESS YEARS

PATRICK Joyce was not to lead the Chicago Great Western in the post-war era. Suffering from an advanced case of Parkinson's disease, he stepped down from the presidency on May 21, 1946, although he continued to head the Executive Committee until his death that November. Joyce's successor was a man who knew the Great Western well — Harold W. Burtness.[58]

Like his predecessor, the sixth president of the Corn Belt Route came from Chicago. Born there on November 16, 1897, Harold William Burtness received a high school and business college education. Yet before he finished his formal training, he followed in the footsteps of his older brother, Thorstein (later Secretary of the Milwaukee Road), and entered railroading. The future Great Western official accepted a clerk's job at the Burlington in 1914 but left after a year to join the traffic department of the Pennsylvania system. Burtness's career with the CGW began in 1922, and he held the position of secretary to the president for the next eleven years. From 1925 to 1930 he also served as secretary to the chairman of the board and secretary to the chairman of the Western Association of Railway Executives. A major change in Burtness's duties took place in 1933; he became both assistant to the president in charge of transportation and corporation secretary. During the receivership years, Burtness remained in these capacities, and then when reorganization occurred, he assumed a vice-presidential

The end of steam on CGW passenger service is near, as train #24, *Mill Cities Limited,* pauses at Hampton, Minnesota, in the summer of 1947. The artifacts of the "railroad corridor" are readily evident. (Howard S. Reinmuth, Jr., Photograph)

slot, but he continued to head the transportation sector.[59]

Harold Burtness seemed to be cut from the same cloth that produced Samuel Felton. He was a very precise individual of the old school of manner and behavior. A devout Lutheran, he proudly and loyally served on the boards of the Waverly, Iowa-based Lutheran Mutual Life Insurance Company and Chicago's Lutheran Deaconess Home and Hospital. Even though staid and colorless, Burtness was bright, honest, and hard-working, qualities which his subordinates respected.[60]

The Burtness regime lasted only twenty-eight months. Yet, this proved to be an eventful period. Although freight and especially passenger volume had dropped from the peak war years, the Great Western was not drowning in a sea of red ink. Quite to the contrary, earnings were adequate, and the future looked promising. The administration knew that to be successful it had to find ways to maximize profits. It tried to the best of its abilities to meet these challenges.

One place where an obvious economy could be realized was the retirement of the DeKalb branch. Fortunately, the Great Western could remove the six-mile line and continue to serve its principal ship-

The *Minnesotan,* train #2, is shown at Damen Avenue in Chicago, two miles from its destination at Grand Central Station. In this October 1947 photograph, the run carried a coach from the Twin Cities, a Pullman from Rochester, and several mail and baggage cars. (Robert Milner Photograph; H. Roger Grant Collection)

pers. Not only did the Chicago & North Western willingly grant trackage rights over its parallel Syca-more to DeKalb segment, but the ICC quickly sanc-tioned the idea. The Commission received the for-mal abandonment petition on February 17, 1947, and then gave the green light to dismantle this small appendage three months later.[61]

Major savings, however, came not from branch line removals but from dieselization. The decision to use this technological breakthrough made the great-est positive impact in the Great Western's history. While the Burtness administration's determination to retire the steamers was not an industry first, it placed the company in the forefront of the diesel revolution. It is not at all odd that the CGW opted for this form of motive power; the road had embraced internal-combustion engines decades earlier for certain pas-senger, switching, and maintenance-of-way assign-ments. The smooth-talking diesel-electric salesmen who knocked on the Great Western's doors came at the right time. The firm's aging and ailing steam locomotives had barely pulled the tonnage through the war years. No one denied that this power fleet badly needed to be replaced. In May 1944 the roster listed 156 steamers, with only 77 equipped with mechanical stokers and two oil-fired.[62]

The Great Western's pioneer diesel, #2, an 800-horsepower Westinghouse switcher acquired in 1934, works in Minneapolis on May 18, 1952. Number 2 had the distinction of being the first diesel locomotive in America to be repowered. In December 1941, Electro-Motive gave it a new 720-horsepower engine. (W. H. Applegate Collection)

The Great Western conducted crucial diesel tests in November 1946. The road willingly allowed General Motors, the automotive giant that had acquired diesel-engine manufacturer Electro-Motive in 1930, to bring its gleaming "F3" locomotive set #291 for a two-week trial. On the maiden run, the F3's left the Chicago yards on November 7 with a ninety-one-car consist (61 loads and 30 empties) bound for Oelwein. The diesels also pulled the business car of the Vice-President of Operations, Samuel Golden. When the train tied up in the Hub City, a good-sized crowd, braving steady rain, gathered around the engines to "admire this new post-war creation of power and efficiency." Golden found the demonstration ride exhilarating. He told the *Oelwein Daily Register* that he felt "just like a small boy with a brand new toy!" The vice-president seemed especially impressed with the F3's "rapid take-off on hills from a full stop, and the fact that it is unnecessary to stop during a trip for service."[63]

It did not take long for the Burtness administration to reach a decision. On December 19, 1946, it sent an order to General Motors for a dozen of these powerful diesels. The first six arrived in October 1947; the rest came in early 1948. The company bought another fifty diesels of various types and sizes during 1947 from both GM and the American Locomotive Company. These ranged from 660-horsepower yard switchers to 3,000-horsepower passenger units. At year's end Burtness reported that "upon the placing in service of these locomotives, all road operations on the railway, except on light traffic branch lines and

The Great Western used this shiny unmarked Electro-Motive F unit, built in 1946, to operate a Twin Cities to Omaha passenger run. The demonstrator stands with the train at the Austin, Minnesota, station. (James L. Rueber Collection)

all except a few isolated yard operations, will have been changed over from steam to Diesel-electric power."[64]

The initial outlay of money for dieselization was considerable. The price tag for the locomotives alone exceeded $4,500,000. There were also the expenses associated with the erection of new service and maintenance facilities, installation of longer passing tracks and strengthening of bridges for the now longer and heavier freights, and removal of obsolete equipment associated with the rapidly disappearing "Age of Steam"—coal chutes, water towers, and the like. The road also faced the costs of retraining operating and repair personnel. Unquestionably, though, the investment yielded enormous dividends. Observed a Great Western official, "Transition from steam to diesel power permitted eventual economies never dreamed of, not even by the inventors and manufacturers of the latter." The CGW could enjoy more powerful and efficient motive power and at the same time benefit from the cost savings of a significantly reduced work force. The diesel, of course, was much less labor-intensive than steam.[65]

Although wisely embarking on a dieselization program, the Burtness people committed a blunder of sorts, one common to the industry. In their haste to scrap the steamers, "they bought every diesel locomotive they could find." And by allowing the traffic department to dictate equipment purchases, the Great Western ended up with a hodgepodge of makes and types, or, as William N. Deramus III, future company president, flippantly concluded, "a conglomeration of nothing in the way of diesel power."[66]

With its fleet of smartly painted, albeit assorted, diesel-electric locomotives, the Chicago Great Western sported adequate motive power, but there were other concerns. The overall condition of the physical plant was not particularly good, and competition from rival carriers between the five principal gateways—Chicago, Omaha, Kansas City, St. Joseph and Minnesota Transfer (Twin Cities)—and rubber-tired vehicles continued to be keen. Nevertheless, the Corn Belt Route caught the eyes of a group of aggressive Kansas City investors; it became for them an "interesting situation."[67]

COMING OF THE KANSAS CITY GROUP

OCTOBER 19, 1948, marked the dawn of a new era for the Chicago Great Western. On that day the Board of Directors, meeting at the company's Chicago headquarters, named coal magnate Grant Stauffer as seventh president. Described by the press as "short and stocky with a generous amount of general good nature," the Great Western chief lacked an extensive railroad background. Board membership on the Kansas City Southern constituted his principal experience with the industry. Technically, the position Stauffer filled was vacant because several months earlier Harold W. Burtness had resigned not only as president but also as chairman of the Executive Committee and as a director. He had not done so freely. The so-called Kansas City Group, which included Stauffer, had forced him out of office: "Burtness just didn't fit into the new picture." By mid-1948 only six of the Board's fifteen members owed their appointments to the rapidly fading old guard, and they lacked the wherewithal to save their man.[1]

An assortment of highly resourceful individuals made up the guiding force behind the Great Western. The group consisted of the Kelce brothers, L. Russell, Merle C., and Ted L., officials of the Kansas City–based Sinclair Coal Company; Grant Stauffer, Sinclair's president; William G. Parrott, who worked closely with the Kelces in their varied and immensely profitable mining activities; and Edward Marsh (Ned) Douthat, a former Sinclair officer and head of the enormously profitable Locke Stove Company. Also participating were R. Crosby Kemper and his son, R. Crosby Kemper, Jr., executives with the City National Bank & Trust Company of Kansas City, Missouri, and another father-son pair, William N. Deramus, president of the Kansas City Southern, and William N. Deramus III, assistant to the KCS's general manager.[2]

Several reasons prompted the Kansas City Group to invest heavily in the Corn Belt Route. Most of all, it looked like a way to earn a long-term profit. Admittedly the property needed major rehabilitation, but it held promise. A program of speedy and intensive modernization theoretically could realize financial rewards. As Stauffer himself said, "You can't make money with a poor [quality] railroad." Of course, there was an element of risk in the Great Western venture. But these capitalists, particularly Russell Kelce, described by a long-time associate as a "superb businessman," fully understood gambles. Together they had made far-ranging and usually winning investments in such areas as farms, ranches, oil fields, construction, and farm-machinery con-

Members of the CGW Board of Directors assemble in Kansas City, Missouri, in December 1949 to consider stock dividend payments. They are, from left to right: Ivan A. McKenna, W. G. Parrott, William C. Engle, W. G. Kellogg, William N. Deramus III, L. Russell Kelce, Guy Gladson, Harold O. Washburn, Paul A. Nehring, and Andy C. O'Donnell. (James L. Rueber Collection)

cerns. And the Great Western seemed to have the right characteristics: it carried a relatively small debt and thus a low level of fixed charges and sold its stock at bargain-basement prices. Finally, the Kansas City Group members wanted the CGW under their thumb to protect their position in the Kansas City Southern. If the Great Western were to fall into unfriendly hands, traffic might be diverted from KCS rails. In fact, elements within the rival Missouri-Kansas-Texas Railroad (MKT) had recently pressured the Great Western's largest single stockholder, Sherman Hoar Bowles, a wealthy and eccentric Springfield, Massachusetts, newspaper publisher, to work for merger of the CGW with the MKT and the Chicago & Eastern Illinois. He refused, but the KCS still had some reason for concern.[3]

Selection of Grant Stauffer as chief executive officer did not mean that this coal man actually ran the railroad. He functioned merely as a figurehead. Decisions that related to daily matters rested mostly with the Deramuses. The senior Deramus regularly advised the Great Western, usually through his thirty-three-year-old son, who served as Stauffer's assistant. Indeed, syndicate members from the start saw the younger Deramus as the Corn Belt Route's future president. "I guess that they figured that [he] was a little bit too young to take him right off of practically no experience and put him on a job like that without any background," recalled a company official. "So Stauffer went in as a front."[4]

This strategy worked only temporarily. On March 31, 1949, just five months after assuming the presidency, the sixty-year-old Grant Stauffer died of cancer. The Kansas City Group decided that the time obviously had come to elevate the junior Deramus to the Great Western's top post.[5]

The CGW had its share of wrecks. A spectacular one happened on the morning of October 3, 1950, at Rinard, Iowa, when a Fort Dodge–bound Great Western freight plowed through a Fort Dodge, Des Moines & Southern (electric) train. (James L. Rueber Collection)

DERAMUS TAKES CONTROL

Not since Samuel M. Felton had a Chicago Great Western president been so well educated. Born into a Pittsburg, Kansas, railroad family on December 10, 1915, William N. Deramus III earned his bachelor's degree from the University of Michigan in 1936 and an LL.B. from the Harvard University Law School three years later. Rather than practicing this profession, he entered railroading in 1939 as a transportation apprentice on the Wabash and remained in that capacity until 1941. For the next two years Deramus served as an assistant trainmaster on the Wabash's St. Louis Division before entering the Army's Transportation Corps. During this tour of duty with the 726th Operating Battalion he helped to operate a rail line through India and

Burma to the famed Ledo Road. Said Deramus, "Burma is the only place I wouldn't want to run a railroad." And he quipped, "Another year of that and I'd have been ready to drive a bus." After the war he became Assistant to the General Manager on his father's railroad.[6]

The tenure of William N. Deramus III started on May 17, 1949, with considerable national attention. The *Chicago Daily News,* for example, carried a feature story on May 18 with a three-column headline, "Rails' Youngest President at Great Western's Throttle." No one questioned Deramus's overall ability to run the road, and, of course, he would continue to have access to his father's counsel. Those who knew Deramus well realized that he was also a "workaholic." As he admitted, "[My] only hobby is railroading." The notion soon spread that the Chicago Great Western was on the comeback trail. Perhaps it could repeat the best days of the Felton era.[7]

William Deramus knew he faced a formidable task at the CGW; he saw the property as a virtual transportation slum. "The railroad had not been maintained. They had done nothing during the Second World War." And there existed another serious matter: "They had everything scattered. They had the accounting department, for example, in two places." The early solutions involved considerable spending and took various forms. In the 1949–1951 period, capital expenditures for track, bridges, and structures amounted to $6.9 million and for equipment, $15.7 million. The company ordered the reworking of much of the Chicago to Kansas City and Oelwein to Omaha lines and major repairs on the Mississippi River bridge at St. Paul and the Des Moines River viaduct at Fort Dodge. During this time Des Moines received both an impressive combination office, passenger and freight facility and a new 1,600-capacity car yard; Fort Dodge and Marshalltown each got attractive brick stations, and Oelwein witnessed construction of an icing plant and major yard improvements. The firm also replaced nine obsolete wooden depots with highly utilitarian metal ones. By late 1949 operations be-

One improvement that the Deramus regime accomplished was to construct a modern ice plant at Oelwein. Designed to supply the needs of refrigerator cars, the facility had the capability of producing either chunk ice (as shown) or crushed ice. (F. Stewart Mitchell Collection)

came entirely dieselized and new rolling stock started to arrive: 600 boxcars, 300 gondolas, 150 flats, and 75 covered hoppers.[8]

The Great Western became even better. The management, throughout the Deramus tenure, continued to improve the property, although the level of rehabilitation was not maintained to the initial degree. For instance, workers constructed a two-story brick and concrete office building in Kansas City and a combination office and freight house in Minneapolis. Oelwein received a modern car repair shop, new store buildings, and a reclamation plant. And attractive depots appeared in St. Joseph and Council Bluffs while five other communities got smaller, though functional, ones. Literally hundreds of thousands of creosoted cross ties and millions of tons of

The Deramus regime authorized construction of this functional office building in Kansas City, Missouri. The photograph dates from about 1956. (D. Keith Lawson Collection)

The company during the fifties regularly replaced original small-town depots with ugly, yet utilitarian cinder-block ones. When fire destroyed the wooden station at Lidderdale, Iowa, this tiny one replaced it. (H. Roger Grant Photograph)

chat and slag ballast upgraded scores of miles of track. And the process of laying heavier rail, often 115-pound steel, continued. The company also modernized its automatic block signal system.[9]

PASSENGER CUTBACKS, LONG FREIGHTS, AND LINE ABANDONMENTS

WHILE the general public probably failed to notice much of the Deramus regime's rebuilding program, its drastic paring down of the quantity and quality of passenger train service caught people's attention. Yet the Great Western management was merely responding to the realities of intercity travel. The immediate post–World War II period witnessed soaring automobile traffic. Although the federal government would not launch its massive interstate highway building program until 1956, Americans took to the roadways in larger numbers every year. In 1945 about 31 million vehicles of all sorts were registered. By 1950 the figure reached 49 million. Unlike most of its sister Granger roads, the CGW never seriously thought of acquiring sleek stream-

liners to lure travelers back to the rails. Historically, Great Western patrons had been of the "short-haul" type, and if they were going a hundred miles or so, they likely would opt for the convenience of their own cars. Logically, freight, not people, would be the company's mainstay. Thus there existed no sound reason to upgrade the existing passenger trains, except to substitute diesel power for steam.[10]

The ax began to fall on Great Western varnish in March 1949. The road discontinued motor trains 41 and 42 that operated between Rochester and McIntire; it dropped the *Minnesotan*'s name-train status (the trains became simply 1-23 from Chicago and 24-2 out of the Twin Cities), and it removed all club-lounge cars. Soon thereafter the company pulled off the remaining sleeping and dining equipment. Another change occurred on July 26, 1950. On that peaceful summer evening, train 36, the clanking old McKeen motor car, tied up at the Oelwein depot after completing its final run from Clarion. This piece of aging rolling stock had been a fixture on this 99-mile route for decades. The *Oelwein Daily Register* duly noted, "the train . . . was killed by cars." Then, a few weeks later, a more modern "doodlebug," train 44, ended service between Randolph, Red Wing, and Rochester. Unlike

The last southbound run of the Rochester to McIntire motor train gets a "highball" at the Rochester station on March 3, 1949. The "goodbyes" are forever. (Olmsted County Historical Society)

other more typical discontinuances, this one finished with considerable fanfare. Several adventuresome souls staged a mock holdup near Hay Creek, and the Goodhue High School marching band and fire truck met the twenty or so passengers when the train pulled into town. All of this resembled the commotion six decades before when service began.[11]

By the early 1950s, the Deramus administration had cut passenger operations to the bone. The public timetable effective October 31, 1951, showed only one movement each way on the Twin Cities to Kansas City, Twin Cities to Omaha, and Chicago to Oelwein routes. Going from Chicago to the Twin Cities was still possible, but it was a trip for tena-cious travelers. Patrons changed from number 3 to number 12, the *Mill Cities Limited,* after a two and one-half hour layover in Oelwein. Like the *Nebraska Limited,* this consist was indeed "limited," usually a single air-conditioned coach that tagged behind several mail and express cars. But this offered ample room, for in May 1951, the *Mill Cities* carried an average of only 14.4 persons daily. However, a healthy "head-end" business of mail and express made these runs financially feasible. And, too, the company creatively coupled freight equipment, often piggyback flats and refrigerator cars, to these passenger trips.[12]

As varnish disappeared from the Great Western,

Only months remain before the final run of the elderly McKeen motorcar #1003. It is seen here coming onto the main track at Hampton, Iowa, on December 30, 1949. (W. L. Heitter Photograph)

freight movements lengthened. Management discovered that it could successfully lash six, and occasionally more, diesel locomotives together to produce the high horsepower required for consists that frequently exceeded 150 cars. A few trains even approached the 275 mark. Attempting to haul the biggest possible payload was not new on the CGW. In October 1894, for instance, "a mammoth freight train, consisting of 83 cars, hauled by two engines, pulled out of [Oelwein] . . . for St. Paul." The road's subsequent acquisition of the monster Mallets and Texas-type locomotives came about in order to utilize crews efficiently and economically over the busiest trackage. By the early fifties, multiple-unit diesel

power that pulled huge loads emerged as the visible symbol of Deramus's rule.[13]

The extra-long freights were not without their problems, however. The delivery of cars often took longer; the company commonly waited until it had enough tonnage in its yards before ordering a trip. While these movements necessitated the extension and relocation of numerous sidings, even these improvements did not always prevent the lengthy delays caused by the absence of suitable passing tracks at logical meeting points. And, too, these trains regularly undertook local switching chores between terminals, for management frowned on expensive way-freight runs. Cutting cars in and out of a one- or

"Cow and calf" diesel, #61, built by Electro-Motive in 1949, gets refueled in Oelwein. This TR2-type locomotive handled switching chores in the larger yards. (H. Roger Grant Collection)

two-mile train meant that it took considerable time to pump-up the air before moving. (An official of the Great Northern jokingly referred to the Deramus road as "the nation's longest rip-track!") These gigantic, slow-moving freights meant that engine and train crews faced greater responsibilities and more arduous duties, factors that triggered a bitter strike in 1953.[14]

As had been the trend on the Great Western and other roads for decades, lightly used feeder lines faced retirement. By the time Deramus took control, little trackage remained to be trimmed; after all, mostly trunk, not branch, blessed the carrier. Still, some paring was possible. In 1950 the CGW received regulatory permission to abandon nearly five miles between Bremer and Waverly on the twenty-two-mile Sumner line. Both Waverly and Bremer continued to be served; the company merely severed the branch. Without doubt the line was "neither necessary nor desirable." In fact, dangerous track conditions had blocked train service (freight only) over this section since November 1946. Two years later the road scrapped the six-mile Belle Chester, Minnesota, spur. Like the Waverly to Bremer piece,

this appendage was in extremely poor physical condition. Its fifty-six-pound rail, rolled in 1886 and installed in 1910, seemed more appropriate for a museum than a common carrier. And business was terrible on this line; in 1950 the company handled just forty-four cars.[15]

MODERNIZATION

ALTHOUGH the renaissance of the Great Western involved line abandonment, it also included consolidation and modernization at the road's historic center of operations, Oelwein. During the closing years of the nineteenth century, Oelweinites excitedly watched a modern railroad shops complex and roundhouse take shape in their midst. Once it was completed, citizens mostly took for granted the facility that largely sustained their hometown. While gyrations in the economy produced good and bad times for the Hub City, the trend after 1930 seemed to be that improvement dollars were more likely to

The diesel most commonly associated with the Great Western during the Deramus years is the F3. Manufactured by Electro-Motive in 1947, these particular units sport the company's origi-nal paint scheme and the famous Corn Belt Route logo. (H. Roger Grant Collection)

be spent here than elsewhere. This orientation toward Oelwein became even more pronounced with the ascendancy of William N. Deramus III.

In its desire for economy of operations, the Great Western leadership pushed hard for the centralization of facilities. The process began in 1949 when it consolidated all train dispatching in a new building next to the Oelwein passenger station. No longer did Des Moines, Iowa, St. Paul, Minnesota, and Stockton, Illinois, have such employees. Then two years later the company launched a more extensive unification drive. The principal work focused on relocating the operating, accounting, purchasing, freight claims and engineering departments from Chicago. By 1953 the only major units not situated in the Iowa community were the industrial, personnel and treasury departments, based in Kansas City, and the traffic department and the offices of the president, general manager, and legal counsel in

Chicago. The latter three, however, would move to Kansas City by 1956.[16]

The consolidation process worked reasonably well. Savings occurred and productivity increased. While some Chicago employees refused to transfer or came only temporarily to Oelwein, their places were filled easily. Deramus recalled that "most of the people we hired at Oelwein were college graduates from the surrounding territory." He added, "That amazed me that you could find that sort of talent out there." The company paid good wages; in fact, "they were more than competitive for the area." Turnovers were rare.[17]

The work force in Oelwein enjoyed modern equipment in Spartan although usually comfortable quarters. The introduction of data processing units attracted the most attention. "Vistors are awed by the IBM machines 'which do everything but talk.'" For one thing, the road sought to reduce the num-

Although this photograph of a westbound CGW freight detour-
ing over the Illinois Central near Dubuque dates from April 1966,
the enormous amount of headend power became a company
hallmark during the Deramus era. (Mark Nelson Photograph)

ber of clerical steps required in producing daily
"wheel reports." By having yard and train crews use
"sense-marked" cards, they easily recorded such information as freight-car destination, month, day,
time, train number, and so forth and then sent the
cards to the accounting department for processing.
The company utilized similar key punch cards for
timekeeping and other statistical chores. Once more
it adopted a path-breaking technology. "The Chicago Great Western has progressed rapidly in the
application of new techniques and new machines to
its accounting problems," reported *Modern Railroads* in 1954. "The Great Western intends to
maintain an efficient, up-to-date Accounting Department which is thoroughly conversant with modern methods."[18]

State of the art technology likewise found a place
on the operating side. During this time immediate
and dramatic improvements in communications
emerged as the foremost change. Installation of car-

rier telephone circuits, teletypes and radios, with
the latter placed in locomotives and cabooses,
worked splendidly, as did the walkie-talkies for
yard clerks. Once again the Great Western was an
industry leader.[19]

Perhaps undetected by outsiders, these better
means of communications allowed management to
attain its goal of a highly centralized system of go-
vernance. These tools unquestionably weakened the
established chain of command among employees.
The use of carrier telephones, in particular, permitted trainmasters and other minor officials to call the
Director of Personnel and other top officers directly
and at any time to obtain immediate answers to
their problems. This practice, which Deramus encouraged, permitted "fishing expeditions" that
sought the reversal of decisions made previously by
immediate and intermediate supervisors. Naturally,
disruptions occurred. Explained one unhappy executive, "Emasculation of authority at the division level

Train #95 moves near the Indiana Harbor Belt Railroad interchange at Bellwood, Illinois, in March 1951. Powered by four Electro-Motive F3's, this freight heads toward Oelwein. (Robert Milner Photograph; H. Roger Grant Collection)

resulted in loss of respect for division officers and consequent loss of morale."[20]

The steadily growing list of improvements tended to overshadow any problem areas. As long as employees did their jobs, Deramus and his associates considered other matters. The leadership had good reason to feel self-satisfied. The Great Western was no longer the "dog" it had been a few years earlier. Its operating ratio (operating expenses divided by operating revenues) dropped significantly from 75.36 percent in 1949 to a respectable 67.7 percent in 1953. For example, in 1953, two of the nation's premier carriers, the Santa Fé and the Illinois Central, reported operating ratios of 71.9 and 71.7 percent, respectively.[21]

Even though many outsiders understandably praised the young railroad executive, William Deramus made some bad decisions. At times his brash ways cost the company heavily. The Des Moines station fiasco illustrates his limitations. Completed in November 1950 this magnificent structure seemed at first to be another Deramus triumph; it represented nicely the theme of centralization with its considerable benefits. Heretofore, the road had its employees scattered throughout the Capital City: traffic department people worked out of expensive downtown quarters; the dingy Union Station housed division personnel; and the roundhouse and yard "shacks" accommodated still others. Thus, consolidation of the work force in a single place that would also serve as a dual freight and passenger station made sense. Not only was Deramus "bullish" on the idea, he personally got involved in site selection. He wanted the facility to be on 9th Street near the Raccoon River, in spite of the fact that local engineers warned him that this was an extremely poor choice; the area had once been a public landfill. The spongy, garbage-laden soil lacked stability. Deramus, however, ignored the advice and ordered construction. Soon after completion, the building began

The Des Moines station, opened in November 1950, soon settled badly and caused the company considerable grief and expense. The Des Moines Chamber of Commerce commissioned this photograph on December 13, 1950. (Iowa State Historical Department)

to settle badly. "The floor just started to drop out. . . ." This dramatic event ruptured the hot-water heating pipes, making the facility virtually worthless. Repairs were possible, yet the situation necessitated use of an enormously expensive "floating foundation," the cost of which equaled about one third of the original price tag for the structure. The company also had to replace the heating system at further expense.[22]

THE STRIKE OF 1953

Bᴜᴛ the event that proved much more costly to the railroad than any faulty building was the strike of operating personnel in 1953. This work stoppage shut down the Great Western for forty-two days, and it took several months before traffic levels returned to normal.

Since the ascendancy of Deramus the road's overall labor-management relations had not been particularly smooth. Hard feelings existed over the deep reductions in the work force. In 1947, during the Burtness tenure, the company employed 4,584; but at the end of 1949, Deramus's first year, the figure stood at 3,631, a 20.7 percent drop. By 1951, the number reached 3,105. In 1949, for example, fifty of the firm's 110 employees in Rochester, Minnesota, got pink slips. Dieselization made scores of slots unnecessary, but sentiment grew that cuts were frequently drastic, at times impairing safe operations.[23]

Initially, however, employee unrest related directly to national matters. In 1949, operating unions demanded that the industry grant them a forty-hour week with forty-eight hours' pay, overtime rates on Sundays and holidays for yard crews, and modifications of certain work rules. When collective bargaining failed, a Presidential Emergency Board attempted to solve the dispute. But its recommenda-

This 1952 company photograph catches the staff of the Comptroller's office in Oelwein. (H. Roger Grant Collection)

tions infuriated the Switchmen's Union of North America, and the members of this small union struck the Great Western and four other carriers on June 25, 1950. Because the government threatened punitive action, workers returned to their posts on July 7. By fall, the Switchmen's Union won substantial concessions, including a twenty-three cent per hour pay raise. The leadership of other operating brotherhoods accepted similar arrangements and formally signed a "Memorandum of Agreement" on December 21, 1950. Soon thereafter, though, the rank-and-file refused the settlement, and widespread wildcat strikes ensued. But the Army served notice on all strikers to return to their jobs within forty-eight hours or lose their seniority rights. The mili-

tary entered the dispute because President Harry S Truman's Executive Order of August 25, 1950, had produced federal control of the railroads. Truman commanded Secretary of the Army Frank Pace, Jr., to run the carriers in the face of a threatened national strike by the Brotherhood of Railroad Trainmen and the Order of Railroad Conductors. The dispute between labor and management dragged on until May 23, 1953, when workers finally accepted agreements substantially like those that the switchmen had received in late 1950. With the May settlement, the government relinquished control.[24]

Just over six months passed before labor troubles flared again. This time the Great Western alone faced a major confrontation with the operating

In Oelwein, Steve McGuinnis, the road's top communications specialist, checks a test board of the recently installed carrier telephone system. (F. Stewart Mitchell Collection)

The outside yard clerk at Oelwein, Russell Shippey, takes his newly acquired Motorola portable radio to work. (F. Stewart Mitchell Collection)

crafts. The unrest centered on an accumulation of grievances related to the road's type of operations, namely those not-so-speedy long freights. While specific complaints numbered into the hundreds, the conflict boiled down to this: "No management should be allowed to intentionally set up train runs which will keep employees away from home for days on end at their own expense and on duty more than sixteen hours a day." The company, of course, saw it differently. As Deramus told the press, "These claims involve, for the most part, additional payments ranging up to a full day's pay for a few minutes' work and payment for services performed by other employees who were fully compensated for the work done."[25]

When the operating unions walked out on January 25, 1953, their leaders realized that some question existed over the legality of a strike based on "claims and grievances." The collective charges fell largely into the category of "minor disputes." Unlike the so-called major disputes that involved negotiation of a new or significantly altered contract, minor disputes centered on controversies that dealt with the meaning of an existing collective bargaining agreement and generally involved only one employee. In fact, several years after the 1953 job

A major Deramus triumph occurred with the establishment of the Roseport Industrial District near St. Paul. This development gen-erated enormous volumes of carload traffic. (H. Roger Grant Collection)

action ended, the Supreme Court in *Brotherhood of Railroad Trainmen* vs. *Chicago River & Indiana Railroad Company* decided once and for all that minor issues were not strike material and must go to the National Railroad Adjustment Board (NRAB) for adjudication.[26]

At the time of the 1953 stoppage, the courts had not decided the major versus minor controversy, even though the NRAB had existed since 1934 to deal with labor problems. The body had the power to settle disagreements over long-standing contracts that related to working conditions, rules, and pay. What the CGW dissidents were then doing was striking in order to obtain a change in the work

agreement without going through the legally pre-scribed process. Indeed, this had been a common tactic used by railroad labor before it lost the Chi-cago River & Indiana decision.[27]

William Deramus's tough stand against union de-mands took courage. His predecessor, Harold Burt-ness, would likely have conceded defeat. The indus-try itself seemed fearful of offering assistance, even moral support. "I think the 43-day strike was a perfect example of why the railroads in this country have failed to prosper as they should," observed Deramus in 1982. "During that period of time, I did not receive a single call from the head, or any of-ficer, of any of the railroads of this country." Dera-

Roadswitcher #55, purchased from Alco-GE in 1949, leaves the Fort Dodge yards for Harlan, Iowa, about 1950, with the after-noon way-freight. (Basil W. Koob Photograph; Mrs. R. C. Kepler Collection)

mus rightfully felt that his administration was fighting the battle of all rail managements to retain control over their property.[28]

Deramus's tenacity led to a shutdown that proved costly to both sides, especially labor. Workers lost wages, and the company faced a drastic drop in revenues and longer-term traffic disruptions. The timing of the strike, though, favored management, for trains stopped running during the most adverse weather conditions, "which are costly and generally run into red ink." And the Deramus forces ultimately got the upper hand: long freights continued but with some special considerations to their train crews. The official statement simply announced that "the settlement did not provide any wage increase but was a complicated compromise of a long docket of grievances involving alleged violations of working rules." But as the General Chairman of the Brotherhood of Locomotive Engineers frequently complained, "We didn't win anything by the strike." Fortunately for both parties and the service territory, too, the dispute produced none of the violence

that had characterized the nasty shopmen's strike of 1922.[29]

The end of the operating craft's walkout on March 8, 1953, did not mean that an era of good labor feelings had arrived. Nonoperating personnel threatened to strike between 1956 and 1958 over a plethora of "minor" matters, but injunctive court action aborted any walkouts. Moreover, the Deramus regime skillfully used another weapon. It imaginatively reactivated its wholly owned subsidiary, the Iowa Townsite Company, not to peddle Hawkeye State real estate but to outflank the Brotherhood of Railway and Steamship Clerks and the other nonoperating unions. In 1956, the Clerks demanded to be allowed to represent nearly all of the employees in the traffic department, both "on" and "off" lines. Already the Interstate Commerce Commission had given its stamp of approval, for it held that various positions in the traffic department below the rank of General Agent were eligible for union representation. Unless this issue between the Great Western management and the Clerks could be resolved amicably, the way for a legal strike would open. Consequently, members of other brotherhoods, who would enthusiastically honor the Clerks' picket lines, could gain powerful leverage to force settlement of their own list of minor disputes and thus avoid the NRAB.[30]

Officials of the Brotherhood of Railway and Steamship Clerks knew that they would surely win if the National Mediation Board conducted a representation election. Board policy dictated that an entire class or craft participate. In other words, instead of the hundred or so employees in the traffic department balloting, all others represented or eligible for representation by the Clerk's Union—numbering several hundred—would cast their votes. If these individuals did not back ratification, they would lose union protection.[31]

Management eagerly sought to resist the Clerks. It saw no other option. "Unionization of subordinate officials and solicitors in the Traffic Department would practically nullify their useful function and was unthinkable." So the company pushed the Iowa Townsite ploy in 1957. All on- and off-line employees in the traffic department below the rank of General Agent not then represented by the Clerks' Union were required to resign from the railroad and transfer to the townsite subsidiary. As the Great Western's personnel officer explained, "This would not prohibit the Brotherhood from serving notice on the Iowa Townsite Company to represent said employees, but the Off-Line situation and legal technicalities involved made the proposition impractical and expensive for the Brotherhood, which subsequently abandoned the notice."[32]

Much of this labor unrest lay with widespread worker unhappiness about Deramus himself. Those who prospered under his tenure, of course, liked him: "Mr. Deramus, the man, possesses the innate qualities of a gentleman, compassionate, charitable, altruistic, interested in the welfare of all employees," wrote one such person. "His sense of fairness brought dignity to the railroad." But this seems to be the exceptional point of view. In the eyes of many, on the other hand, the "big boss" functioned much differently. His arrogance, snap decisions, and profanity produced terror and anger. "He was hard to work for. . . . I hated that man," recalled one station agent. Even a close financial adviser admitted that "young Bill was not diplomatic" and that "he lacked the charm of his father." The dismissal of one Oelwein worker helps to explain why Deramus's popularity sank to low levels.[33]

Rosalie O'Hara worked as a receptionist and switchboard operator for the superintendent of motive power. She was single and cared for her invalid father. "One day Deramus came into the office and she apparently didn't have a big smile on her face. . . . He walked right on by her and into the Superintendent's Office [and said] 'FIRE HER!' " So Rosalie O'Hara lost her job. Immediately, the Brotherhood of Railway Clerks filed a claim that demanded reinstatement and back pay. As usual, the appeal process dragged on for nearly a year. Finally, the personnel officer, who knew that the company had no defense ("I couldn't make up a story that would fit in as any reason"), succeeded in reaching a compromise with the general chairman of the union: Rosalie O'Hara would be transferred to the accounting department, although she would not receive her lost wages. She performed admirably in her new position. Said her boss later, "She's the best clerk I've ever had."[34]

Perhaps to compensate for sagging morale, Deramus endorsed creation of two projects that lifted workers' spirits. The first was a mimeographed employee's magazine, Great Western Safety News. Explained editor Walter J. Murphy, an Oelwein train dispatcher, in the maiden copy of January 1955, "We hope to bring you news . . . [and] other items of interest to the entire Great Western family." The popular paper carried safety tips, personal items, and features on shippers and reinforced the company's tradition of being a "big family." Unlike either The Maize or the Great Western Magazine, this publication was solely an in-house organ. Beginning with the April 1956 issue, Safety News became a printed and illustrated monthly. Perhaps Deramus also thought that the publication might serve as an effective propaganda vehicle for management's view.[35]

Paralleling the appearance of *Safety News,* Deramus sanctioned the notion of a company-sponsored annual picnic. Ostensibly the gathering was to promote safety practices, but it emerged as a "tribute to the Great White Father's image" and as an enormously treasured social function. The first picnic, held on September 19, 1955, at the Oelwein City Park, attracted 2,102 participants (only 500 were expected). Some came on special trains and chartered buses; all enjoyed themselves immensely. Bingo, checkers, ball games, horseshoe pitching, three-legged races, pie-eating contests, pony rides, and merry-go-rounds furnished entertainment for various ages, tastes, and temperaments. The second picnic a year later drew 3,540 participants. Commented the *Oelwein Daily Register,* "One of the most effective projects developed by any Iowa industry on the public and employer-employee relations side has been the two Great Western picnics held the last two years."[36]

THE FINAL DERAMUS YEARS

The Chicago Great Western prospered during the boom years of the Eisenhower administration. Nationally, personal consumption of durable goods reached record heights, and industries buzzed with activity. The CGW benefited from the larger trends. By the 1950s its traffic patterns were more heavily oriented toward manufacturing than at any previous time. From 1953 through 1956 the company's operating revenues grew steadily from $31,436,397 to $35,626,656 and net operating revenues rose from $10,166,127 to $11,256,112. In 1953 the Board eliminated the arrearages that had been building since 1946 on preferred stock. This came about not only because of these healthy earnings but also because of a successful suit by some preferred stockholders who demanded settlement. "The Kansas City Group didn't like to pay dividends." Yet pay it did. During this time the road voted a regular $2.50 per share on preferred and began to declare dividends on common. In December 1954 the company gave a 75-cent payment, the first since the 1940 reorganization. The next year common stockholders got $1.375 in cash and a 2.5 percent common stock dividend. A year later they received $1.40 and another stock dividend. The value of Great Western securities increased nicely. During the first half of 1948 common stock traded in a $6 to $12 range and preferred sold from $12 to $21.50. By 1956 the former varied from $36.50 to $50 and the latter, $36.50 to $41.75.[37]

As part of the Deramus administration's smart financial guidance the road decided to incorporate under the more favorable laws in Delaware. On May 13, 1955, the firm, Chicago Great Western, Inc., emerged. In November the ICC sanctioned the statutory merger of the Chicago Great Western Railway Company, an Illinois corporation, and the Delaware one. On December 31, 1955, union between the two became official, but the Delaware corporation then changed its name to that of the now dissolved Illinois unit, Chicago Great Western Railway Company. This juggling came about according to Deramus for the "simple reason that the so-called 'Insull Acts' passed during the '30's, which in some instances could be most restrictive, were thought to perhaps apply to a chartered Illinois railroad company." He added, "Discretion was the better part of valor." But there was also the chance to save on taxes: "The advantages were so pronounced that this step was finally decided upon." And, too, the official headquarters could now be moved formally from Chicago to Kansas City.[38]

A much more visible and significant development that bolstered earnings came about with the creation of a large industrial district at Roseport, Minnesota, about a dozen miles south of St. Paul. Deramus's acquaintance with a Louisiana oilman, Sylvester Dayson, led to the erection of the $25 million Great Northern Oil Company refinery. Subsequently, St. Paul Ammonia Products, Inc., constructed a $16 million plant, and other concerns eventually selected this magnificent 5,000-acre site. All, of course, were served exclusively by the CGW.[39]

The ubiquitous railfan found the CGW in the 1950s. On Sunday, June 3, 1956, the Minnesota Railfans' Association sponsored "Great Western Day" over the 190 miles between Minneapolis and Oelwein, the first such "buff" trip ever operated over the road. Riders explore the Hayfield, Minnesota, station. (Basil W. Koob Photograph; Mrs. R. C. Kepler Collection)

On January 8, 1957, William N. Deramus III resigned as president of the Chicago Great Western Railway Company and assumed the throttle of the sickly Missouri-Kansas-Texas Railroad Company. As with the Great Western, Deramus announced that his primary objective was "to get the railroad back on its feet." He believed that the ideal time had come to leave the CGW. "The rehabilitation program is well along and the present management team is highly qualified to carry forward the progressive program of the Great Western." Apparently, too, the antics of one director, Robert F. McAteer, greatly annoyed Deramus. "I acquired him through the behest of my Father and not through my own good judgment. He was probably the poorest director I have ever seen and in looking back, he

may have hastened my departure from the Great Western."[40]

The departing Deramus selected the road's Vice-President and General Manager, Edward T. Reidy, as the firm's ninth and, as it turned out, last president. "The Kansas City interests had a lot of money invested and they wanted to be sure who was going to run things. . . . Deramus figured that Reidy was going to do everything he said." The new head, in fact, was a loyal lieutenant, at least initially. Deramus gave one piece of parting advice to Reidy, a Roman Catholic. "I'll fry your ass if you give any mackerel snapper special breaks!" This suggested two things: Deramus recognized the road's Protestant heritage, and he did not plan to forget about the Chicago Great Western.[41]

CHAPTER EIGHT
THE FINAL DECADE, 1957–1968

E. T. REIDY'S TENURE

THE Kansas City Group made a good choice when it selected Edward T. Reidy as president in January 1957. He knew railroading and the peculiarities of the Chicago Great Western. Recalled one fellow railroad president, "In my trips over the CGW, it soon became evident that its success at that time was in large part due to Reidy's intense knowledge of the property and his 'on hands' management of it." Reidy, moreover, possessed considerable intelligence and drive. Born in Chicago on April 4, 1903, the company's final chief executive lacked the quality formal education of Felton or Deramus; he attended college for only one semester. As was customary for the times, though, Reidy entered the industry when he was merely a teenager. His first position came in June 1921 when he accepted a clerk's job with his hometown Baltimore & Ohio Terminal Railroad. He stayed with this switching road for five years before joining the Great Western in a similar capacity. Reidy did well with his new employer. He moved up the corporate ladder and in December 1929 began serving as secretary to the operating vice-president. Then, Patrick Joyce picked him to be his personal secretary in July 1933. Beginning in February 1941, Reidy acted for

nearly eight years as the assistant corporate secretary until he became secretary in December 1948. After fourteen months, the future head won the general manager's position and in November 1952 got the nod to be vice-president and general manager. Differing dramatically from his predecessor, this "big, good-hearted Irishman" enjoyed fine rapport with employees and did much to restore the road's traditional heritage of being one big happy family.[1]

The Spartan simplicity of the Deramus era, however, likewise characterized the Reidy regime. As he himself noted in 1960, "Although we have operated economically for many years, we are not and will not be content with our performance and are continuing to press for greater efficiency and better results." The Chicago Great Western remained its spunky, no-nonsense self.[2]

Understandably, innovations continued. While the company could not claim any transportation "firsts," it did embrace up-to-date equipment. The road acquired powerful locomotives in the tradition of those celebrated Mallet- and Texas-type engines. In 1963 it took delivery of eight 2,250-horsepower GP-30 diesels from the Electro-Motive Division of General Motors and three years later received nine 3,000-horsepower SD-40's from the same manufacturer. The latter allowed the CGW to operate 21,304 more train miles with 135,205 fewer locomotive-unit miles. Less obvious to the casual observer, the company continued to improve its handling of paperwork. In April 1964 the Oelwein offices saw installation of an ultra-modern International Business Machines 1440-type data processing system.[3]

The Great Western's determination to tap available sources of business led to the strengthening of its piggyback operations. Said Reidy, "[It is] an effort to regain further traffic from the highways." In the two decades since the road had popularized this concept, it remained an industry leader. By the mid-1950s, the CGW ranked in fourth place (behind the Southern Pacific, Pennsylvania, and New Haven) among those carriers who were participating, although its position dropped as other larger roads entered the field. During Reidy's tenure the company rented more than 250 refrigerated semi-trailers, which it assigned to meat service, and it equipped twenty-five flat cars with multilevel racks to transport new automobiles. The CGW also added ramp sites in Dubuque and Harlan, Iowa, and Red Wing and Winona, Minnesota. In 1960 the Great Western joined Trailer-Train Company, a Chicago-based firm that developed a successful flatcar leasing program.[4]

One other significant development in the Great Western's freight picture during the final decade was the movement of long iron-ore trains. Cars hauling this low-grade rock originated at Ostrander, Minnesota on the Rochester-McIntire line and travelled over the company's rails to Galena Junction (Dubuque). There the Burlington picked them up for the final lap into Alton, Illinois.[5]

To improve the earnings picture, the Reidy management chopped off the remaining passenger trains. At the beginning of the 1960s, the road operated only trains 5 and 6 between the Twin Cities and Kansas City and 13 and 14 between the Twin Cities and Omaha. Trains 5 and 6 died first. By 1961 the Kansas City runs carried less than a half dozen passengers per trip, and the amount of "head-end" business failed to offset growing losses. At the April 23, 1962, meeting of the Board of Directors, Reidy happily announced that regulatory authorities had allowed the final runs to be made four days later

Edward T. Reidy, elected to the presidency of the Chicago Great Western Railway in January 1957, served as the company's chief officer until the merger with the Chicago & North Western. (W. A. Vaughn Collection)

and that termination would save about $150,000 annually. Publicly, however, the Great Western head said that "we hated to discontinue the service" and claimed losses of more than twice the actual amount.[6]

Trains 13 and 14 lasted longer because they were financially much more viable. With the abandonment in 1959 of the only other competing mail-passenger train between the Twin Cities and Council Bluffs, the C&NW's *North American,* the Great Western gained considerable mail and express traffic from and for the Union Pacific connection. And there existed a small yet steady stream of riders. In fact, in March 1961, just at the time when the road was beginning the legal work to remove the Kansas

Four Great Western GP-30's wait at Central Avenue, Chicago, on May 1, 1966. (Joseph Piersen Photograph)

City runs, it bought two Milwaukee Road chair cars, built in 1934 for the *Hiawatha*. This comfortable rolling stock accommodated patrons' needs splendidly for the duration of service. In time the familiar factors of high costs and low revenues halted these trains. The end came on the evening of September 29, 1965, when number 14 (diesel, baggage car, combine and coach) unceremoniously pulled out of Omaha's Burlington Station bound for its last early morning arrival in Minneapolis.[7]

Just as passenger trains vanished, so did fifty-six miles of trackage. Unlike the massive abandonments that would take place in the 1970s and 1980s, the pieces retired during the Reidy years were short, lightly used, and almost always in terrible physical condition. In July 1961 the Board agreed to push for the end of the ten-mile Utica-Altura branch. This Minnesota trackage generated only $23,692 in 1959, and one of its bridges urgently needed $50,000 worth of repairs. Regulators responded

favorably, and service was stopped on May 29, 1962. Two years later, the Reidy administration decided to scrap another Minnesota line. The thirty-one miles between Red Wing and Pine Island were "badly in need of rehabilitation." Income from this route was even worse than from the Altura trackage: $22,460 in 1962 and $19,023 in 1963. Furthermore, the company estimated that the price tag for upgrading the line approached $700,000. This abandonment, unlike the earlier case, would end through movements; it would sever the secondary main line between McIntire and Randolph via Rochester. The Great Western was thus about to employ again the practice of "stubbing"—a technique it had used successfully on the Waverly-Sumner line fifteen years earlier. The CGW got the green light to dismantle, and the last freight train carefully made its way over the route on March 5, 1965. The final retirement of the Reidy regime was the 15.75-mile segment between McIntire and Osage. By 1966, service on this

Only recently arrived from Electro-Motive, these four GP-30's pull tonnage near Sumner, Iowa, in September 1963. (W. S. Kuba Photograph)

A typically long freight, powered by four GP-30's, rolls through Elma, Iowa, in 1967. (Charles W. Bohi Photograph)

weedy Iowa appendage consisted of a weekly local that crept along a dangerously deteriorated track. Since the Illinois Central also served Osage, no major objections from shippers materialized at the abandonment hearings. So on April 10, 1967, the Great Western withdrew from still another "Middle Border" community.[8]

While the Chicago Great Western gained considerable savings from terminating its last four passenger trains and removing three Minnesota and Iowa pieces of trackage, even greater economies came with reductions in the work force. Not only did the closings of small-town depots continue, but other positions disappeared owing to a national agreement in 1964 on the highly charged issue of "featherbedding." The rail industry called for the elimination of what it considered nonessential workers, in this case, firemen on diesel-electric locomotives. The CGW quickly released sixty-seven enginemen. This act cost $322,000 in severance allowances, yet it promised major long-term returns.

By 1967, the lean and efficient Great Western counted only 1,643 employees.[9]

Notwithstanding hustle and frugality, the overall health of the Great Western slipped from the time of Reidy's inaugural and the Chicago & North Western takeover a decade later. Revenues remained generally flat, averaging $32,317,000 annually. They peaked at $36,820,000 in 1957 and dropped to $28,686,000 in 1967, both recession years. Perhaps a better barometer of the CGW's economic condition was its operating ratio. For the first five-year period it boasted one of the lowest in the industry, an envious 68.28 percent in 1957 and a still respectable 74.97 percent in 1961. But then the ratio crept upwards and hit 80.78 percent in 1967. Still, the Great Western was not a Rock Island or some other business basket case. Throughout the decade the Board of Directors was able to vote the customary $2.50 payment on preferred stock, and it skipped the common dividend only twice, in 1965 and 1967, although the latter shareholders got only fifty cents in 1962, 1963, 1964, and 1966. Earlier they had

A year after their arrival on the property, three SD-40's, each boasting 3,000 horsepower, idle in the Oelwein yards. These diesels were the most powerful that the company ever owned. (W. S. Kuba Photograph)

received remunerations that averaged $1.77, and in 1957, 1959, and 1960 they also got an extra 2.5 percent stock award. These facts of economic life, though, made the CGW a likely candidate for merger.[10]

THE MOVE TOWARD MERGER

Railroad consolidation has undergone distinct phases since the appearance of the first companies in the 1830s. Some united before the Civil War; many more merged between the depressions of the 1870s and 1890s; and still others joined together early in the twentieth century. Most of this activity then stopped until the late 1950s. Although the Interstate Commerce Commission formulated its master unification plan in the twenties, leading lines failed to embrace it. Similarly, the ICC blocked those proposals that did not fit its blueprint. Even though most carriers experienced difficult days during the Great Depression, they generally believed that mergers were not necessary for their economic survival; the nation's railroad map remained largely unaltered.

Conditions, however, changed dramatically after mid-century. The reasons are complex, but the worsening financial positions of numerous roads convinced their owners and the ICC as well that the time was ripe for consolidation. Air, land, and water competitors took a steadily increasing amount of business, and the spectacular impact of reduced costs brought about through dieselization had nearly run its course. "What had once spelled dramatic savings was now a lot less dramatic, and it was time to look beyond the diesel," observed historian Richard Saunders. "Merger was one answer." If properly executed, unification created an enterprise with more gateways, longer hauls, better routes, and reduced labor costs, especially in terminals.[11]

The "merger madness" that infected the railroad industry during the 1960s began in 1957 when the

In the last years of passenger operations between the Twin Cities and Kansas City, mail provided the principal source of revenue. A Star Mail Route carrier receives a sack of letters from train #5 at Diagonal, Iowa, circa 1960. (Liz Wiley Collection)

1,049-mile Nashville, Chattanooga & St. Louis Railway united with the 4,765-mile Louisville & Nashville Railroad. Designed to save $3.75 million in annual operating expenses, this was the first merger whose principal objective was retrenchment. In the years that followed, the industry was abuzz with news of consolidations. In 1960 alone the Canadian Pacific fused together its three American properties, the Minneapolis, St. Paul & Sault Ste. Marie ("the Soo"); the Duluth, South Shore & Atlantic; and the Wisconsin Central into the Soo Line Railroad. The Chicago & North Western gobbled up the Minneapolis & St. Louis, and the Erie joined with the Delaware, Lackawanna & Western. While the decade witnessed the consolidation of such important carriers as the Atlantic Coast Line and the Seaboard Air Line; Baltimore & Ohio and Chesapeake & Ohio; and the Norfolk & Western, Nickel Plate and Wabash, *the* merger was the Pennsylvania and the New York Central. The 19,000-mile Penn Central Transportation Company, which included the sickly New Haven within a year, made its historic debut on February 1, 1968. The age of the "mega-merger" had dawned.[12]

Whether the Chicago Great Western wished to or not, it could not avoid the national phenomenon of

It is a cloudy April 27, 1962, as the last northbound Chicago Great Western passenger train, #6, calls at New Hampton, Iowa.

A small crowd gathers to say good-bye to a long-time friend. (Don L. Hofsommer Photograph)

consolidation. Even though the ICC had mandated that merging roads must maintain "all routes and channels of trade via existing junctions and gateways" and "all present traffic and operating relationships" (the so-called Detroit, Toledo & Ironton conditions), the Great Western realized that in all likelihood it would be adversely affected. Government guarantees did not always work. The road depended heavily on bridge traffic through its five

principal gateways, and its owners worried, of course, about merger proposals in their own back yard. The announcement that came in February 1963 of the planned marriage between the Union Pacific and the Rock Island looked especially ominous; the CGW fed daily at the Union Pacific's troughs in Council Bluffs and Kansas City; and the Rock Island, a keen competitor, also interchanged heavily with the Union Pacific at these points. The

Train #5, the counterpart of #6, leaves the Diagonal, Iowa, station for the final time on the morning of April 27, 1962. (Liz Wiley Collection)

The friendly faces of Conductor Marv Clopton and Brakeman Pat Patterson greet a late-night traveler at Manning, Iowa. (H. Roger Grant Photograph)

realities were such that an old interchange partner might be far less considerate, or outright hostile.[13]

At the start of the 1960s the leaders of the Great Western seemed fully aware of the consolidation phenomenon. Indeed, the road had long toyed with the possibilities of a merger. In 1946 Edward N. Claughton, a Miami, Florida, financier whose investment activities included railroads, theaters, and hotels, sought to fuse together the CGW, Missouri-Kansas-Texas (Katy), and the Chicago & Eastern Illinois (C&EI). A major Katy stockholder, Claughton had also acquired large blocks of CGW and C&EI securities. "I am hoping that a merger agreement may be worked out by the stockholders," he told the press. "A merger is possible and practical and ought to be done." While the three roads would fit together well (the Great Western connected with the Katy at Kansas City and the C&EI in Chicago and the Katy and C&EI met in St. Louis), discussions soon collapsed. For one thing, Sherman Hoar Bowles, a powerful Great Western stockholder,

showed little interest in the scheme. The Katy, correctly sensing difficulties, withdrew.[14]

Not long after the three-way talks ended, the introduction of the Kansas City Group seemed to herald the future fusion of the Great Western with the Kansas City Southern. For a decade or so, employees, shippers, industry observers, and investment analysts assumed that this sensible "end-to-end" merger would take place eventually. While the two companies developed a close operating relationship, no serious efforts were made to do anything more. The Deramuses flatly rejected any union. They probably backed off from fear of other roads diverting traffic from the KCS in retaliation for such an act. Syndicate members, moreover, began to liquidate their Great Western holdings not long after Reidy's ascendancy, in part because of the death of Russell Kelce, a leading stockholder.[15]

As the scramble for corporate partners commenced, the Chicago Rock Island & Pacific approached the Great Western. The Rock Island was

The last CGW revenue train on the sixteen-mile McIntire to Osage branch nears its Osage destination on April 10, 1967. Soon the salvageable rails and ties will be removed. (Don L. Hofsommer Photograph)

not a financial rock of Gibraltar; this old Granger road was experiencing falling revenues and escalating costs. (Unmerged, it collapsed in 1980.) Unlike the earlier road unification possibilities, this potential mate had trackage that paralleled, at times closely, the CGW; in fact, the two roads interchanged carload freight at twenty-nine points. If the companies were to combine, most of the Great Western's lines would be either downgraded or scrapped. The Rock Island seemed most interested in the Oelwein to Des Moines segment and in certain large customers, for example, those at Roseport, Minnesota. Still, Reidy and his associates listened: "We are anxious to merge with somebody." So the CGW made a preliminary study; but the Rock Island lost interest, and the talks sputtered and fizzled.[16]

On the heels of the ill-fated Rock Island deliberations, the Great Western found a new suitor, the Soo Line. This promised to be a much better arrangement; the Soo enjoyed good financial health, and it complemented rather than duplicated the Great Western. The two roads connected only at the Twin Cities and in the Chicago area through the Belt Railway. The marriage, if consummated, would create a 6,200-mile rail network spanning eleven upper Midwestern states. Informal contacts started in mid-1962 between Reidy and the Soo Line President Leonard H. Murray. Their chats led to a formal joint study in October. Then on March 29, 1963, the two heads discussed the preliminary findings. At that time Murray informed Reidy that his firm did not intend to extend a bid, "but would consider any offer that the Great Western might like to make to the Soo Line." This lukewarm response to merger centered on five areas. President Murray admitted that the CGW provided competitive freight sched-

Flames engulf the Oelwein car-repair shop in January 1960. Fortunately, no employee was seriously hurt, and insurance covered much of the financial loss. (H. Roger Grant Collection)

ules between Chicago and the Twin Cities, but he questioned the viability of the Chicago to Kansas City service because of the longer mileage between those points. There was also the matter of the Great Western's outstanding preferred stock; too many of these securities existed to suit him. The Soo Line chief, furthermore, challenged the joint study's suggestion that $2 million in anticipated additional revenues could be realized quickly, and he believed that the $500,000 in yearly savings in labor costs were several years away, largely because of the likely provisions that the ICC would impose for protection of employees. Finally, the Soo Line executive seemed troubled by the fact that the Great Western had already reduced its work force to such a point that he felt that they would be unable to make further reductions to offset future wage increases.[17]

The Great Western thought that the reservations of the Soo Line were largely unwarranted. Reidy later responded point by point. He told Murray that while the CGW faced the longest mileage from Chicago to Kansas City, "nevertheless, the Great Western is able to retain certain traffic between these points and such traffic would not be jeopardized by the merger with the Soo Line." As for the matter of the securities, Reidy believed that it would not become a roadblock either. "The difficulty with respect to the outstanding preferred stock could be handled by conversion of that issue to debentures as part of a plan of merger or possibly might be handled by the Great Western's own action before a formal plan was presented." The CGW chief disagreed that it would take a long time before a merged property would generate those anticipated addi-

Providing railroad service to the Midwest during winter frequently meant serious operating problems. Crews fight to free a stalled freight train west of Hampton, Iowa, in 1965. (James L. Rueber Collection)

tional revenues, "if a concerted solicitation effort was carried out." While the Commission might order employee protection, Reidy suggested reducing the number of workers in the affected classifications before the formal consolidation process began. In this final rebuttal, Reidy argued cogently that the size of the work force of the combined companies could be scaled down further "if the operating policies presently in effect on the Great Western were adopted [by the Soo]."[18]

At the Great Western's board meeting held on November 11, 1963, President Reidy took great pains to relate the overall status of the merger talks with the Soo Line. Unquestionably, the CGW would need to make a "most generous" offer. This did not happen. The directors agreed with Reidy that the "Great Western's operation ratio was con-

siderably better than the Soo Line's and that its earnings were relatively more stable over a longer period of time than those of the Soo Line and that from an over-all point of view the Soo Line needs the Great Western more than the Great Western needs the Soo Line." The directors flatly refused to place the CGW on the defensive. Reidy told Soo officials that his company would withdraw immediately from further negotiations.[19]

Although the press announced on November 12, 1963, suspension of the Great Western and Soo Line talks, more behind the scenes discussions with other roads soon followed. The St. Louis–San Francisco, better known as the Frisco, a 5,000-mile mid-South carrier, also made an overture. As with the Katy and the KCS, the CGW's connection with this possible partner was through the Kansas City gateway. But little came of this; rather, the Great Western quickly found a determined suitor, the Chicago & North Western, and so terminated its contacts with the Frisco.[20]

The 10,642-mile North Western was an old foe. For decades the two companies battled for traffic at Chicago, Omaha, the Twin Cities, and various points in between. Their close competitiveness increased markedly in 1960 when the Minneapolis & St. Louis came under the C&NW's banner; by the time merger talks began, the two rivals connected at twenty-eight points. Although Ben W. Heineman, the aggressive chairman of the North Western board of directors, had his eyes on other properties, most notably the Rock Island and then the Milwaukee, he

A common sight on the Great Western during the diesel era was six F units lashed together and pulling a lengthy freight train. The place is Randolph, Minnesota, and the time is shortly before the merger. (Don L. Hofsommer Photograph)

The breathtaking scenery of northwestern Illinois is captured in this photograph of an eastbound Great Western freight about to enter the Winston tunnel. The Iowa bluffs on the west bank of the Mississippi River loom in the background. (Mark Nelson Photograph)

Several F units idle at the diesel engine house, opened in 1957, at Council Bluffs, Iowa. The photograph dates from around 1960. (W. H. Applegate Collection)

GP-30 #206 heads westbound train #91 with 175 cars through the west portal of the Winston tunnel, the longest manmade bore in Illinois, on March 13, 1966. The abandoned fan house stands on the left. (Mark Nelson Photograph)

found the possibilities of acquiring the Great Western intriguing. Heineman got involved through Great Western director Robert F. McAteer. This associate of Richard J. Buck & Company, a New York City investment firm, claimed to represent the interests of several shareholders who controlled about five percent of the CGW's stock. In all probability, McAteer told Heineman that the Soo Line negotiations had soured and that the Great Western eagerly wanted a merger partner. A gadfly in the classic mold, McAteer seemed entirely independent of the Deramus interests, individuals who had no liking for either the North Western or Chairman Heineman.[21]

Progress on a potential merger began in earnest in May 1964. At a meeting held on the seventh of that month in the North Western's Chicago headquarters, Heineman asked Reidy how the Great Western would feel about consolidation. Heineman revealed that his company had already made a preliminary examination of the CGW but that it would not extend an offer unless Reidy thought his road would be receptive. The North Western board chairman told his guest that his carrier was particularly anxious to have the Great Western's Marshalltown to Kansas City trackage because "the North Western has business originating and terminating in Wisconsin which would give both lines the long haul."

The spectacular scenery of the Mississippi River Valley near Dubuque is captured in this view of train #192, led by four GP-30's, at Portage, Illinois, on May 16, 1964. (W. S. Kuba Photograph)

He suggested, too, that consolidation would yield substantial savings, conservatively estimated at $5 million annually. (These would result largely through united general offices and the elimination of duplicate operating facilities.) Prior to leaving, Reidy agreed to take the matter to the Great Western board, which was scheduled to meet on May 19, twelve days later.[22]

Before the Great Western directors gathered, McAteer and Heineman discussed on several occasions details of the merger proposal. In a May 18 telephone conversation, Heineman told McAteer that he wanted to give .75 shares of C&NW preferred stock for each comparable Great Western certificate and .7 shares of C&NW common stock for each share of CGW common. He also pointed out that he was not anxious to obtain the Great Western's industrial real estate or the stock assets held by Great Western subsidiaries. Heineman closed with

one request: he wanted an indication of interest by the Great Western before he would submit the matter to the North Western's board. Since both governing bodies were scheduled to meet the next day, he asked McAteer to have the subject brought up by the Great Western in the morning and to report back to him so he could discuss the topic with his board that afternoon.[23]

McAteer carried out Heineman's wish. The Great Western directors seemed genuinely interested, even anxious to move on a merger. They wholly agreed with their colleague that the "Great Western is a fine property but that it is being squeezed by increased competition, rate cuts and higher labor costs and that merger with another railroad is the ultimate solution." Yet the Board thought that McAteer should retire from the negotiations and that the North Western should make a formal proposal directly to Reidy as company president. There were

Train #192 leaves Illinois Central trackage at Portage tower, south of East Dubuque, Illinois, on May 28, 1966. (W. S. Kuba Photograph)

On a July day in 1966, train #192, with four GP-30's and 142 cars, marches east of Portage, Illinois. (Mark Nelson Photograph)

some directors (and shareholders, too), who expressed concerns about the North Western as a suitable partner. The road's numerous light-density branches and its short-average hauls looked bad. And the C&NW possessed an erratic pattern of earnings. To complicate matters further, the possibility of a North Western and Rock Island or Milwaukee consolidation might adversely affect the long-run value of C&NW securities.[24]

The Great Western was not about to make any financial blunders. To protect its investors, the Board of Directors sought outside advice. It engaged the services of the investment banking firm of Kuhn, Loeb & Company. The CGW leadership soon received its study, dated July 17, 1964, recommending merger with the North Western and generally approving the Heineman offer. The Board then sent two of its members, headed by the highly knowl-

edgeable John Hawkinson, President of Supervised Investors Services, and F. Stillman Elfred, Chairman of the Board of Peabody Coal, together with the Great Western's Assistant General Counsel Edmund J. Kenny to review further the details with Heineman's representatives. The Great Western wanted to increase the percentage of the North Western common stock for similar Great Western securities, but the C&NW refused, although it made a concession of sorts. If the Great Western would surrender the assets of the Iowa Development Company (Roseport), the Heineman road would allow the CGW to declare a special dividend, aggregating $3 million, to its common stockholders before an official merger.[25]

Once Great Western and North Western representatives hammered out a preliminary agreement, the internal process of consolidation moved smoothly and swiftly. The Great Western Board approved in

Led by four GP-30's, train #192 with 134 cars, is seen on May 28, 1966, from the cab of the lead engine of six F-units that powers train #91 near East Dubuque, Illinois. (Mark Nelson Photograph)

principle the revised proposal on July 24, 1964, and then each company, meeting separately, ratified a formal "Plan and Agreement of Merger." Two months later, stockholders of both roads overwhelmingly backed the union. The CGW balloting produced an 83 percent favorable response, and the C&NW received an 83.1 percent approval rate.[26]

The final roadblock that the CGW–C&NW merger faced was the Interstate Commerce Commission. Even though this all-powerful regulatory body had been regularly approving rail consolidations, especially those that promised to achieve considerable savings, it often took years to decide a case. The paper work with the Commission started officially on November 13, 1964, when the two companies filed a joint application of merger. Public hearings on the merger began in Chicago on March 1, 1965, in the stately Palmer House hotel. For twenty-two days, the talks ran intermittently there and in Iowa

and Minnesota before concluding on July 30. While the testimony gathered by ICC Examiner Lester R. Conley attracted mostly local press coverage, those parties that had a financial stake to protect paid close attention.[27]

The ICC examiner heard and read a number of viewpoints, pro and con. Naturally, the principals offered the argument that the union would be in the combined firm's own interest and the public interest as well. And there were those shippers who heartily agreed. As Harold O. Moe of the Public Utility Department for the City of Rochester, Minnesota, viewed the matter, "Because we are a governmental agency and because the CGW pays local taxes, they have demanded a share of our business. However, delivery by CGW has been slow and erratic, upsetting our schedules of inbound coal, and actually increasing our coal unloading costs. Merger will completely solve this problem." Most railroads who participated

Train #192, consisting of four GP-30's and 167 cars, travels through the hills and dales west of Dubuque on April 2, 1966. The freight is about to reach milepost 177, the distance from Chicago. (Mark Nelson Photograph)

in the sessions sought to obtain traffic conditions and operating concessions from the combined company rather than to block the merger itself.[28]

However, serious opposition materialized. In fact, a majority of the Great Western patrons believed that eventually the overall quality of service would decline. Observed Richard O. Shirk, of Oelwein, owner of the Shirk Oil Company, a Texaco affiliate, "All of our package lubricants must ... come in carload rail freight from Port Arthur, Texas. We feel strongly that the proposed merger would, despite statements to the contrary on the part of the affected railroads, ultimately result in a serious deterioration of service to us." The regulatory commissions of Iowa and Minnesota and the City of Oelwein likewise blasted the proposal. These groups agreed with Shirk that shippers would suffer from reduced attention and that the Fayette County community, in particular, would experience a sizable drop in its employment rate. Railroad labor, represented by the Railway Labor Executives' Association and the Brotherhood of Locomotive Engineers, similarly voiced disapproval, arguing that hundreds of their members, many of whom lived in Oelwein, would eventually lose their jobs.[29]

What would prove to be the most effective opposition came from two other carriers, the Minneapolis, Northfield & Southern, a Minneapolis-based

Time freight #92, led by Electro-Motive F-3A unit #111-A, swirls the snow between South St. Paul and St. Paul on a wintry day in February 1968. Merger with the C&NW is only a few months away. (F. Stewart Mitchell Photograph)

Train #192, six F units and 125 cars, roars out of the east portal of the crumbling Winston tunnel on a snowy March 23, 1967. The destination is Chicago. (Mark Nelson Photograph)

The lead unit, #101-C, of train #192 pokes its nose out of the east portal of the Winston tunnel on March 13, 1966. The deteriorating condition of the tunnel, caused in part by ever-present ground water (ice to the left of the locomotive), attests to the long-standing burden of maintenance. (Mark Nelson Photograph)

switching pike, and the Soo Line, the Great Western's earlier suitor. Both roads complained loudly and with some justification that consolidation would hurt them badly. They feared traffic diversions; thousands of cars that heretofore had moved from the Great Western to their rails would travel automatically from the former CGW to the North Western. The Soo offered a case in point. Under the current arrangements, the Soo regularly got covered hopper cars of corn from a Minneapolis elevator switched exclusively by the Great Western for shipment to a Milwaukee, Wisconsin, milling company served by the C&NW. The CGW willingly gave some of this traffic to the Soo because it could not obtain any line-haul revenue from this business. An expanded North Western would capture the entire payment, since the shipper would not be likely to ask that the corn be switched to the Soo, thereby incurring unnecessary delays.[30]

The slow process of regulatory consideration continued. Arguments at last were heard before the Interstate Commerce Commission in Washington, D.C., on October 12, 1966; and then on April 20, 1967, the body finally announced its verdict: unani-

Sections of some branch lines deteriorated badly during the company's closing years. The trackage near Bremer, Iowa, on the seventeen-mile Sumner-Bremer line, required a six mile per hour speed restriction in May 1967. (Philip R. Hastings Photograph)

mous approval of the merger. But the ICC stipulated several protective features, mostly to satisfy the principal opponents. Generally speaking, employees would be protected; interchange points would remain; and the Soo could gain access to both the North Western's Railway Transfer Company in Minneapolis and the Great Western's sprawling Roseport facility to serve a refinery whose coke shipments it already handled between St. Paul and Wisconsin points.[31]

The Soo Line, however, found the Interstate Commerce Commission's decision wholly unacceptable, even with special considerations. The company charged that interchange losses would still cost it millions of dollars annually and argued that the ICC seriously misjudged the impact of the pending merger. The Soo emphasized that the Commission erred in describing the property as a "corporate child and operating affiliate" of the Canadian Pacific and in making the assumption that its relationship with the Canadian Pacific was such that it

could help the Soo prevent merger-caused traffic diversions. (The Canadian Pacific at the time owned about 56 percent of the Soo's stock.) So on May 26, 1967, lawyers for the Soo Line filed a petition for reconsideration with the ICC. This occurred five days before the anticipated consolidation and therefore postponed it. But the ICC rejected the Soo Line's request on September 27. Undaunted, the Soo sought relief from the federal courts. Much to the surprise and horror of the Great Western and the North Western, the three-member United States District Court in Minneapolis voted two to one to remand the case back to the Commission.[32]

Officials of the Great Western and the North Western had to reassess their strategy. The roads had thought, prior to the judges' decision, that they could combine on December 1, 1967, and in fact had made such preparations. But now additional delays seemed inevitable. The merger might take years to accomplish. Of course the costs in lost savings, litigation fees, and possibly lower security

The shabby condition of the Sumner-Bremer branch shows in this May 1967 view of the depot, privy, section house, and yards at Tripoli, Iowa. The once-a-week freight is setting out and picking up cars. (Philip R. Hastings Photograph)

values would be considerable. Negotiations with the aggrieved party seemed the only logical recourse. Fortunately, the Soo was willing to talk, and the two sides reached an agreement in April 1968. The tenacious Soo had won. While granting concessions on several interchange matters, the accord's central feature gave the Soo *unrestricted* access to the Roseport district. The monopoly that the Great Western had created and enjoyed would end. So the "highball" for merger at last came. At one minute past midnight on July 1, 1968, the Chicago Great Western

Railway Company disappeared. The road of Stickney, Felton, and Deramus was no more.[33]

V. Allan Vaughn, editor of *Safety News,* penned an appropriate and nostalgic epilog in the final issue of that publication. He wrote,

• • •

I remember the motive power which evolved the task of moving steel over steel—the mighty 2-10-4 Texas, the undisputed lord of the iron. The CGW is far from one of the largest railroads entering Chicago . . . , but its 800s [2-10-4's] were never chal-

The official end of the Chicago Great Western was only hours away when James L. Rueber, a dispatcher in Oelwein, photographed business car #100 leaving town on a Kansas City-bound freight. President E. T. Reidy and his grandchildren were aboard the company's finest piece of rolling stock. (James L. Rueber Photograph)

lenged as the biggest steam power operating in and out of Railroadtown.

I remember the first maroon and chocolate brown Diesels, at first a sheet metal monster along side the mighty 2-10-4. Progress being what it is and always will be gave the steamer her deserved niche in railroad lore and crowned the Diesel king. . . .

I remember a 1500-mile hauler of meat and packing house products, a hauler of ore and ingots, a hauler of lumber and grain — the harvests of an abundant Mother Nature.

I remember a legion of Great Westerners spanning the half-century mark in cab and caboose, in office and section gang. Such a tribute to one's company is a record any railroad accepts as honor indeed, that its men devote their entire working days to its service.

I remember the railroad itself, winding through hill and farm, along river and streams of Iowa and the other states served by the Great Western. Winston Tunnel, Nerstrand [Minnesota] Hill, the bluffs along the Missouri, the lakes and forests in Minnesota and the little country stations with their distinctive CGW depot design.[34]

• • •

AFTERWORD

FIFTEEN years have proved that the merger of the Chicago Great Western with the Chicago & North Western yielded mixed results. (The firm became the Chicago & North Western Transportation Company in 1972 when Ben W. Heineman's holding company, Northwest Industries, sold the railroad to the employees.) Corn Belt Route personnel, whether blue or white collar, adjusted reasonably well. Some retired, others left the industry, still more found similar positions in the sprawling North Western system. Disruptions did occur, mostly in Oelwein. Virtually all those employees who held operating and office jobs left that Iowa community by the mid-1970s. Shopmen, though, generally stayed. The North Western selected the huge repair facility as the site for major diesel rebuilding, even for units from "foreign" roads. By 1983 several dozen workers still preserved the town's proud railroad heritage. Even so, the morale of ex-Great Westerners never seemed particularly high on the C&NW; the expanded company was not a closely knit family. "I'm not a North Western employee, I'm a Great Western orphan," snapped Karl R. Weber, a former CGW engineer.[1]

Security holders fared better and seemed happier. Not only did merger negotiations run up Great Western stock spectacularly—from a 1963 low of $14.50 for a share of common to a 1967 high of

$105—but the North Western deal was "most profitable." Stock dividends and splits since 1968 have made these shares valuable, largely because the C&NW benefited enormously from a rapidly changing Midwestern railroad scene. Observed one employee in 1980, "The C&NW defeats its competition by destroying it." This statement holds some truth. The road took over both the Minneapolis & St. Louis and the Great Western, major rivals, and it gobbled up chunks (through lease) of the defunct Rock Island and smaller portions of the steadily shrinking Milwaukee Road, two other old adversaries. The North Western profited immensely from the latter two companies' withdrawal from the busy and once highly competitive "central-haul of America route," Chicago to Omaha. Rather than five other competing lines, the C&NW faces only the Burlington Northern (previously, Chicago, Burlington & Quincy) and the Illinois Central Gulf (previously Illinois Central).[2]

Shippers on the former Great Western apparently lost the most. Soon after the North Western assumed control, it pared down freight service, except on the Kansas City line. Then the company began to petition for abandonment of major segments, at times leaving customers without alternative rail connections. By 1983 nearly three quarters of the CGW's trackage had been retired, including its busiest section, Oel-

Although the track remains in place, the C&NW has stopped running trains into Harlan, Iowa. The depot, built around 1903, has been sold to a local restaurateur. (Charles W. Bohi Photograph)

wein to Chicago (twenty miles remain in operation, Elmhurst to Fox River, Illinois). Even the vital Kansas City stem has an uncertain future; presently, the C&NW is renting and will likely acquire the largely parallel Rock Island property between the Twin Cities and the Missouri metropolis, an artery that is shorter and better engineered.[3]

Patrons frequently complained about the contraction of the former Great Western. Yet, the Interstate Commerce Commission offered little help; it regularly, even speedily, approved abandonment requests, especially of late when the spirit of decontrol has permeated the regulatory bureaucracy. The North Western, however, could truthfully tell the Commission that business did not warrant continuation of certain trackage, usually because it had driven away as many shippers as possible. This was done by reducing train movements, cutting maintenance, and

In February 1973 a crew busily dismantles the former CGW line near Woodbine, Illinois. (Philip R. Hastings Photograph)

closing depots. For example, the C&NW might retire the middle of a line; once stubbed, the remaining portions withered. Unquestionably, the presence of a tri-weekly or less frequent way-freight hardly stimulated growth and retention of traffic. North Western officials from the start said that they wanted only the Kansas City extension, and they viewed most of the remaining system as expendable. Indeed, these men thought it desirable to liquidate redundant pieces quickly. Thus, the railroad willingly left those communities that it had once so vigorously promoted.[4]

In two instances, shippers who had failed to get regulatory support adopted the concept of self-help. Shortly before the last revenue freight rumbled over the historic 146-mile stretch between Randolph, Minnesota, and Oelwein on November 6, 1981, certain Hawkeye State patrons organized the Northeast

On March 31, 1981, the final day the Chicago & North Western operated in Dubuque, Iowa, a staff photographer for the city's *Telegraph Herald* snapped the last employees and engine to work the former Great Western trackage; Tom Goin, station agent (left), and crewmen (left to right on #4481) Chris Anderson, Frank Roe, and Jeff Frazer willingly pose. Reported the newspaper, "The end of the line came with no fanfare, no sudden jolt or blaring horn. Rather the end came with the rusty grind of heavy machinery, the groan of aging wheels." This was a far cry from that memorable November day in 1885 when 2,000 jubilant residents gathered for the beginnings of the Dubuque & Northwestern. (Steve Gustafson Photograph)

Iowa Transportation Association. They sought to create an independent short line in order to maintain service; otherwise, they confronted the prospects of higher truck charges. The organization's efforts, however, fizzled; it simply lacked the financial wherewithal to enter railroading. Recently, Minnesota customers along the Dodge Center to Sargeant segment and the Hayfield to Waltham portion of the abandoned Hayfield to Mason City line have formed the Hayfield Northern Railroad. While this company is not yet operating, it has prevented the North Western from ripping up these nineteen miles of rusting track. Generally speaking, these types of responses have been common nationally; but in their lack of success, they also parallel the vast majority of similar schemes, for such consumer-backed endeavors either never turn a wheel or quickly fold.[5]

Yet even with major retrenchments, the Chicago & North Western has usually offered some benefits to one type of former Great Western customer, the grain shipper. This company has led the industry with its economical multiple-car and unit-train pricing for those willing to use main line elevators. For example, eastern Carroll County, Iowa, farmers can

Only one mile remains before this North Western freight train enters the Oelwein yards on November 6, 1981, for the last trip from Minnesota. The company had received regulatory permission to abandon the 146 miles of the ex-Great Western between Randolph, Minnesota, and Oelwein. (Richard Wilkinson Photograph)

no longer drive the few miles to Lanesboro or Lidderdale to load boxcars but must go ten to twenty miles further to Ralston. But the inconvenience and extra expense in trucking are often more than compensated by the bargain-basement rail rates from this point.

Even though much of Chicago Great Western vanished after 1968, there is no reason to assume that merger with a different road would have preserved it totally. Admittedly, if consolidation with the Soo Line had occurred, more of the now abandoned trackage would likely have remained. The

The final revenue train to roll north out of Oelwein is photographed on November 6, 1981, by Richard Wilkinson of the *Oelwein Daily Register*. Within a year, the rails and ties would be gone. (Richard Wilkinson Photograph)

Soo would probably have retained access to both the Kansas City and Omaha gateways. (The CGW enjoyed the shortest distance between the Twin Cities and the Nebraska city.) And perhaps the Oelwein to Chicago line also would have survived.

While the amount of Great Western mileage that might have lived is debatable, there is little likeli-hood that the road could have completely escaped merger pressures. As Great Western director Robert F. McAteer correctly observed in 1967, "If CGW was to be left alone with all surrounding railroads in the process of merger, it could ultimately have only one result, beset as it is with constantly rising costs in both labor and materials, and that is, I believe,

The sun sets on Chicago & North Western service from the north into Oelwein, Iowa. (Richard Wilkinson Photograph)

bankruptcy. . . ." The inroads of truck, barge and air transportation and their subsidies would also eventually contribute to its ultimate finish."[6]

Although the wreck of the Penn Central in June 1970 and the collapse of the Erie-Lackawanna two years later caused skepticism about mergers as the remedy for industry ills, the desire to consolidate remained keen. By the 1980s, roads that had often expanded through merger in the sixties continued to do so. Present leaders are the big new carriers — Burlington Northern, CSX, and Norfolk Southern. These giants, which in some cases cover 25,000 miles in twenty states, have benefited more from a favorable regulatory milieu than from the savings derived through joint facilities and the like. The Staggers Rail Act of 1980, in particular, appears to have done much to improve conditions by significantly deregulating the pricing structure. This legislation gave railroads greater freedom to raise and lower rates, especially when transporting fresh fruits and vegetables, thus meeting the competition from trucks.[7]

While the current environment would have considerably helped an independent Chicago Great Western, the road's size by the 1980s would have made it a transportation anachronism. Class I roads of fewer than 1,500 miles simply are the exceptions and not the rule. Yet for decades the Great Western

A C&NW scrap train heads toward Oelwein on June 11, 1982. The place is near New Hampton, Iowa, the then end-of-tracks. The company will use these materials elsewhere on the system. (Philip R. Hastings Photograph)

harmonized well with the national railroad picture: it could admirably serve patron needs (particularly when their alternatives were slow-moving vehicles on poor-quality roads or erratic steamboat schedules) and its special features created an outstanding tradition of innovation and modernization. The

In early October 1981, shortly after removal of the rails on the Oelwein to Dubuque line east of Dyersville, Iowa, only usable ties need to be collected. Nearby, the Illinois Central Gulf closely parallels the former Great Western right-of-way. (H. Roger Grant Photograph)

The naked grade of the Chicago Great Western west of St. Charles, Illinois, has become a hiking and biking path, appropriately called the "Great Western Trail." (H. Roger Grant Photograph)

By July 7, 1982, the C&NW had located part of its track removal operations on the Randolph-Oelwein line at Fredericksburg, Iowa. The crew is inactive for the weekend. (Philip R. Hastings Photograph)

The deteriorating west portal of the Winston tunnel basks in the autumn sun. By 1981, portions of the bore had collapsed, and water covered much of the floor. (H. Roger Grant Photograph)

The former Chicago Great Western line east of Stillman Valley, Illinois, awaits scrappers in October 1981. Ironically, a corn stalk has grown between the rusty rails—a fitting reminder of the once vigorous "Corn Belt Route." (H. Roger Grant Photograph)

CGW fit nicely into the evolving railroad structure. It forged a multistate system when the puny, independent carriers faded, and it disappeared as the industry blossomed forth into massive units of interregional stems. Because the nature of intercity travel has changed dramatically since World War II, tens of thousands of miles of trackage have been abandoned; indeed, the nation's railroad map no longer needs to be a nearly solid blotch of black lines.

Some of the "ferrocide" of the recent past is logical, but not all of it can be fully justified. The concept of progress is difficult to grasp when a road like the Corn Belt Route has been mostly junked. Much of Stickney's glory has either been left in a state of decay or has reverted back to nature or has been put to agricultural use. In a few cases, the rights-of-way have even been adapted for recreational purposes. (The DeKalb County, Illinois, Forest Preserve Commission, for one, maintains approximately eighteen miles of the former main line between St. Charles and Sycamore. This naked grade is fittingly called the "Great Western Trail," an ironic finale for a property intended to "run forever" as a railroad.)

Two nagging questions persist: Can the railroad enterprise be creative without the smaller, scrappy companies like the CGW? And will the service territory in time be hurt severely by the dismantlement of so many miles of former Great Western roadway? No matter what the answers, the Chicago Great Western is gone, never again to be a separate entity and not likely to be rebuilt.

APPENDIX

COMPONENTS OF THE CHICAGO GREAT WESTERN RAILROAD CO.

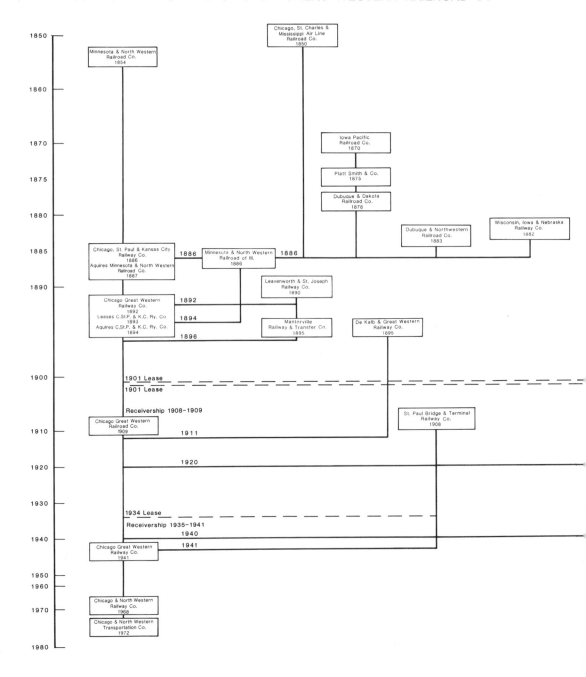

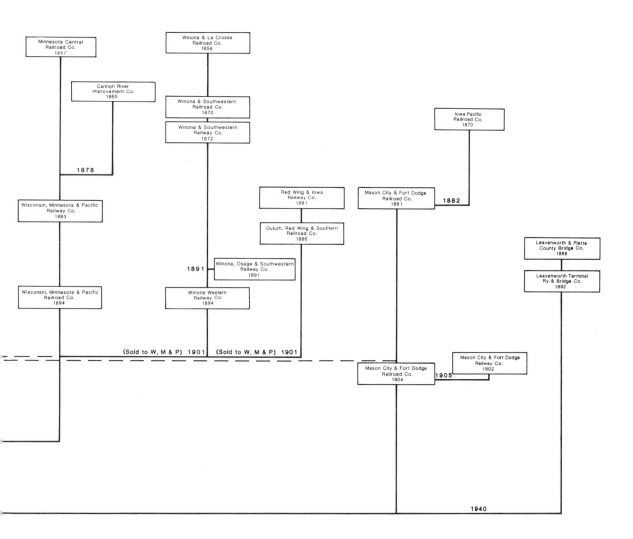

Minnesota Central
Railroad Co.
1857

Cannon River
Improvement Co.
1865

Winona & La Crosse
Railroad Co.
1856

Winona & Southwestern
Railroad Co.
1870

Winona & Southwestern
Railway Co.
1872

Iowa Pacific
Railroad Co.
1870

1878

Wisconsin, Minnesota & Pacific
Railway Co.
1883

Red Wing & Iowa
Railway Co.
1881

Mason City & Fort Dodge
Railroad Co.
1881

1882

Duluth, Red Wing & Southern
Railroad Co.
1886

Leavenworth & Platte
County Bridge Co.
1888

1891

Winona, Osage & Southwestern
Railway Co.
1891

Leavenworth Terminal
Ry. & Bridge Co.
1892

Wisconsin, Minnesota & Pacific
Railroad Co.
1894

Winona Western
Railway Co.
1894

(Sold to W, M & P) **1901**   (Sold to W, M & P) **1901**

Mason City & Fort Dodge
Railway Co.
1902

Mason City & Fort Dodge
Railroad Co.
1904

1905

1940

— — — —   **Indicates Lease**

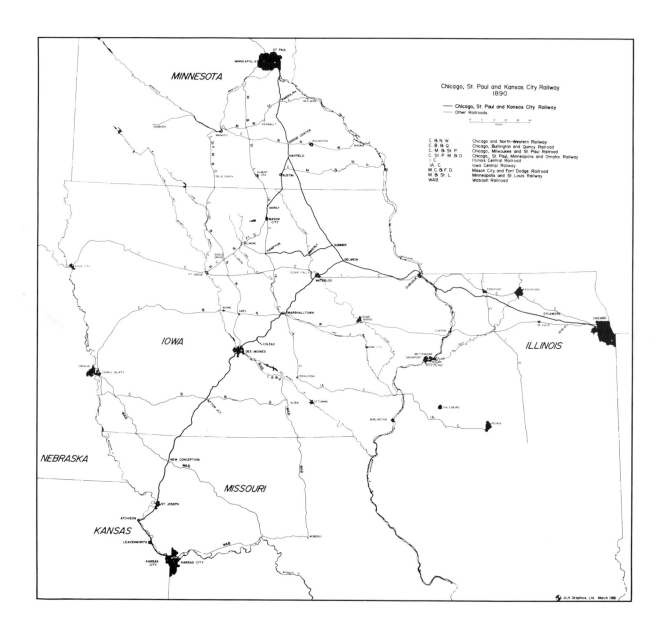

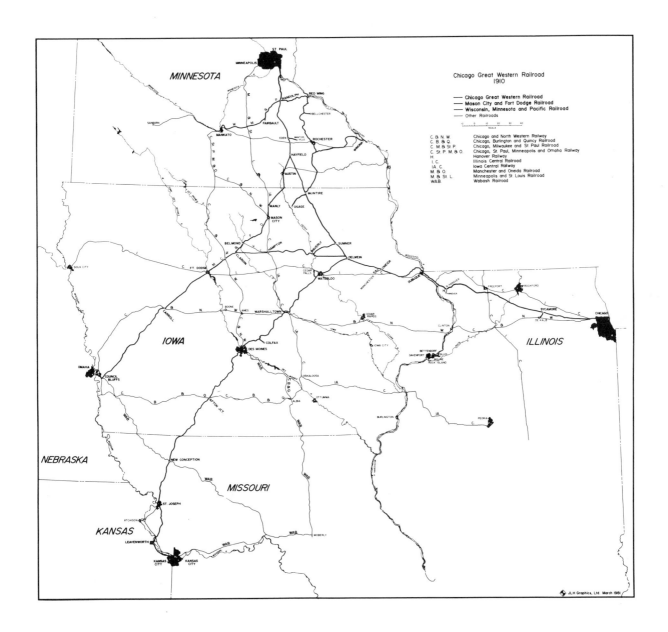

Chicago Great Western Railroad
1910

— Chicago Great Western Railroad
— Mason City and Fort Dodge Railroad
— Wisconsin, Minnesota and Pacific Railroad
— Other Railroads

C. & N. W.   Chicago and North Western Railway
C. B. & Q.   Chicago, Burlington and Quincy Railroad
C. M. & St. P.   Chicago, Milwaukee and St. Paul Railroad
C. St. P. M. & O. Chicago, St. Paul, Minneapolis and Omaha Railway
H.   Hanover Railway
I. C.   Illinois Central Railroad
IA. C.   Iowa Central Railway
M. & O.   Manchester and Oneida Railroad
M. & St. L.   Minneapolis and St. Louis Railroad
WAB.   Wabash Railroad

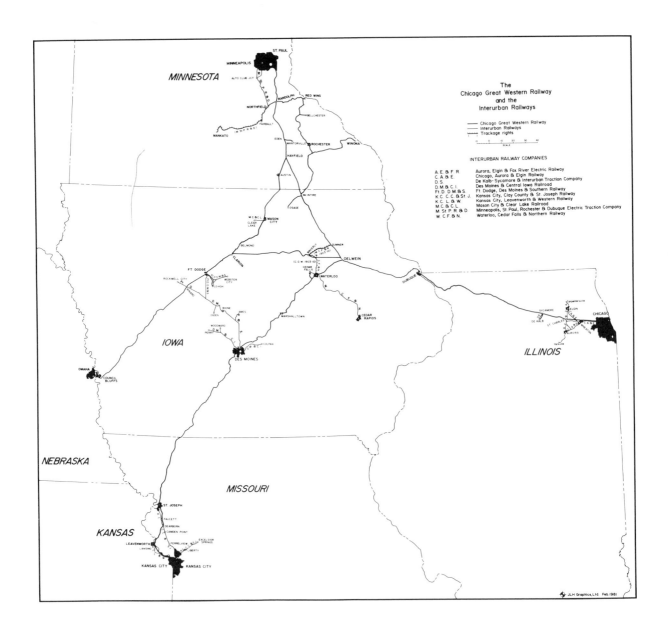

The
Chicago Great Western Railway
and the
Interurban Railways

——— Chicago Great Western Railway
——— Interurban Railways
——— Trackage rights

INTERURBAN RAILWAY COMPANIES

A.E.&F.R.   Aurora, Elgin & Fox River Electric Railway
C.A.&E.   Chicago, Aurora & Elgin Railway
D.S.   De Kalb- Sycamore & Interurban Traction Company
D.M.&C.I.   Des Moines & Central Iowa Railroad
Ft.D. D.M.&S.   Ft. Dodge, Des Moines & Southern Railway
K.C.C.C.&St.J.   Kansas City, Clay County & St. Joseph Railway
K.C. L.&W.   Kansas City, Leavenworth & Western Railway
M.C.&C.L.   Mason City & Clear Lake Railroad
M.St.P.R.&D.   Minneapolis, St. Paul, Rochester & Dubuque Electric Traction Company
W.C.F.&N.   Waterloo, Cedar Falls & Northern Railway

JLH Graphics, Ltd. Feb 1981

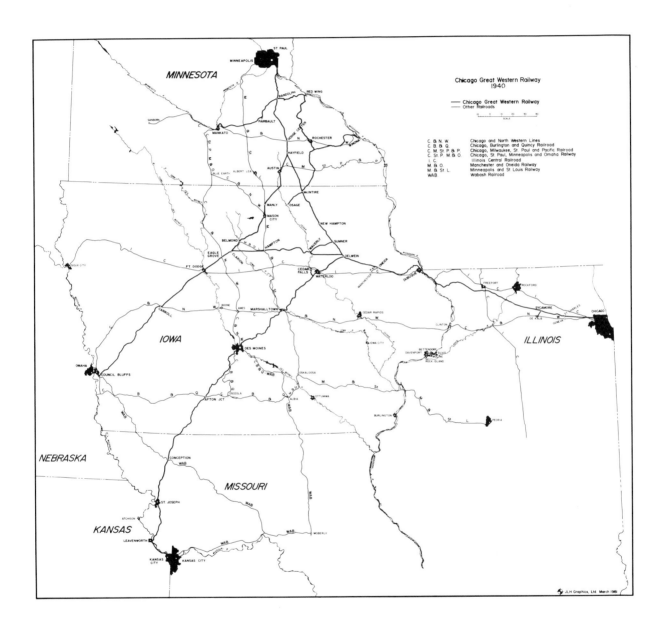

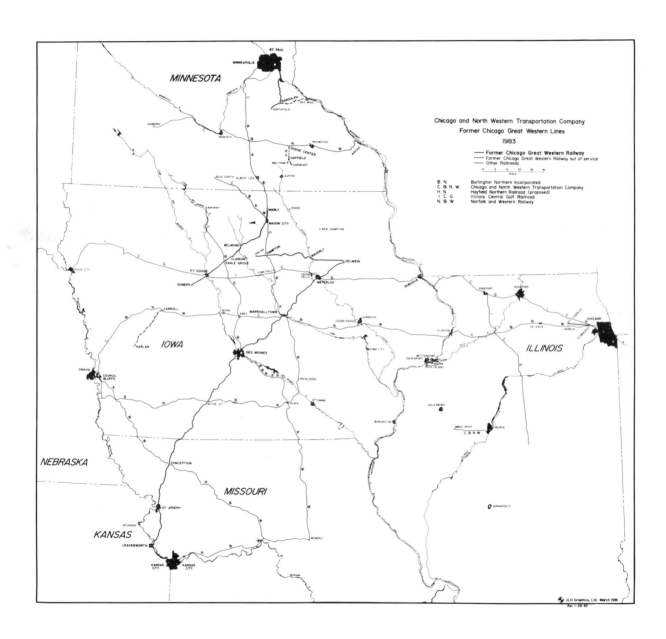

NOTES

CHAPTER ONE

1. *Statistical Abstract of the United States, 1916* (Washington, D.C., 1917), 292; *Report on Population of the United States at the Eleventh Census, 1890* (Washington, D.C., 1895), I: 2.

2. *The Chicago & North-Western Line* (Chicago, 1881), 2.

3. See Hallie Farmer, "The Railroads and Frontier Populism," *Mississippi Valley Historical Review,* 13(December 1926):387–97; Lawrence Goodwyn, *Democratic Promise: The Populist Moment in America* (New York, 1976), 115–17.

4. Marion D. Shutter and J. S. McLain, *Progressive Men of Minnesota* (Minneapolis, 1897), 178; *Oelwein* (Iowa), *Register,* August 16, 1916.

5. T. A. Busbey, ed., *The Biographical Directory of the Railway Officials of America* (Chicago, 1893); Dumas Malone, ed., *Dictionary of American Biography,* 20 vols. (New York, 1936), 18:15–16; *New York Times,* August 10, 1916; Frank P. Donovan, Jr., and W. B. Davids, "A. B. Stickney: Spokesman for Progress," *Railway Progress* (December 1952), 16; A. B. Stickney Papers, Minnesota Historical Society, St. Paul (hereafter cited as Stickney Papers).

6. Stickney Papers; *Fort Dodge* (Iowa) *Messenger,* December 28, 1903.

7. Pierre Berton, *The Impossible Railway: The Building of the Canadian Pacific* (New York, 1972), 252, 264, 302; W. Kaye Lamb, *History of the Canadian Pacific Railway* (New York, 1977), 78, 82–83.

8. Lamb, *History of the Canadian Pacific Railway,* 78, 82–83; *National Cyclopedia of American Biography,* multivolume series (New York, 1926), 19:33; *Poor's Manual of Railroads* (New York, 1884), 740; Frank P. Donovan, Jr., *Mileposts on the Prairie: The Story of the Minneapolis & St. Louis Railway* (New York, 1950), 63–64.

9. Minnesota & Northwestern Railroad Company, Minute Book Two, Chicago & North Western Transportation Company, Chicago (hereafter cited as M&NW Minute Book 2).

10. M&NW Minute Book 2; "Charter & Amendments, Minn. & NW RR," Chicago & North Western Transportation Company, Chicago; Stock affidavit, March 27, 1883, Chicago & North Western Transportation Company, Chicago; "Memo. of Stock Subscriptions & Transfers of Shares of Minn. & N.W. R.R. Co.," December 19, 1883, Chicago & North Western Transportation Company, Chicago.

11. *Dubuque* (Iowa) *Daily Times,* August 18, 1886.

12. Ibid., June 18, September 22, 1885; M&NW Minute Book 2.

13. M&NW Minute Book 2; "Corporate History of the Chicago Great Western Railroad Company as of the Date of Valuation June 20, 1916" (Chicago, 1920), 8–9(hereafter cited as "Corporate History of the CGW"); *Railroad Gazette,* May 15, 1885; *Dubuque Daily Times,* July 6 and August 11, 1885; *The Maize* (February 1916), 6. Even before the M&NW's first revenue train entered service between Randolph and the Twin Cities, the Minneapolis & St. Louis Railway operated freights 98 and 99 over the 32.8 miles between Randolph and West St. Paul starting June 1, 1885. This arrangement, however, was temporary.

14. M&NW Minute Book 2.

15. *Railway World,* June 13, 1885; *Dubuque Daily Times,* May 22, August 20, August 29, 1885.

16. *Oelwein Register*, February 14, 1895; *St. Paul Pioneer-Press*, August 29, 1885. For a useful overview of the larger railroad strategies of the late nineteenth century, see Chapter 5, "System-Building, 1880s–1900s," in Alfred D. Chandler, Jr., *The Visible Hand: The Managerial Revolution in American Business* (Cambridge, 1977), 145–87.

17. M&NW Minute Book 2.

18. John F. Stover, *History of the Illinois Central Railroad* (New York, 1975), 133–35; *Dubuque Daily Times*, June 17 and June 22, 1883; *Iowa State Register* (Des Moines), September 16, 1883.

19. *Oelwein* (Iowa) *Daily Register*, July 21, 1948; *Dubuque Daily Times*, June 13 and July 7, 1883, October 1, 1885.

20. *Dubuque Daily Times*, July 26, 1883, May 18, 1884.

21. Ibid., May 7, 1885.

22. Ibid.; *Railroad Gazette*, June 19, 1885; *Poor's Manual of Railroads* (New York, 1886), 343.

23. *Dubuque Daily Times*, July 22, July 30, August 12, August 16, 1885; *Railroad Gazette*, July 31, 1885.

24. *Railroad Gazette*, November 20, 1885.

25. *Dubuque Daily Times*, November 10, 1885.

26. *Poor's Manual of Railroads* (New York, 1886), 343; *Dubuque Daily Times*, April 29, June 17, July 27, July 31, August 21, August 31, September 4, October 20, October 22, 1886; *Historical Atlas of Chicksaw County, Iowa* (Chicago, 1915), 6; *St. Paul Pioneer-Press*, July 9, 1886; *Railroad Gazette*, July 2, July 19, 1886; *Fort Dodge Messenger*, August 19, 1886.

27. *Byron* (Illinois) *Express*, December 3, 1886; *Dubuque Daily Times*, November 30, 1886, February 10, 1887.

28. "Corporate History of the CGW," 16; *Railroad Gazette*, November 26, 1886.

29. *Byron Express*, January 22, March 4, March 16, April 2, April 19, May 28, 1886; "Corporate History of the CGW," 10; *Dubuque Daily Times*, March 19, 1886.

30. *Aurora* (Illinois) *Beacon*, September 12, 1850, May 8, 1851; *Aurora* (Illinois) *Guardian*, November 9, 1853; *Sycamore* (Illinois) *Republican-Sentinel*, December 28, 1854, February 22, 1855; *Byron Express*, March 24 and August 6, 1886, January 14, 1887; *Dubuque Daily Times*, December 23, 1886.

31. *Byron Express*, July 2, 1886; "Corporate History of the CGW," 10; Stover, *History of the Illinois Central Railroad*, 201.

32. "Contract: Minnesota & Northwestern R. R. of Ill. and Minn. Loan & Debenture Co., June 28, 1886," Chicago & North Western Transportation Company, Chicago; M&NW Minute Book 2. See also *Byron Express*, July 2, 1886; *Dubuque Daily Times*, October 28, 1886.

33. Quoted in the *Byron Express*, June 25, July 2, July 23, September 10, 1886. See also *Dubuque Daily Times*, September 21, 1886.

34. *Byron Express*, July 16, July 23, July 30, September 3, 1886, October 24, 1890.

35. O. T. Willard, "First Eastern Division Train Order," *The Maize*, (June 1915), 9; *Valley Chronicle* (St. Charles, Illinois), October 15, 1886; *Byron Express*, November 12 and December 10, 1886, January 7, January 14, May 27, 1887.

36. *Oelwein Register*, June 3 and August 5, 1887; *Byron Express*, June 17 and August 5, 1887; *Valley Chronicle*, August 5, 1887; *Railroad Gazette*, August 5, 1887; *Stockton* (Illinois) *Herald-News*, July 28, 1937.

37. *Railroad Gazette*, February 11 and March 18, 1887; *Dubuque Daily Times*, February 24, 1887; *Byron Express*, February 25 and November 25, 1887, February 10, 1888.

38. Richard C. Overton, *Burlington Route: A History of the Burlington Lines* (New York, 1965), 190–96; *Oelwein Register*, January 27, 1888, *Byron Express*, February 3, 1888; *Second Annual Report of the Chicago, St. Paul and Kansas City Railway Company* (St. Paul [?], 1888), 6.

39. *Oelwein Register*, September 2, 1887; *Byron Express*, September 9, 1887; *Dubuque Daily Times*, August 31, 1887; C. W. Finch, "The Winston Tunnel," unpublished ms.; *Second Annual Report of the Chicago, St. Paul and Kansas City Railway Company* (1888), 6.

40. Donovan, *Mileposts on the Prairie*, 105–21; "Corporate History of the CGW," 8; *Dubuque Herald*, December 15, 1886; *Railroad Gazette*, December 4, 1885, February 14, 1890; *Northwestern Railroader*, September 16, 1887.

41. Donovan, *Mileposts on the Prairie*, 113–14; *Rand McNally Official Railway Guide* (Chicago, 1887), 383.

42. "Corporate History of the CGW," 13–14.

43. Ibid., 11; *American Railroad Journal*, May 27, 1871.

44. Ibid.; Marshall B. Craig, "The Chicago Great Western's Oldest Miles," unpublished ms., State Historical Society of Iowa, Iowa City; *Allison* (Iowa) *Tribune*, January 27, 1954.

45. George M. Craig, "The 'D. & D.' Railroad," *Great Western Magazine* (May 1922), 8; *American Railroad Journal*, September 13, 1873.

46. Iowa Vol. 19, 408, R. G. Dun & Co. Collection, Baker Library, Harvard University Graduate School of Business Administration; *Fort Dodge Messenger*, May 30, 1906.

47. Letter from J. B. Dumont to W. K. Ackerman, July 21, 1877, Illinois Central Papers, Newberry Library, Chicago (hereafter cited as IC Papers).

48. "Corporate History of the CGW," 13; *Poor's Manual of Railroads* (New York, 1881), 708; *Report of the Board of Railroad Commissioners* (Des Moines, 1880).

49. Ibid.; *Dubuque Daily Times,* July 26 and November 1, 1879, July 22, 1880; Craig, "The Chicago Great Western's Oldest Miles"; *Allison Tribune,* January 27, 1954.

50. Craig, "The 'D. & D.' Railroad," 8; Donovan, *Mileposts on the Prairie,* 112; letter from Stuyvesant Fish to M. K. Jesup, July 12, 1880, IC Papers.

51. *Dubuque Daily Times,* September 24, 1879, December 14, 1886; Craig, "The 'D. & D.' Railroad," 8–9.

52. *Dubuque Daily Times,* April 7 and December 14, 1886; letter written by Stuyvesant Fish (addressee unidentified), n.d., IC Papers.

53. *St. Paul Pioneer-Press,* December 3, 1885; *Oelwein Register,* July 29, 1887; *Byron Express,* August 5, 1887; *Northwestern Railroader,* August 5, 1887; *Railroad Gazette,* May 2, 1885; November 11, 1887. The Minnesota & Northwestern did acquire access to valuable trackage in the Twin Cities. In 1886, it won admittance as an equal partner in the multiowned Minnesota Transfer Railway Company. See Frank P. Donovan, Jr., *Gateway to the Northwest: The Story of the Minnesota Transfer Railway* (Minneapolis, 1954), 24.

54. *Railroad Gazette,* September 23, 1887. Two other rumors of M&NW expansion appeared in the press during 1887, which included a Dubuque to Davenport–Moline–Rock Island line and one from Dubuque to Milwaukee, Wisconsin. See *Dubuque Daily Times,* August 18 and November 17, 1887.

55. *Byron Express,* August 19, 1887.

56. *Waterloo (Iowa) Courier,* April 29, 1887.

57. *Oelwein Register,* October 13, 1915.

58. *Railroad Gazette,* November 5, 1886; *Tenth Annual Report of the Board of Railroad Commissioners* (Des Moines, 1888), 434.

59. *Tenth Annual Report of the Board of Railroad Commissioners,* 436, 438; C. S. McCloud, "Tales of an Old Timer," *The Maize,* (December 1915), 16; *Byron Express,* September 9, 1887, July 20, 1888.

60. Letter from Jno. Alloway to James J. Hill, April 20, 1886, James J. Hill Papers, James Jerome Hill Reference Library, St. Paul, Minnesota. Although the M&NW was not involved directly in townsite promotion, communities sprang up at trackside, including the Illinois settlements of Kent, Stockton, Woodbine, and Yellow Creek. In Stockton, for example, the inaugural issue of the *Herald* (May 11, 1888) noted that "fortunately for the new town, the land was owned by men of enterprise who saw no gold dust creeping through the soul, and who were willing to dispose of lots on a common sense basis."

The other roads that competed with the M&NW between the Twin Cities and Chicago were the Chicago & North Western–Chicago, St. Paul, Minneapolis & Omaha; Chicago, Burlington & Northern–Chicago, Burlington & Quincy; Chicago, Milwaukee & St. Paul; and the Wisconsin Central. Later, the Minneapolis & St. Louis and the Illinois Central forged a direct line through the Albert Lea gateway.

61. H. E. Lamb, "Reminiscences of Yesteryear on the Minnesota & Northwestern: The Story of the Building of the Great Western," *The Great Western Magazine* (March 1926), 3; J. W. Losey, *In the Matter of the Chicago, St. Paul & Kansas City Railway Co.: Brief in Behalf of the Chicago, Burlington & Northern, 1888,* 1–29(In collection at the Newberry Library, Chicago).

62. *The Review* (Mankato, Minnesota), August 2, 1887; *Northwestern Railroader,* August 5, 1887; *Dubuque Daily Times,* August 18, 1886.

63. *Byron Express,* August 26, 1887.

64. *Dubuque Daily Times,* February 8, 1887.

65. *Northwestern Railroader,* August 19, 1887.

CHAPTER TWO

1. *Democrat* (Savannah, Missouri), September 23, 1887.

2. *Statistics of the Population of the United States at the Tenth Census* (Washington, D.C., 1883), 169; *Iowa Official Register* (Des Moines, 1960), 7–9. Des Moines would continue to grow rapidly. In 1890 its population stood at 50,093, a 44.7% increase over the previous decade. See *Report on the Population of the United States at the Eleventh Census* (Washington, D.C., 1895), 138.

3. *Dubuque Daily Times,* November 14, 1880; *Iowa State Register* (Des Moines), April 29, 1883; *Railroad Gazette,* September 19, 1884. Dr. George Glick (1827–1906), the guiding light behind the emerging "Diagonal" road, was a typical small-town booster and entrepreneur. After selecting Marshalltown as his home, this German immigrant worked first as a dry-goods merchant and grocer, later as a druggist, and then as a banker. Even though he probably lacked a medical degree, Glick always used the title of doctor, a familiar practice for pharmacists during the nineteenth century. In addition to his work as head of the First National Bank of Marshalltown, he served as an organizer and long-time board member of the Des Moines-based insurance firm, The Bankers Life Association.

4. *Poor's Manual of Railroads* (New York, 1885), 745; *Railroad Gazette,* October 26, 1883.

5. Quoted in the *Dubuque Daily Times,* September 22, 1882.

6. *Iowa State Register,* May 27 and July 10, 1883; *Dubuque Daily Times,* April 11, 1882; *Railway World,* April 22, 1882; William Batten and F. A. Moscrip, *Past and Present of Marshall County, Iowa* (Indianapolis, 1912), 206.

7. *Dubuque Daily Times,* January 18, 1883; *Railroad Gazette,* February 2, December 7, December 23, 1883; *Iowa State Register,* March 10, November 8, November 13, November 29, 1883; *Waterloo Courier,* April 23, 1883; C. E. Rambo, "Early Days on the C.G.W.," *The Maize* (April 1916), 28.

8. *Railroad Gazette,* May 2 and June 27, 1884; *Poor's Manual of Railroads* (New York, 1884), 783.

9. Quoted in the *Iowa State Register,* April 12, May 18, May 26, May 27, 1883.

10. Promoters of the Wisconsin, Iowa & Nebraska apparently had their eyes set on an even more grandiose objective. "We learn from sources in New York," reported the *Iowa State Register,* March 24, 1883, "that this company is now seeking a line from the Mississippi east to Janesville, Wisconsin or some other point in that region, with lines beyond that both to Chicago and Milwaukee, and that the money has been raised and is now ready for call to build the road from Chicago and Milwaukee, to and through Iowa to Nebraska City."

11. *Railroad Gazette,* April 11 and July 11, 1884; *Dubuque Daily Times,* August 28, 1885. Even though the WI&N never acquired title to the DMO&S, it briefly fashioned a close, working relationship with the narrow-gauge road. Between 1884 and 1885 the Diagonal and the "Osceola Line" (its popular nickname) shared the same general manager and publicized their operations jointly. The difference in track width, of course, prevented the interchange of rolling stock.

12. *Iowa State Register,* September 23 and November 21, 1883; *Report of the Iowa Improvement Company Operating the WI&N Railway Company to the Board of Railroad Commissioners of Iowa, for the Year Ending June 30, 1885,* 8, 12.

13. *Railroad Gazette,* August 28 and September 25, 1885.

14. *Iowa State Register,* September 23, 1883; *Railroad Gazette,* October 26, 1883.

15. *Railroad Gazette,* June 18, 1886; July 1, 1887; *Poor's Manual of Railroads* (New York, 1886), 822; ibid., (New York, 1887), 1000; *Dubuque Daily Times,* June 8 and August 27, 1886; *Oelwein Register,* June 10, 1887.

16. *Second Annual Report of the Chicago, St. Paul and Kansas City Railway Co. for the Year Ending June 30, 1888,* 8–9; *St. Paul Pioneer-Press,* December 6, 1887.

17. *Second Annual Report of the Chicago, St. Paul and Kansas City Railway Co. for the Year Ending June 30,* 1888, 9; *Dubuque Daily Times,* February 4, 1887; *Byron (Illinois) Express,* August 19, 1887; *Iowa State Register,* March 6, 1887; *Railroad Gazette,* October 14 and November 4, 1887.

18. *Railroad Gazette,* February 25, 1887; *Democrat,* November 4, 1887; January 6, 1888.

19. *Democrat,* January 13, 1888. The editor of the Savannah *Democrat* was naturally overjoyed at his community's triumph. Since 1883 there had seemed to be the possibility of a much-needed north-south railroad. Residents had hoped for the completion of efforts started by the ill-fated La Crosse, Iowa & Southwestern, which had planned a line from the Mississippi River town of La Crosse, Wisconsin, through Charles City, Iowa, to St. Joseph, Missouri. Only survey work, however, occurred in the Savannah area, but it was the route that the Diagonal generally followed. See *Democrat,* November 23 and December 27, 1883; March 28, May 9, 1884; December 25, 1885; May 26, 1886; January 28, 1887.

20. *Oelwein Register,* May 25, 1888; *Railroad Gazette,* April 20 and August 3, 1888.

21. "Corporate History of the CGW," 19; *Report on the Population of the United States* (1890), 216; *Fourth Annual Report of the Chicago, St. Paul and Kansas City Railway Co. for the Year Ending June 30, 1890,* 3; *Democrat,* January 27 and March 7, 1890; "History of the Chicago Great Western Railway Company," unpublished ms., personal possession, 6.

22. *Annals of Platte County, Missouri* (Kansas City, 1897), 930; *Oelwein Register,* February 5, 1891.

23. *Report on the Population of the United States* (1890), 211; Mrs. B. M. Lesan, *Early History of Ringgold County, 1844–1937* (n.p., 1937), 96; *Ravenwood (Missouri) Gazette,* December 16, 1926.

24. "Corporate History of the CGW," 17; *Railroad Gazette,* September 20, 1889.

25. *Oelwein Register,* March 24, 1892; *Railroad Gazette,* May 9, 1890.

26. *Oelwein Register,* May 8, 1890.

27. Quoted from Ibid; *Democrat,* April 11, 1890.

28. *Oelwein Register,* May 8, 1890.

29. Ibid., July 24, 1890; *Democrat,* May 2 and September 19, 1890.

30. *Oelwein Register,* April 6, 1888; *Railroad Gazette,* April 13, 1888.

31. *Oelwein Register,* March 2, 1888.

32. *Report on the Population of the United States* (1890). 117; quoted in the *Byron Express,* March 27, 1891; *Stockton (Illinois) Herald,* December 7, 1888.

33. *St. Joseph Gazette,* August 22, 1889; quoted in the *Oelwein Register,* July 19, 1889.

34. Larry P. McAdam, "Early Days at St. Paul," *The*

Maize (February 1915), 20. *Kansas City Times,* October 3, 1891; *Stockton Herald,* January 9, 1890.

35. *Wabash, St. Louis & Pacific Railway Co. v. Illinois,* 188 U.S. 557. See Solon Justus Buck, *The Granger Movement* (Cambridge, Mass., 1913); D. Sven Nordin, *Rich Harvest: A History of the Grange, 1867–1900(Jackson, Miss., 1974); and Ari and Olive Hoogenboom, A History of the ICC: From Panacea to Palliative* (New York, 1976).

36. Albro Martin, *Enterprise Denied: Origins of the Decline of American Railroads, 1897–1917* (New York, 1971), 111–14.

37. *Stockton Herald,* December 28, 1888; *Northwestern Railroader,* May 2, 1890; A. B. Stickney, *The Railway Problem* (St. Paul, 1891). One of the progressive era's most renowned railroad reformers, Wisconsin Governor Robert M. La Follette, Sr., considered Stickney's 249-page work to be one of the three best books on regulation. See Stanley P. Caine, *The Myth of a Progressive Reform: Railroad Regulation in Wisconsin, 1903–1910* (Madison, 1970), 72.

38. George Brown Tindall, ed., *A Populist Reader* (New York, 1966), 93.

39. Stickney, *The Railway Problem,* 6, 26, 32.

40. Ibid., 180, 195.

41. See Robert H. Wiebe, *The Search for Order, 1877–1920* (New York, 1967).

42. *Sixth Annual Report of the Chicago, St. Paul and Kansas City Railway Co. for the Year Ending June 30, 1892,* 5, 9, 20; Paul E. Miller, "A Financial History of the Chicago Great Western Railroad Company," unpublished M.A. thesis, Northwestern University, 1924, 13; *First Annual Report of the Chicago Great Western Railway Company for the Year Ending June 30, 1893,* 3.

43. *Oelwein Register,* October 12, 1888; I. L. Sharfman, *The American Railroad Problem* (New York, 1921), 37; *Commercial and Financial Chronicle,* September 21, 1889; *Second Annual Report of the Chicago, St. Paul and Kansas City Railway Co. for the Year Ending June 30, 1888,* 7; *Third Annual Report of the Chicago, St. Paul and Kansas City Railway Co. for the Year Ending June 30, 1889,* 14.

44. *Third Annual Report of the Chicago, St. Paul and Kansas City Railway Co. for the Year Ending June 30, 1889,* 5–7, 24–28; *Commercial and Financial Chronicle,* September 13, 1890; October 3, 1891.

45. Miller, "A Financial History of the Chicago Great Western Railroad Company," 10.

46. *Dubuque Daily Times,* July 10, 1885; December 17, 1886; Dorothy R. Adler, *British Investment in American Railways, 1834–1898* (Charlottesville, Va., 1970), 149, 186–88.

47. A. B. Stickney, *A Western Trunk Line Railway Without a Mortgage: A Short History of the Finances of the Chicago Great Western Railway Company* (New York, 1900), 6–7.

48. In an analysis of the CGW's debenture stock, the *Railway Age Gazette,* August 18, 1916, pointed out that "this theory of railroad financing has been successful in England, but did not prove to be a success in the United States." This trade publication argued that two factors worked against it: "The earning power of the CGW did not increase as time went on as rapidly as it had been estimated and investors abroad did not come forward as ready to buy American railroad securities unsecured by a mortgage as had been expected."

49. Stickney, *A Western Trunk Line Railway Without a Mortgage,* 6.

50. Ibid., 8.

51. The reason for the selection of the Chicago Great Western name is a mystery. Perhaps the Stickney management wished to capitalize on both America's greatest railroad center—Chicago—and a premier English carrier—The Great Western. Or perhaps the Chicago-area terminal company, the Chicago & Great Western Railroad, with which the M&NW of Illinois (CStP&KC) connected, served as the inspiration. One problem the Chicago Great Western banner caused throughout its lifetime (1892–1968) was that people repeatedly called it the Chicago *and* Great Western. Indeed, one employee noted in 1912 that the company lost revenue "by error of shippers and billers showing 'C.&N.W.' or 'C.&G.W.' instead of C.G.W."

52. *Commercial and Financial Chronicle,* January 23 and March 26, 1892.

53. *Railroad Gazette,* March 25 and July 22, 1892; "Corporate History of the CGW," 22; *First Annual Report of the Chicago Great Western Railway Company for the Year Ending June 30, 1893,* 10; Stickney, *A Western Trunk Line Railway Without a Mortgage,* 4–5.

54. *Commercial and Financial Chronicle,* March 10 and April 21, 1894.

CHAPTER THREE

1. For a review of the impact of the depression of the 1890s, see Charles Hoffman, *Depression of the Nineties: An Economic History* (Westport, Conn., 1970), especially chap. 2; Douglas W. Steeples, "Five Troubled Years: A History of the Depression of 1893–1897," unpublished Ph.D. dissertation, University of North Carolina, 1961; and Gerald T. White, *The United States and the Problem of Recovery after 1893* (University, Alabama, 1982), 1–7, 21–32, 71–81.

2. *Second Annual Report of the Chicago Great Western Railway Company for the Year Ending June 30, 1894*, 5, 12; *Third Annual Report of the Chicago Great Western Railway Company for the Year Ending June 30, 1895*, 4–5; *Fourth Annual Report of the Chicago Great Western Railway Company for the Year Ending June 30, 1896*; 5; *Fifth Annual Report of the Chicago Great Western Railway Company for the Year Ending June 30, 1897*, 6.

3. Quoted in the *Mantorville* (Minnesota) *Express*, February 28 and March 20, 1896; *Railroad Gazette*, February 14, 1896.

4. *Oelwein* (Iowa) *Register*, June 21, 1915; *Oelwein Daily Register*, June 6, 1923.

5. Ibid., July 21, 1948; *Oelwein Register*, March 23, 1888.

6. James Thomas Craig, "Great Western Builds Oelwein Shops," *Annals of Iowa*, Third Series, 26 (October 1944):90; *Third Annual Report of the Chicago Great Western Railway Company for the Year Ending June 30, 1895*, 9; *Oelwein Register*, January 11, May 4, June 7, 1894; *St. Paul Pioneer-Press*, June 3, 1894; *St. Paul Dispatch*, June 30, 1894.

7. James Thomas Craig, "Oelwein Secures the Machine Shops of the Chicago Great Western Railway Company, 1894," *Annals of Iowa*, Third Series, 24(January 1943):222; *Oelwein Register*, June 7, 1894.

8. Craig, "Oelwein Secures the Machine Shops of the Chicago Great Western Railway Company, 1894," 214.

9. Ibid., 216–21.

10. *Oelwein Register*, April 26, 1894; *St. Paul Dispatch*, May 28, 1894; Craig, "Oelwein Secures the Machine Shops of the Chicago Great Western Railway Company, 1894," 227–28; Craig, "Great Western Builds Oelwein Shops," 95.

11. *Oelwein Register*, June 20 and July 4, 1895; Craig, "Great Western Builds Oelwein Shops," 97–98.

12. Craig, "Great Western Builds Oelwein Shops," 101–6.

13. Ibid, 108–9, 110–12, 115–17; *Oelwein Register*, May 24, 1899; *Twelfth Census of the United States Taken in the Year 1900, Population, Part I* (Washington, D.C., 1901), 150; *Railway Age*, October 6, 1899. The Great Western did not permanently close the South St. Paul shops. The facility continued to provide minor repair services. Oelwein's population fell far below predictions: 6,028 in 1910 and 7,455 in 1920.

14. *Oelwein Register*, February 23, 1898; March 22, 1899; *Railroad Gazette*, June 21, 1901; *American Engineering and Railroad Journal*, July 1900; *Railway and Engineering Review*, April 16, 1898. In addition to construction of the shops complex, the Chicago Great Western replaced its earlier engine facility with a magnificent roundhouse that opened in fall of 1904. The *Oelwein Register* of September 5, 1906 noted: "It may not be generally known, but [the roundhouse] is one of the largest circular roundhouses in the world and the largest in the West. It is about a fifth of a mile in the semicircuit, and has forty stalls for locomotives, besides a machine shop, plant for steam heating, and the foreman's office."

15. *Sixth Annual Report of the Chicago Great Western Railway Company for the Year Ending June 30, 1898*, 5–7; *Seventh Annual Report of the Chicago Great Western Railway Company for the Year Ending June 30, 1899*, 5–6; *Railroad Gazette*, October 2, 1896; *Oelwein Register*, April 4, 1899.

16. *Eleventh Annual Report of the Chicago Great Western Railway Company for the Fiscal Year Ending June 30, 1903*, 17; Albro Martin, *Enterprise Denied: Origins of the Decline of American Railroads, 1897–1917* (New York, 1971), 61.

17. *Oelwein Register*, September 1, 1897; June 8, July 20, October 5, 1898; *Sheridan* (Missouri) *Advance*, July 15, 1898; *Parnell* (Missouri) *Sentinel*, December 8, 1898; *Review* (Mankato, Minnesota), April 30, 1901; Ed Gardner, *Chicago Great Western Scrapbook* (Mountain Top, Pa., n.d.), 1, 3, 5. The *Oelwein Register* of April 13, 1898, took considerable pride in reporting the swiftness of one regularly scheduled freight: "Train #60 between here [Oelwein] and Dubuque makes the fastest time of any freight train on the entire system, its time being two hours and forty minutes, 71 miles, with at least two stops, and hauling a load of from 660 to 675 tons." While the 26.69 mph average by #60 may seem slow, it was an impressive speed by the standards of the 1890s.

18. *Oelwein Register*, May 23 and July 11, 1895; *Railway Age*, February 9, 1900.

19. *Oelwein Register*, September 10, 1896; February 9, 1897; *Railroad Gazette*, February 19, 1897; *First Annual Report of Chicago Great Western Railroad Company for the Ten Months Ending June 30, 1910*, 16; A. B. Stickney, *Omaha as a Market-Town* (St. Paul, 1903), 15–18; "History of the Chicago Great Western Railway Company," 11–12. Stickney's grain development activities in Omaha worked well. Reported the Fort Dodge *Messenger* of April 18, 1905: "We [the railroad] pointed out the possibilities of the city as a grain market, the initial step toward which was the organization of a grain exchange. There was none there. It was established forthwith. The city was not then known as a grain market. In one year from last February [1904] it has taken rank as the fourth grain market in the country following in order Chicago, Minneapolis and St. Louis." See also Lawrence H. Larsen and Barbara J. Cottrell, *The Gate City: A History of Omaha* (Boulder, Colo., 1982), 137–40.

20. Sig Greve, "Buccaneering Days," *Railroad Magazine,* 34(November 1943):78–79. See also *Railroad Gazette,* October 20, 1905.

21. *Railroad Gazette,* August 15, 1902.

22. *Great Western Magazine,* 5(March 1926):5; *Sheridan Advance,* October 14, 1897; *Oelwein Register,* September 26, 1900. Stickney himself commented on the stock-purchase program in 1900: "I am obliged to confess that it has not made much of a success. Forty or fifty employees made small investments, but soon got tired of saving and as the stock advanced in price many sold out. It is certainly an uphill job to induce working men to try to save."

23. *Third Annual Report of the Chicago Great Western Railway Company for the Year Ending June 30, 1895,* 4; Stanley Buder, *Pullman: An Experiment in Industrial Order and Community Planning, 1880–1930* (New York, 1967), 157–62, 179–87; *Stockton Herald,* July 19, 1894; James Thomas Craig, "The 'Big Strike' at Oelwein Shops," *Annals of Iowa,* 3rd series, 28 (October 1946): 116–38.

24. *Railroad Gazette,* August 6, 1897; *Oelwein Register,* May 11, 1898.

25. Richard C. Overton, "Ralph Budd: Railroad Entrepreneur," *Palimpsest,* 36(November 1955):434–35; Walter P. Chrysler, *Life of an American Workman* (New York, 1950), 98–99; *Oelwein Daily Register,* August 19, 1940. Paralleling most sister carriers, the Great Western hired female employees, but almost exclusively as agents for its smallest stations. In 1903, the company had such workers at Douglas, Minnesota; South Freeport, Illinois; Kidder, Iowa; Laird, Minnesota; Lowther, Iowa; and Talmage, Iowa. This represented a mere 2.3 percent of the total agent force. Earlier, however, the CGW did hire Dora Newall, a former agent, as a dispatcher in Des Moines.

26. *Messenger,* February 21, 1905.

27. *Twelfth Annual Report of the Chicago Great Western Railway Company for the Fiscal Year Ending June 30, 1904,* 5; *Thirteenth Annual Report of the Chicago Great Western Railway Company for the Fiscal Year Ending June 30, 1905,* 5,7; *Fourteenth Annual Report of the Chicago Great Western Railway Company for the Fiscal Year Ending June 30, 1906,* 5.

28. Edward Sherwood Meade, "The Chicago Great Western," *Railway World,* 49(August 25, 1905):675–76; *Review,* December 2, 1903; January 6, 1903; November 29, 1904; *Messenger,* October 26 and October 27, 1904; *Parnell Sentinel,* April 4, 1901; *Oelwein Register,* November 6, 1901; May 14 and September 10, 1901.

29. *Railroad Gazette,* September 22, 1905; September 28, 1906; December 6, 1907; *Railway Era,* March 1899.

30. *Messenger,* September 23, 1907; *Railway World,* January 10 and January 17, 1908; "Office of President, Chicago Great Western Railway Co., Private and Confidential, to the Finance Committee of the Chicago Great Western Railway Co., St. Paul, Minn., June 6, 1907"; Directors' Meeting, February 2 and December 4, 1907.

CHAPTER FOUR

1. *Statistical Abstract of the United States, 1916* (Washington, D.C., 1917), 293.

2. *Seventh Annual Report of the Chicago Great Western Railway for the Year Ending June 30, 1889,* 6; *Report on Population of the United States at the Eleventh Census: 1890* (Washington, D.C., 1895), 104; Frederick A. Cleveland and Fred Wilbur Powell, *Railroad Promotion and Capitalization in the United States* (New York, 1909), 203–4.

3. *Railroad Promotion and Capitalization in the United States,* 203–4; *Railroad Gazette,* March 29, April 5, July 19, October 4, 1895; "History of the Chicago Great Western Railway Company," unpublished ms., 3; "Corporate History of the CGW"; "Chicago Great Western Railway Suburban Trains" timetable, July 1, 1897.

4. *Railroad Gazette,* April 1 and April 15, 1904; *Fort Dodge* (Iowa) *Messenger,* March 19, 1904; Chicago Great Western Railway Company, Minute Book, Chicago & North Western Transportation Company, Chicago, February 13, 1903.

5. "Corporate History of the CGW," 17; *Mantorville Express,* March 27, April 10, December 1, 1896.

6. *Mantorville Express,* May 22, August 7, October 30, November 27, 1896; *St. Paul Dispatch,* December 12, 1896.

7. "Corporate History of the CGW," 20; *Mantorville Express,* August 7, 1896.

8. *Mantorville Express,* December 4, 1896.

9. "Corporate History of the Wisconsin, Minnesota and Pacific Railroad Company as of the Date of Valuation, June 30, 1916," (Chicago, 1920), 14(hereafter cited as "Corporate History of the WM&P").

10. *Review* (Mankato), November 22, 1881; September 2 and September 9, 1884; "Corporate History of the WM&P," 6, 8.

11. *Review,* May 9, August 8, August 29, September 5, 1882.

12. Ibid., May 15, 1883; August 10 and September 30, 1884; June 22, 1886; *Statistics of the Population of the United States at the Tenth Census* (Washington, D.C., 1883), 224.

13. "Corporate History of the WM&P," 6; *Review,* March 16, 1886; May 3, 1887; *Poor's Manual of Rail-*

roads (New York, 1890), 582; Frank P. Donovan, Jr., *Mileposts on the Prairie: The Story of the Minneapolis & St. Louis Railway* (New York, 1950), 65–66.

14. *Review,* December 15, 1891; November 21, 1893; *Railroad Gazette,* July 21, 1893.

15. "Corporate History of the WM&P," 6; *Review,* April 10, 1894; October 1, 1895; May 12, 1896.

16. *Review,* May 16, May 23, June 6, 1899; May 14, 1901; *Railroad Gazette,* May 26, 1899.

17. "Corporate History of the WM&P," 14; *Railway Age Gazette,* September 13, 1912.

18. *An Exhibit of the Duluth, Red Wing & Southern Railroad; the Most Important Projected Line in the Northwest* (Red Wing, Minn., 1887), 1, 26. The Duluth, Red Wing & Southern technically had a predecessor, the Red Wing & Iowa Railway Company. Organized in 1881, this "paper" road never progressed off the drawing board. Its backers soon turned to the DRW&S project.

19. Ibid., 24; *Railroad Gazette,* December 3, 1886.

20. *Railroad Gazette,* September 30 and October 21, 1887; *Northwestern Railroader,* December 7, 1888.

21. *Railroad Gazette,* October 19, December 7, December 14, 1888; February 1, 1889; *Poor's Manual of Railroads* (New York, 1889), 834.

22. W. B. Harrison, "A Train Order of Yesteryear: Railroading in 1889 on the Old Duluth, Red Wing & Southern R. R.," *Great Western Magazine,* 4(June 1925):9; *Travelers' Official Guide of the Railway and Steam Navigation Lines in the United States and Canada* (New York, 1890), 380.

23. Quoted in the *Zumbrota* (Minnesota) *News,* February 27, 1891.

24. Ibid., July 3, July 24, September 11, 1891.

25. *Railroad Gazette,* August 28, 1891.

26. *Zumbrota News,* December 4, 1891; "Corporate History of the WM&P,"9; "Deed, Duluth, Red Wing & Southern Railroad Company to the Wisconsin, Minnesota & Pacific Railroad Company, July 5, 1901," Chicago & North Western Transportation Company, Chicago; *Railroad Gazette,* July 5, 1901.

27. R. E. Miles, *A History of Early Railroading in Winona County* (Winona, Minn., 1958), 22; "Corporate History of the WM&P," 12.

28. Miles, *A History of Early Railroading in Winona County,* 22; "Corporate History of the WM&P," 11.

29. Miles, *A History of Early Railroading in Winona County,* 22.

30. Ibid.

31. *Northwestern Railroader,* May 20, 1887; *Railroad Gazette,* July 22, September 2, September 16, 1887; November 30, 1888; *Fort Dodge Messenger,* November 29 and December 6, 1888.

32. *Chicago Times,* May 31, 1888; *Rochester* (Minnesota) *Post,* February 7, 1890; *Fort Dodge Messenger,* April 26, 1888; *Railway World,* August 3, 1889.

33. *Fort Dodge Messenger,* January 10, 1889; November 27, 1890.

34. *Poor's Manual of Railroads* (New York, 1889), 880; *Fort Dodge Messenger,* September 12, 1889; *Railroad Gazette,* October 4 and October 25, 1889; January 10, 1890.

35. *Railroad Gazette,* July 27 and November 16, 1888; Michael E. Crowe, "Winona & South-Western Ry.," *Chicago Great Western Historical & Technical Society Newsletter,* 21(1979):1–4.

36. *Rochester Post,* February 7, February 15, June 13, 1890.

37. *Fort Dodge Messenger,* August 14, August 28, December 4, December 11, 1890; *Railroad Gazette,* January 2, 1891; *Rochester Post,* December 26, 1890.

38. *Railroad Gazette,* October 17, 1890; May 15 and June 5, 1891; *Fort Dodge Messenger,* August 21, 1890; June 11, 1891; "Corporate History of the WM&P," 13.

39. *Fort Dodge Messenger,* June 11, 1891; *Railroad Gazette,* August 14, 1891; "Corporate History of the WM&P," 13; Ben Hur Wilson, "Abandoned Railroads of Iowa," *Iowa Journal of History and Politics,* 26 (January 1928):63–64.

40. *Fort Dodge Messenger,* January 22 and June 11, 1891; *Railroad Gazette,* April 1, 1892; June 9, 1883. The Winona & Southwestern also contemplated a line deep into southern Iowa. As the *Oelwein Register* of May 18, 1893, revealed, "The survey . . . has been completed from Osage to Chariton, and the route found to be a very feasible one." Perhaps the road had its eyes set on a St. Joseph or Kansas City destination; Chariton, in fact, offered a direct connection to both Missouri cities via the Chicago, Burlington & Quincy.

41. *Rochester Post,* September 21, 1894; *Record and Union* (Rochester), September 21, 1894; *Railroad Gazette,* November 24, 1893; March 23 and September 7, 1894.

42. *Railroad Gazette,* April 7, 1899; *Post and Record,* September 1, 1899; *Olmsted County Democrat* (Rochester), October 19, 1900.

43. *Post and Record,* August 30 and September 13, 1901; *Oelwein Register,* July 17 and October 2, 1901; June 11, 1902.

44. *Minneapolis Tribune,* October 18, 1890.

45. "Corporate History of the Mason City and Fort Dodge Railroad Company, as of the Date of Valuation, June 30, 1916" (Chicago, 1920), 2–3(hereafter cited as "Corporate History of the MC&FD"); *Mason City* (Iowa) *Express,* November 16, 1871; *Fort Dodge Messenger,* December 23, 1881; November 4, 1886.

46. *Mason City Express,* June 22 and July 27, 1881.

47. *Fort Dodge Messenger,* April 26, 1883; Albro Martin, *James J. Hill and the Opening of the Northwest* (New York, 1976), 113.

48. *Fort Dodge Messenger,* February 4, March 25, April 8, 1886; *Belmond* (Iowa) *Herald,* May [?], 1886.

49. Letter from Hamilton Browne to James J. Hill, April 16, 1886, James J. Hill Papers, James Jerome Hill Reference Library, St. Paul, Minnesota (hereafter cited as Hill Papers); *Railroad Gazette,* May 21, 1886.

50. *Fort Dodge Messenger,* June 24, July 1, September 9, October 10, October 28, 1886, letter form Hamilton Browne to James J. Hill, August 8, 1886, Hill Papers; *Railroad Gazette,* November 12, 1886; February 11, 1887.

51. Martin, *James J. Hill and the Opening of the Northwest,* 329; *Fort Dodge Messenger,* November 4 and November 18, 1886; *Des Moines Leader,* April 30, 1897; "Memorandum in re Sale of Iowa Properties to Mason City & Fort Dodge R.R. Syndicate (A. B. Stickney, President)," Hill Papers.

52. *Fort Dodge Messenger,* February 25 and August 5, 1886; March 10 and March 17, 1887.

53. Ibid., April 4, 1889; letter from Hamilton Browne to James J. Hill, May 27, 1886, Hill Papers.

54. Martin, *James J. Hill and the Opening of the Northwest,* 409; *Railroad Gazette,* January 18, 1889; *Oelwein Register,* March 20, 1901.

55. *Evening Messenger* (Fort Dodge), May 1 and 10, 1899; April 19, 1900.

56. Ernest R. Sandeen, *St. Paul's Historic Summit Avenue* (St. Paul, 1978), 25, 42–46; Martin, *James J. Hill and the Opening of the Northwest,* 242, 309, 487; H. Roger Grant, "A. B. Stickney and James J. Hill: The Railroad Relationship," *Railroad History,* 146(Spring 1982):9–22. James J. Hill had little desire to help the CM&StP. For one thing, this ambitious rival had already invaded the Red River Valley of the North, which Hill considered his exclusive domain.

57. *Oelwein Register,* June 15, 1893.

58. *Thirteenth Census of the United States Taken in the Year 1910* (Washington, D.C., 1913), Vol. 2, 604; Vol. 3, 28; *Railroad Gazette,* June 17, 1898; August 11, 1899; *Oelwein Register,* April 6 and May 18, 1897; June 8, July 27, September 7, October 4, 1898; *Sheridan Advance,* August 5, 1898; *Fort Dodge Messenger,* August 6, 1895; *Evening Messenger,* May 11, 1897; John F. Stover, *History of the Illinois Central Railroad* (New York, 1975), 142–43. Apparently A. B. Stickney showed some interest in a bizarre "self-help" proposal made by a group of Iowa Populists headed by Des Moines reformer T. R. Green. In 1895 and 1896 these embattled farmers sought relief from

high and discriminatory transportation rates through the organization of the American Railway Company (ARyCo), a consumer-oriented and operated enterprise. Initially the road would link Omaha with Chicago, paralleling closely the Chicago, Rock Island & Pacific. But when the ARyCo seemed unable to manage such a plan, Green looked toward the Maple Leaf for help. "I believe we can build from Council Bluffs to connection with C&GW [sic] Ry. this Fall [1896]." Continued problems with financing and a return of prosperity prevented the ARyCo from ever converting into reality its dreams of a 180-mile Council Bluffs to Hampton, Iowa, line. See *Progressive Thought and Dawn of Equity* (Olathe, Kansas), November 1896, and H. Roger Grant, *Self-Help in the 1890s Depression* (Ames, 1983), 82–83.

59. "Corporate History of the MC&FD," 6; Marshall B. Craig, "The Chicago Great Western's Oldest Miles," unpublished manuscript, 6; *Oelwein Register,* May 1, June 19, October 23, 1901. The actual lengths of the six competing roads between Chicago and Omaha are as follows: Chicago & North Western, 488 miles; Chicago, Milwaukee & St. Paul, 488; Chicago, Rock Island & Pacific, 493; Chicago, Burlington & Quincy, 496; Chicago Great Western, 508; and Illinois Central, 515. See Michael Conant, *Railroad Mergers and Abandonments* (Berkeley, 1964), 17.

60. *Evening Messenger,* May 16, 1901; Donovan L. Hofsommer, "A Chronology of Iowa Railroads," *Railroad History,* 132(Spring 1975):78, 81.

61. *Herald* (Carroll, Iowa), May 7, 1902; *Daily Nonpareil* (Council Bluffs), April 8 and June 25, 1902; *Oelwein Register,* May 1, 1901.

62. *Ninth Annual Report of the Chicago Great Western Railway Company for the Fiscal Year Ending June 30, 1901,* 19; "Corporate History of the MC&FD," 6–7; Chicago Great Western Railway Company, Minute Book, April 29, 1901; April 14, 1902; *Messenger,* October 19, 1903.

63. *Herald,* February 12, 1902; *Daily Nonpareil,* February 5, 1902.

64. *Daily Nonpareil,* February 5, 1902.

65. Ibid., June 22, 1901.

66. *Herald,* October 22 and November 19, 1902; *Oelwein Register,* May 13, 1903.

67. *Evening Messenger,* December 13, 1902; *Oelwein Register,* March 18 and October 28, 1903; "Twenty-Fifth Anniversary of Building of Great Western Viaduct at Fort Dodge," *Great Western Magazine,* 7(April 1928):8, 40.

68. *Herald,* May 6 and July 22, 1903; *Daily Messenger,* August 31, 1903; *Messenger,* April 18, 1905; *Daily Nonpareil,* November 7, 1903; *Oelwein Register,* July 29, 1903.

69. *Herald*, June 17, 1903; *Daily Nonpareil*, November 7, 1903; *Sheridan Advance*, December 24, 1903.

70. *Herald*, September 16, 1903; *Messenger*, March 31, 1903; April 18, 1905; *Oelwein Register*, September 23, 1903.

71. "Articles of Incorporation of Iowa Townsite Company," State of Minnesota, Office of the Secretary of State, 1901, 218–19. See also H. Roger Grant, "Iowa's New Communities: Townsite Promotion Along the Chicago Great Western Railway's Omaha Extension," *Upper Midwest History* 2(1983): 53–63.

72. *Messenger*, September 2, 1904.

73. *Herald*, February 12, September 3, October 8, 1902; *Evening Messenger*, March 4, 1902; January 21, 1903; "Plat of Town of Lanesboro, Carroll County, Iowa," October 4, 1902, Office of the Carroll County Recorder; *Oelwein Register*, March 18, 1903.

74. *Herald*, July 22, 1903; *Ravenwood* (Missouri) *Gazette*, August 28, 1903; *Messenger*, September 9 and October 21, 1903; *Mixed Train*, 30(May 1981):1. The Iowa Townsite Company (ITC) also became involved in Moorland. This Webster County hamlet owed its creation to the coming of the Des Moines & Fort Dodge Railroad in 1882, but in August 1902, the ITC platted the "Iowa Town Site Company's Addition" on the north end of the existing community and adjacent to the soon-to-be completed Omaha Extension. Incorporated officially in 1902, Moorland's population reached 137 by the 1910 census.

75. *Railroad Gazette*, September 22, 1905.

76. *Oelwein Register*, March 31, 1892; February 2, 1893; June 13, 1895; May 22, April 24, December 4, 1901; *Evening Messenger*, April 3, 1901; *Herald*, October 22, 1902; *Tenth Annual Report of the Chicago Great Western Railway Company for the Fiscal Year Ending June 20, 1902*, 1.

77. *Herald*, July 30, 1902; *Railroad Gazette*, February 20, 1903; *Messenger*, June 7, 1904; July 21, 1906.

78. *Messenger*, July 17, 1902; March 25, 1904; Wilson, "Abandoned Railroads of Iowa," 57–59.

79. *Oelwein Register*, March 29, 1905; *Herald*, March 21, 1906; *Railroad Gazette*, April 28, 1905.

80. *Evening Messenger*, August 21, 1901; *Messenger*, October 7, 1903; *Oelwein Register*, December 18, 1901; *Railroad Gazette*, October 23, 1903.

81. *Messenger*, April 1, 1903; *Oelwein Register*, April 8, 1903; William Edward Hayes, *Iron Road to Empire* (New York, 1953), 181.

82. *Oelwein Register*, May 27, 1903; *Railroad Gazette*, June 5, 1903. See also *Messenger*, November 25, 1905.

83. *Messenger*, July 7, 1905; *Oelwein Register*, July 11, 1906.

84. Robert G. Athearn, *Rebel of the Rockies: A History of the Denver and Rio Grande Western Railroad* (New Haven, Conn., 1962), 201–5; Steven F. Mehls, "Westward from Denver: The Obsession of David Moffat," *Railroad History*, 146(Spring 1982):29–40.

85. *Thirteenth Census of the United States*, 2(Washington, D.C., 1913):590; *Oelwein Register*, August 23, 1916.

86. *Oelwein Register*, April 18, 1900; April 17, 1901; August 2, 1905; Frank P. Donovan, Jr., "The Manchester & Oneida Railway," *Palimpsest*, 38(September 1957): 337–46; Record of the Board of Directors, March 28, 1901, Manchester & Oneida Railway Company Papers, Iowa State Historical Department, Division of the State Historical Society, Iowa City.

87. *Railroad Gazette*, August 18, 1905; *Herald*, August 2, 1905; *Stockton* (Illinois) *Herald*, March 27 and October 23, 1907; June 3, 1908; *Byron* (Illinois) *Express*, March 11, 1898. The closeness of the CGW with the Waterloo & Cedar Falls Rapid Transit Company (W&CFRTCo) is seen in the latter's lease of the Waverly-Sumner branch on August 14, 1902. In order for the W&CFRTCo to operate directly from Waterloo to Sumner, it constructed an electric line north from Denver to Denver Junction and a connection with the CGW. Then the W&CFRTCo obtained trackage rights from there over the Maple Leaf into Waverly. The interurban abandoned this arrangement on August 1, 1909, when it decided to quit the Waverly-Sumner line and build its own electric access into Waverly. See Norman Carlson, ed., *Iowa Trolleys* (Chicago, 1975), 197; George W. Hilton and John F. Due, *The Electric Interurban Railways* (Stanford, 1960), 360.

CHAPTER FIVE

1. A. B. Stickney, *In the Matter of the Minnesota Railroad and Warehouse Commissioner's Proposed Schedule of the Classified Rates, Argument on Behalf of the Chicago Great Western Railway Company* (St. Paul, March 1906), 46; *Railway World*, January 17, 1908.

2. *Wall Street Journal*, March 9, 1909; *Railway World*, January 17, 1908.

3. *Oelwein* (Iowa) *Register*, April 29 and July 8, 1908; David Byrn-Jones, *Frank B. Kellogg: A Biography* (New York, 1937), 82–83.

4. *Railroad Gazette*, December 25, 1908; *Oelwein Register*, August 25, 1909; *Wall Street Journal*, August 23, 1909.

5. *Railway World*, January 17, 1908; "Report on the Chicago Great Western Ry., March-1909," Samuel M. Felton Papers, Baker Library, Harvard University Graduate School of Business Administration, hereafter cited as

Felton Papers; *Railway Maintenance of Way Employes Journal* (March 1923), 5–6.

6. *Oelwein Register,* December 23, 1908; June 9 and September 8, 1909; *Minneapolis Tribune,* December 24, 1908; unidentified newspaper clipping, Chicago & North Western Transportation Company Papers, Chicago (hereafter cited as C&NWTCo Papers).

7. *Oelwein Register,* July 28, 1909; *Review* (Mankato, Minnesota), June 15, 1909; unidentified clipping, C&NWTCo Papers; *Plan and Agreement for the Reorganization of the Chicago Great Western Railway Company* (New York, June 1, 1909); S. M. Felton, "The Development of the Chicago Great Western Railroad," *Great Western Magazine* 3(February 1924):5.

8. Felton, "The Development of the Chicago Great Western Railroad," 5; "The Chicago Great Western RR; Seven Years of Progress," Felton Papers.

9. *Oelwein Register,* August 18, 1909; *Railway Age,* March 15, 1930.

10. *Evening Bulletin* (Philadelphia), March 12, 1930.

11. Norman W. Gregg, "Samuel Morse Felton: A Brief History of the Distinguished President of the Great Western," *Great Western Magazine* 1(February 1922):5–6.

12. Letter from E. H. Harriman to S. M. Felton, December 14, 1907, Felton Papers.

13. "Our President," *The Maize* (February 1912), 4.

14. Walter P. Chrysler, *Life of an American Workman* (New York, 1937), 113–15.

15. *Ravenwood* (Missouri) *Gazette,* September 24, 1909; *Oelwein Register,* July 20, 1910; January 18 and October 18, 1911; *Railway Age Gazette,* May 12, 1911; *First Annual Report of the Chicago Great Western Railroad Company for the Ten Months Ended June 30, 1910,* 10; *Second Annual Report of the Chicago Great Western Railroad Company for the Year Ended June 30, 1911,* 8–10; *Stockton* (Illinois) *Herald,* February 8 and March 15, 1911; *East Peru*(Iowa) *Mail,* September 8, 1916. See also H. Roger Grant, "Courting the Great Western Railway: An Episode of Town Rivalry," *Missouri Historical Review* 76(July 1982):405–20.

16. *Oelwein Register,* September 14, 1910; *First Annual Report of the Chicago Great Western Railroad Company for the Ten Months Ended June 30, 1910,* 4; *Second Annual Report of the Chicago Great Western Railroad Company for the Year Ended June 30, 1911,* 5–6; *Railway Age Gazette,* March 17, 1911; October 30, 1914; *Oelwein Daily Register,* July 21, 1948.

17. *Second Annual Report of the Chicago Great Western Railroad Company for the Year Ended June 30, 1911,* 11; *Parnell* (Missouri) *Sentinel,* October 6 and December 1, 1910; *Oelwein Register,* August 10 and August 24, 1910; June 14, 1911. The Great Western even experimented with a battery-electric passenger car. Built by Federal in 1912, this largely wooden vehicle drew its power from a 220-cell Edison battery. The contraption performed poorly, and the railroad returned it to the manufacturer the next year.

18. *Railway Age Gazette,* March 15, 1912; *Second Annual Report of the Chicago Great Western Railroad Company for the Year Ended June 30, 1911,* 11; *Fifth Annual Report of the Chicago Great Western Railroad Company, Being for the Year Ended June 30, 1914,* 19.

19. *Oelwein Register,* February 15, 1911; *Stockton Herald,* April 26, 1911; *The Tale of Our Limited* (Chicago, 1911); *Railway Age Gazette,* August 8, 1911.

20. *Oelwein Register,* June 29, 1910. Patrons of the Great Western also noted the disappearance of the inferior and dangerous acetylene gas lighting in passenger coaches. In early 1910 President Felton ordered that all cars have either a Pintsch gas or axle system of electric illumination. See *Oelwein Register,* March 9, 1910.

21. *Stockton Herald,* October 18, 1911; *Oelwein Register,* August 24, 1910; *Railway and Locomotive Engineering,* September 1916.

22. *Stockton Herald,* February 8, 1911.

23. *First Annual Report of the Chicago Great Western Railroad Company for the Ten Months Ended June 30, 1910,* 8; *Dearborn* (Missouri) *Democrat,* May 6 and May 15, 1910; *Parnell Sentinel,* May 12, 1910; "History of the Chicago Great Western Railway Company," unpublished manuscript, 6 (hereafter cited as "History of CGW Ry."); letter from J. O. Brinkerhoff to A. L. Mohler, July 29, 1910, Leavenworth Depot and Railroad Company Papers, Kansas State Historical Society, Topeka; letter from S. M. Felton to J. O. Brinkerhoff, August 20, 1910, ibid.

24. *First Annual Report of the Chicago Great Western Railroad Company for the Ten Months Ended June 30, 1910,* 9; *Fifth Annual Report of the Chicago Great Western Railroad Company, Being for the Year Ended June 30, 1914,* 17.

25. *Oelwein Register,* September 28, 1910; January 24, 1912; *Oelwein Daily Register,* September 13, 1923; *Omaha World-Herald,* March 18, 1956; Ben Hur Wilson, "Abandoned Railroads in Iowa," *Iowa Journal of History and Politics,* 26(January 1928):23–26, 46–47. Limited talk, too, occurred in 1916 of the Great Western acquiring or at least underwriting the woebegone Creston, Winterset & Des Moines Railroad. Built primarily by Macksburg, Iowa, residents and neighboring farmers in 1912–1913, the twenty-one mile pike connected this Madison County village with Creston, the Union County seat. Even though the company passed into the hands of a receiver in 1914, it hoped to push track either to Winterset and a connection with the Rock Island for Des Moines or to East Peru

and a tie-in with the CGW. Both would involve about fifteen miles of construction. Nothing happened, and the CW&DM was scrapped in 1918. See *East Peru Mail,* October 10, 1916, and Wilson, "Abandoned Railroads in Iowa," 36–38.

26. Russell L. Olson, *The Electric Railways of Minnesota* (Hopkins, Minnesota, 1976), 502–19.

27. Ibid.; *Review,* April 29, 1913; July 7, 1914; February 8 and June 6, 1916; *Fifth Annual Report of the Chicago Great Western Railroad Company Being for the Year Ended June 30, 1914,* 21. The Great Western and the Minneapolis, Northfield & Southern, successor to the Dan Patch Lines, reestablished a lease arrangement in 1925. In that year, MN&S passenger trains began to operate over CGW rails between Faribault and Mankato and between Northfield and Randolph, Minnesota. The Great Western suspended its own passenger operations on the Mankato branch and collected a paltry $1,192 in rental charges. This agreement lasted through the remainder of the twenties. See *Sixteenth Annual Report of the Chicago Great Western Railroad Company Year Ended December 31, 1925,* 9.

28. George W. Hilton and John F. Due, *The Electric Interurban Railways in America* (Stanford, 1960), 113, 143; *Dearborn Democrat,* November 10, 1911; *Faucett* (Missouri) *Democrat,* March 20, 1914.

29. A. Kneubuehl, "The Work of Employees Off the Line," *The Maize* 1(December 1912):5–6; S. A. Baker, "Short Reminiscence of Thirteen Years Solicitation for the 'Great Western,'" *Great Western Magazine* 2(November 1923):9, 34–37; *Railway Age Gazette,* January 12 and May 17, 1912.

30. Unidentified clipping, Felton Papers; *Railway Age Gazette,* October 6 and October 13, 1911; October 18, 1912.

31. *Oelwein Register,* August 17, 1910.

32. *Railway Age Gazette,* November 3, 1911; January 12, 1912; May 16, 1913; J. H. Ambruster, "The Age of Safety," *The Maize* (July 1912), 9.

33. *Railway Age Gazette,* May 15, 1914.

34. *Seventh Annual Report of the Chicago Great Western Railroad Company Being for the Year Ended June 30, 1916,* 17; *Railway Age,* April 21, 1921.

35. See Albro Martin, *Enterprise Denied: Origins of the Decline of American Railroads, 1897–1917* (New York, 1971), 173–318.

36. K. Austin Kerr, *American Railroad Politics, 1914–1920: Rates, Wages, and Efficiency* (Pittsburgh, 1968), 39–100; Richard Saunders, *The Railroad Mergers and the Coming of Conrail* (Westport, 1978), 35–38.

37. Unidentified clipping, Felton Papers; *Stockton Herald,* July 28, 1915; *Oelwein Register,* September 12,

1917; *The Maize* (August 1917). The greatest concentration of Italian workers was in Oelwein. By 1915 the colony numbered about 500. See Thomas M. Shaw, "Oelwein's Italian Neighborhoods: Italian-Americans of Oelwein, Iowa, 1901 to the Present" (unpublished M.A. thesis, University of Northern Iowa, 1978), 30, 34, 61.

38. *The Maize,* (October 1917), 14–15.

39. *Oelwein Register,* October 9, 1918; *Sheridan* (Missouri) *Advance,* October 31, 1918.

40. *Byron* (Illinois) *Express,* July 12, 1918.

41. Ibid., January 18, 1918; *Oelwein Register,* December 10, 1919.

42. Kerr, *American Railroad Politics,* 204–21; S. M. Felton, "Federal Versus Private Railway Control," *Military Engineer* (November 12, 1926), 18.

43. Saunders, *Railroad Mergers and the Coming of Conrail,* 40–41.

44. Ibid., 41–42; William Norris Leonard, *Railroad Consolidation Under the Transportation Act of 1920* (New York, 1946), 4–63; I. Leo Sharfman, *The American Railroad Problem* (New York, 1921), 384–85.

45. Sharfman, *The American Railroad Problem,* 384–85; Kerr, *American Railroad Politics,* 204–27.

46. Kerr, *American Railroad Politics,* 204–27; S. M. Felton to "STOCK AND BOND HOLDERS," July 1, 1926, personal possession; hereafter cited as "Felton letter"; *Dayton–Goose Creek Railway Co. vs. U.S.,* 263 U.S. 456 (1924).

47. Saunders, *Railroad Mergers and the Coming of Conrail,* 44–54; Walter M. W. Splawn, *Consolidation of Railroads* (New York, 1925), 95–97; Stuart Daggett, *Railroad Consolidation West of the Mississippi River* (Berkeley, 1933), 162–65, 207–29; *Consolidation of Railroads* 63 ICC 455 (1921); *In the Matter of Consolidation of Railway Properties in the U.S. into a Limited Number of Systems,* 159 ICC 522 (1929); *Oelwein Daily Register,* December 21, 1929.

48. "Felton letter;" *Fourteenth Annual Report of the Chicago Great Western Railroad Company Year Ended December 31, 1923,* 11–12.

49. *Fourteenth Annual Report of the Chicago Great Western Railroad Company Year Ended December 31, 1923,* 11–12; *Thirteenth Annual Report of the Chicago Great Western Railroad Company Year Ended December 31, 1922,* 4–5; *Seventeenth Annual Report of the Chicago Great Western Railroad Company Year Ended December 31, 1926,* 9.

50. *Railway Age,* September 30, 1922; see also John H. White, Jr., *The American Railroad Passenger Car* (Baltimore, 1978), 579–645.

51. *Railway Age,* September 23, 1922; August 18, 1923; "Our New Gasoline Motor Train," *Great Western*

Magazine 2(August 1923):19; *Railway Mechanical Engineer,* September 1923; October 1924; *Railway Review,* January 24 and May 2, 1925; *Oelwein Daily Register,* August 6, 1923; *Byron Express,* September 14, 1928; Edmund Keilty, *Doodlebug Country: The Rail Motorcar on the Class I Railroad of the United States* (Glendale, Calif., 1982), 47–49.

52. *Railway Mechanical Engineer,* May 1929; *The Blue Bird: Premier DeLuxe Motor Train,* 1929; "The Newest Thing on the Rails," *Great Western Magazine* 12(January 1929):7, 27.

53. "New Motive Power," *The Maize* (February 1914), 40; *Oelwein Register,* April 1, 1914; August 16, 1916.

54. *Great Western Magazine* 3(December 1924):14.

55. Frank P. Donovan, Jr., "The Chicago Great Western Railway," *The Palimpsest* 34(June 1953):277–79; Arthur D. Dubin, *More Classic Trains* (Milwaukee, 1974), 348–51; Chicago Great Western public timetable, November 14, 1926.

56. *Byron Express,* June 27, 1924; R. H. M. Falls, "Wanted a New Name for Nos. 1 and 2," *Great Western Magazine* 3(July 1924):9, 40; R. H. M. Falls, " 'The Legionnaire' Wins!" ibid. 3(November 1924):5–8, 14; " 'The Legionnaire' Is Formally Christened," ibid. 3(January 1925):5–6.

57. *Great Western Magazine* 5(October 1926):n.p.; ibid. 6(July 1925):n.p.

58. Donovan, "The Chicago Great Western Railway," 278–79; Patricia Ann Michaelis, "The Development of Passenger Service on Commercial Airlines, 1926–1930," unpublished Ph.D. dissertation, University of Kansas, 1980, 189–90; *Great Western Magazine* 8(February 1929):n.p.; W. G. Lerch, "Traveling Through Thin Air," ibid. 8(April 1929):13, 19; Transcontinental Air Transport, Inc. public timetable, October 15, 1929; *Railway Age,* April 13, 1929.

59. John B. Hoverson, "The Chicago Great Western Railway Company: 'Maple Leaf Route,' September 1, 1884–June 20, 1968," unpublished manuscript, in possession of the Kansas City Southern Railway Company, Kansas City, Missouri.

60. *Twelfth Annual Report of the Chicago Great Western Railroad Company Year Ended December 31, 1921,* 19, 26; *Twentieth Annual Report of the Chicago Great Western Railroad Company Year Ended December 31, 1929,* 16, 27; *Twenty-First Annual Report of the Chicago Great Western Railroad Company Year Ended December 31, 1930,* 27.

61. "Roster of CGW Steam Locomotives," personal possession; *Stockton Herald,* March 1, 1915; *Fifth Annual Report of the Chicago Great Western Railroad Company Being for the Year Ended June 30, 1914,* 6; *Raven-*wood Gazette, October 21, 1920.

62. "Roster of CGW Steam Locomotives," *Twentieth Annual Report of the Chicago Great Western Railroad Company Year Ended December 31, 1929,* 11.

63. *Fifteenth Annual Report of the Chicago Great Western Railroad Company Year Ended December 31, 1924,* 8; *Sixteenth Annual Report of the Chicago Great Western Railroad Company Year Ended December 31, 1925,* 7; *Nineteenth Annual Report of the Chicago Great Western Railroad Company Year Ended December 31, 1928,* 9; Henry L. Brown, *Steam Locomotives of the Chicago Great Western 2-8-0 Consolidation Type* (Minot, N.D., 1977), 9, 11.

64. *Safety News* 2(April 1956):4; ibid. 9(March–April 1963):4; *Sixteenth Annual Report of the Chicago Great Western Railroad Company Year Ended December 31, 1925,* 7; *Nineteenth Annual Report of the Chicago Great Western Railroad Company Year Ended December 31, 1928,* 7.

65. J. B. Forsythe, "Improving the Social Relations between the Officials of the C.G.W. R.R. Co. and the Farmers of Iowa," *The Maize* (June 1912): 11.

66. *Fourteenth Annual Report of the Chicago Great Western Railroad Company Year Ended December 31, 1923,* 27; *Sixteenth Annual Report of the Chicago Great Western Railroad Company Year Ended December 31, 1925,* 23; *Eighteenth Annual Report of the Chicago Great Western Railroad Company Year Ended December 31, 1927,* 27; *Twentieth Annual Report of the Chicago Great Western Railroad Company Year Ended December 31, 1929,* 30.

67. *Oelwein Register,* February 28, 1895; January 12, 1897; Roy V. Scott, "Railroads and Farmers: Educational Trains in Missouri, 1902–1914," *Agricultural History* 36(January 1962):3–15; Roy V. Scott, "American Railroads and Agricultural Extension Techniques," *Business History Review* 39(Spring 1965):74–98; Roy V. Scott, *The Reluctant Farmer: The Rise of Agricultural Extension to 1914* (Urbana, 1970), 176–83.

68. *Ravenwood Gazette,* May 8, 1903; *Oelwein Register,* December 13, 1905; "Great Western Farmers' Institutes Interest Many," *Great Western Magazine* 1(January 1923):10–11; T. A. Hoverstad, "The Development Department: The Farmers' Institute Car," ibid. 6(February 1927):9–10; W. K. Newland, "Any Winter Day in Great Western Coach 222: The Development Department in Action," ibid. 6(August 1927):5, 40; *Fifteenth Annual Report of the Chicago Great Western Railroad Company Year Ended December 31, 1924,* 9; *Byron Express,* December 7, 1928; *Oelwein Daily Register,* February 19, 1929.

69. "Great Westerners Fighting for Business All Along

the Line," *Great Western Magazine* 3(April 1924):8, 37; *Railway Review*, February 25 and March 11, 1922; *Oelwein Daily Register*, September 19, 1928; November 1929.

70. *Parnell Sentinel*, September 22, 1921; *Oelwein Daily Register*, September 18, 1922; December 7, 1929; January 12, 1935.

71. *Fourteenth Annual Report of the Chicago Great Western Railroad Company Year Ended December 31, 1923*, 22, 28; *Sixteenth Annual Report of the Chicago Great Western Railroad Company Year Ended December 31, 1925*, 29; *Eighteenth Annual Report of the Chicago Great Western Railroad Company Year Ended December 31, 1927*, 14, 23; *Twentieth Annual Report of the Chicago Great Western Railroad Company Year Ended December 31, 1929*, 16, 31; *Byron Express*, March 1, 1929; Charles Laynig, "Great Western Keeps Its Cars Moving," *Great Western Magazine* 6(March 1927): 7–8, 40; *Additional Report of the Committee on Interstate Commerce . . . Control of the Chicago Great Western. . . .* (Washington, 1940), 14.

72. *Fourteenth Annual Report of the Chicago Great Western Railroad Company Year Ended December 31, 1923*, 14; *Sixteenth Annual Report of the Chicago Great Western Railroad Company Year Ended December 31, 1923*, 12; *Twentieth Annual Report of the Chicago Great Western Railroad Company Year Ended December 31, 1929*, 17; *Additional Report of the Committee on Interstate Commerce United States Senate. . . .* (Washington, D.C., 1940), 2–3.

73. Robert H. Zieger, *Republicans and Labor, 1919–1929* (Lexington, 1969), 7–16.

74. Robert K. Murray, *The Harding Era: Warren G. Harding and His Administration* (Minneapolis, 1969), 244–45, 248–51.

75. *Oelwein Register*, July 11 and August 8, 1917; *Oelwein Daily Register*, February 21 and April 22, 1921; April 3, 1922; *Byron Express*, March 31, April 7, April 14, 1922.

76. *Oelwein Daily Register*, August 4, 1922; *Des Moines Register*, August 3 and August 4, 1922.

77. James N. Giglio, *H. M. Daugherty and the Politics of Expediency* (Kent, Ohio, 1978), 146–51; Zieger, *Republicans and Labor*, 133–42; *Thirteenth Annual Report of the Chicago Great Western Railroad Company Year Ended December 31, 1922*, 5; *Oelwein Daily Register*, September 15 and October 4, 1922; *Byron Express*, May 12 and July 14, 1922.

78. Interview with D. Keith Lawson, Rogers, Arkansas, October 18, 1980.

79. *The Maize* (June 1913), 18–19; *Great Western Magazine* 5(April 1926):25; *Conception Courier* (Conception Junction, Missouri), April 4, 1935; Eleanor Burke, "Great Western Veterans' Association Formed," *Great Western Magazine* 3(February 1924):11–12; "Western Division Wins Harriman Memorial Medal," ibid. 4(November 1925):9.

80. *Railway Age*, May 14, 1920; *Sixteenth Annual Report of the Chicago Great Western Railroad Company Year Ended December 31, 1925*, 5, 10.

81. "Important Changes in Great Western Executive Personnel," *Great Western Magazine* 4(November 1925):5.

82. Ibid., 5–6; *Oelwein Daily Register*, November 3, 1925.

83. *Oelwein Daily Register*, April 30 and November 15, 1929; *Railway Age*, October 12, 1929; *Who's Who in America* (Chicago, 1950), 1308.

CHAPTER SIX

1. *Who's Who in Railroading* (New York, 1946), 372; *Oelwein* (Iowa) *Daily Register*, November 2, 1931; *New York Times*, November 11, 1946; *Railway Age*, November 7, 1931.

2. Interview with D. Keith Lawson, Rogers, Arkansas, October 18, 1980 (hereafter cited as Lawson interview); *New York Times*, November 11, 1946.

3. Lawson interview; [*Senate*] *Investigation of Railroads, Holding Companies, and Affiliated Companies . . . Control of the Chicago Great Western* (Washington, D.C., 1940), 2 (hereafter cited as *Senate Investigation*).

4. *Senate Investigation*, 2–3.

5. Lawson interview; *Senate Investigation*, 7–16; *Traffic World*, June 5, 1937.

6. *Senate Investigation*, 3–5, 11–12.

7. Ibid., 7, 30.

8. Ibid., 32–33.

9. Ibid., 34–37.

10. Ibid., 38; *Twentieth Annual Report of Chicago Great Western Railroad Company Year Ended December 31, 1929*, 3, 11; *Twenty-First Annual Report of Chicago Great Western Railroad Company Year Ended December 31, 1930*, 3; *Railway Age*, April 19, 1930.

11. *Transportation*, April 1931; "Our New President: Victor V. Boatner," *Great Western Magazine* 8(October 1929):3.

12. *Naperville* (Illinois) *Clarion*, June 25, 1931; *Oelwein Daily Register*, November 15, 1929; November 21, 1930; May 29, 1944; *Twenty-First Annual Report of the Chicago Great Western Railroad Company Year Ended December 31, 1930*, 10–11; *Fort Dodge* (Iowa) *Messenger*, February 4, 1966; Lawson interview; Interview

with V. Allan Vaughn, Chicago, Illinois, December 3, 1980.

13. Lawson interview; *Oelwein Daily Register*, July 11, 1931.

14. [Senate] *Investigation of Railroads, Holding Companies, and Affiliated Companies . . . Chicago Great Western Dividends* (Washington, D.C., 1940), 2–5; *Oelwein Daily Register*, November 11, 1930.

15. [Senate] *Investigation of Railroads, Holding Companies, and Affiliated Companies . . . Chicago Great Western Purchases of Its Own Stock* (Washington, D.C., 1940), 1–10.

16. Ian S. Haberman, *The Van Sweringens of Cleveland: The Biography of an Empire* (Cleveland, 1979), 105–31.

17. *Senate Investigation*, 23–24.

18. Ibid., 24–26.

19. Ibid., 39–49.

20. [Senate] *Investigation of Railroads, Holding Companies, and Affiliated Companies . . . Kansas City Southern Stock Transaction* (Washington, D.C., 1940), 6–8 (hereafter cited as *Senate Investigation KCS Stock Transaction*).

21. *Senate Investigation KCS Stock Transaction*, 2–5.

22. Ibid., 7–9.

23. Ibid., 9–10.

24. Ibid., 10–13, 28–30; *Twenty-Second Annual Report of Chicago Great Western Railroad Company Year Ended December 31, 1931*, 6.

25. *Senate Investigation KCS Stock Transaction*.

26. Ibid., 33–34.

27. Ibid., 35; Haberman, *The Van Sweringens of Cleveland*, 132–50.

28. *Oelwein Daily Register*, February 28 and March 1, 1935.

29. *Senate Investigation KCS Stock Transaction*, 36–38; *Oelwein Daily Register*, October 17, 1935.

30. Richard T. Ruetten, "Burton K. Wheeler of Montana: A Progressive between the Wars," unpublished doctoral dissertation, Universtiy of Oregon, 1961, 200–202; *Senate Investigation KSC Stock Transaction*, 38–41; *Labor*, October 29, 1940.

31. *Traffic World*, April 27, 1929. See also letter from C. L. Darling to R. D. Bedgood, October 28, 1940, personal possession.

32. *Senate Investigation*, 14–15.

33. Interview with William S. Hunter, Des Moines, Iowa, August 25, 1980; Lawson interview; *Oelwein Daily Register*, November 20, 1967.

34. John B. Hoverson, "The Chicago Great Western Railway Company: 'Maple Leaf Route,' September 1, 1884–June 30, 1968," unpublished manuscript, in pos-

session of the Kansas City Southern Railway Company, Kansas City, Missouri, 34; *Oelwein Daily Register*, January 12, 1931.

35. *Ravenwood* (Missouri) *Gazette*, April 23, 1931; *Twenty-Second Annual Report of Chicago Great Western Railroad Company Year Ended December 31, 1931; 12; Thirteenth Annual Report of the Chicago Great Western Railroad Company Year Ended December 31, 1939*, 12; *Oelwein Daily Register*, December 23, 1932.

36. *Oelwein Daily Register*, May 6, 1931; *Twenty-Third Annual Report of Chicago Great Western Railroad Company Year Ended December 31, 1932*, 6; Hoverson, "The Chicago Great Western Railway Company," 32–33.

37. *Mantorville* (Minnesota) *Express*, November 23, 1933.

38. Ibid., December 21, 1933; February 22, March 15, April 26, November 22, 1934; March 28, 1935.

39. Frank P. Donovan, Jr., *Mileposts On the Prairie: The Story of the Minneapolis & St. Louis Railway* (New York, 1950), 199–211; *Oelwein Daily Register*, March 7, 1935; *Traffic World*, April 4, 1936.

40. George W. Hilton and John F. Due, *The Electric Interurban Railways in America* (Stanford, 1960), 134–35; letter from Henry S. Stebbins to Frank A Seiberling, March 23, 1918, Frank A. Seiberling Papers, Ohio Historical Society, Columbus; William D. Middleton, *North Shore: America's Fastest Interurban* (San Marino, Calif., 1964), 93–95; William D. Middleton, *South Shore: The Last Interurban* (San Marino, Calif., 1970), 140; Chicago, South Shore & South Bend Railroad public timetable, September 27, 1931.

41. Letter from John W. Hancock to author, February 15, 1982; letter from L. E. Hilsabeck to author, March 15, 1982; *Who's Who in Railroading*, 260; Lawson interview; *Oelwein Daily Register*, December 31, 1955.

42. Letter from Hilsabeck to author; *Traffic World*, March 7, 1936; *Railway Age*, May 30, July 4, August 22, 1936.

43. H. Roger Grant and L. Edward Purcell, eds., *Years of Struggle: The Farm Diary of Elmer G. Powers, 1931–1936* (Ames, 1976), 115–16.

44. *Twenty-Fifth Annual Report of Chicago Great Western Railroad Company Year Ended December 31, 1934*, 20; *Twenty-Eighth Annual Report of Chicago Great Western Railroad Company Year Ended December 31, 1937*, 22; *Oelwein Daily Register*, February 4 and February 11, 1936; *Stockton* (Illinois) *Herald-News*, February 12, 1936.

45. Lawson interview; *Oelwein Daily Register*, May 28, 1935; October 3, 1936; Robert Koretz, *Statutory History of the United States Labor Organization* (New York, 1970), 110, 119, 125, 134–35; *Report of Emergency*

Board: Chicago Great Western Railroad Company (Washington, D.C., 1937), 2–6; *Railway Age,* October 10, 1936.

46. *Report of Emergency Board,* 7–12; *Traffic World,* January 23, 1937; *Railway Age,* February 13, February 20, April 3, 1937; *Oelwein Daily Register,* March 27, 1937.

47. *Railway Age,* October 3, 1936; March 1, 1941; *Oelwein Daily Register,* February 8 and February 17, 1941.

48. *Oelwein Daily Register,* February 8 and February 17, 1941; *Thirty-First Annual Report, Report of the Trustees, Chicago Great Western Railroad Company Year Ended December 31, 1940,* 4; *First Annual Report of the Chicago Great Western Railway Company Year Ended December 31, 1941,* 8–9.

49. *Railway Age,* March 1, 1941.

50. Claude Moore Fuess, *Joseph B. Eastman: Servant of the People* (New York, 1952), 270–96; *Second Annual Report of the Chicago Great Western Railway Company Year Ended December 31, 1942,* 10.

51. See S. Kip Farrington, Jr., *Railroads at War* (New York, 1944).

52. *Thirty-First Annual Report, Report of the Trustees, Chicago Great Western Railroad Company Year Ended December 31, 1940,* 8, 19; *Third Annual Report of the Chicago Great Western Railway Company Year Ended December 31, 1943,* 25; *Fifth Annual Report of the Chicago Great Western Railway Company Year Ended December 31, 1945,* 14–25.

53. *Third Annual Report of the Chicago Great Western Railway Company Year Ended December 31, 1943,* 10; *Oelwein Daily Register,* April 21, 1943; January 27, 1944; Lawson interview.

54. Interview with Mac K. Hatch, Oelwein, Iowa, January 8, 1980; *Oelwein Daily Register,* August 20, 1945; *Ravenwood Gazette,* October 5, 1944.

55. *Oelwein Daily Register,* March 9, 1942; November 22, 1946; *Fifth Annual Report of the Chicago Great Western Railway Company Year Ended December 31, 1945,* 10.

56. *Oelwein Daily Register,* October 17, 1942; *Fourth Annual Report of the Chicago Great Western Railway Company Year Ended December 31, 1944,* 10; *Third Annual Report of the Chicago Great Western Railway Company Year Ended December 31, 1943,* 15; *Fifth Annual Report of the Chicago Great Western Railway Company Year Ended December 31, 1945,* 8, 15.

57. James MacGregor Burns, *Roosevelt: The Soldier of Freedom* (New York, 1970), 338; Frances Perkins, *The Roosevelt I Know* (New York, 1946), 307; Harry E. Jones, *Railroad Wages and Labor Relations, 1900–1952*

(Washington, 1953), 121–27.

58. *New York Times,* November 11, 1946; Lawson interview.

59. *Who's Who in Railroading,* 96; *Railway Age,* June 1, 1946.

60. *Who's Who in Railroading,* 96; Lawson interview.

61. *Seventh Annual Report of the Chicago Great Western Railway Company Year Ended December 31, 1947,* 9.

62. *Oelwein Daily Register,* March 29, 1944; John B. Hoverson, "The Chicago Great Western Railway Company," 39.

63. *Oelwein Daily Register,* November 7, 1946.

64. Ibid., December 19, 1946; February 17, 1947; April 10, 1948; *Eighth Annual Report of the Chicago Great Western Railway Company for the Fiscal Year Ended December 31, 1948,* 6. In the carriers' hunger for diesels, they commonly employed a "Noah's Ark" philosophy in their purchases (two of every kind). Although the CGW acquired a mixed fleet, its stable of diesels boasted a greater unity than some competitors, most notably the Rock Island.

65. *Oelwein Daily Register,* December 4, 1947; letter from D. Keith Lawson to author, May 20, 1980.

66. Interview with William N. Deramus III, Kansas City, Missouri, October 15, 1980.

67. Ibid.

CHAPTER SEVEN

1. *Oelwein* (Iowa) *Daily Register,* October 19 and October 21, 1948; Lawson interview. Born in Hope, Kansas, on December 1, 1888, Grant Stauffer attended public schools in his hometown and later the nearby College of Emporia. He spent most of his adult life in the coal business, having served as a salesman, jobber, and producer. In 1927 Stauffer joined with L. Russell Kelce in acquisition of mining properties, thus creating the Sinclair Coal Company, later Peabody Coal Company.

2. Letter from D. Keith Lawson to author, May 20, 1980; interview with John Hawkinson, Chicago, Illinois, December 3, 1980 (hereafter cited as Hawkinson interview).

3. *Railway Age,* November 13, 1948; Hawkinson interview; *New York Times,* July 1, 1957; *Oelwein Daily Register,* November 19, 1948; *Railway Progress,* September 1950. According to William N. Deramus III, the Kansas City Group sought only to make money from the Chicago Great Western. "I think the main reason that intrigued all concerned in the Great Western picture was the possibility of making money and no other logical reason," letter from William N. Deramus III to author, October 4, 1982.

4. Lawson interview.

5. *Oelwein Daily Register,* April 1, 1949.

6. Russell F. Moore, ed., *Who's Who in Railroading in North America* (New York, 1959), 155; *Chicago Daily News,* May 18, 1949; *Oelwein Daily Register,* May 18, 1949; *Railway Progress,* September 1950.

7. *Chicago Daily News,* May 18, 1949; *Journal of Commerce* (Chicago), May 18, 1949; Hawkinson interview. Deramus relied heavily on his father's advice and the practices employed by the Kansas City Southern. Remarked a former Great Western official, "It was almost comical the way D-3 [Deramus] followed on the C.G.W. the pattern established by senior on the K.C.S., even down to the filing system in the office, mile post numbering . . . as well as communication system," letter from D. Keith Lawson to author, June 17, 1982.

8. Interview with William N. Deramus III, Kansas City, Missouri, October 15, 1980 (hereafter cited as Deramus interview). Reynolds & Co., Stock Department, "Chicago Great Western Railway," October 22, 1952 (hereafter cited as Reynolds & Co. report); *Ninth Annual Report of the Chicago Great Western Railway Company* (1949), 4; *Tenth Annual Report of the Chicago Great Western Railway Company* (1950), 2, 5; *Eleventh Annual Report of the Chicago Great Western Railway Company* (1951), 10.

9. *Twelfth Annual Report of the Chicago Great Western Railway Company* (1952), 10; *Thirteenth Annual Report of the Chicago Great Western Railway Company* (1953), 10; *Fourteenth Annual Report of the Chicago Great Western Railway Company* (1954), 8; *Fifteenth Annual Report of the Chicago Great Western Railway Company* (1955), 6–7.

10. Mark H. Rose, *Interstate: Express Highway Politics, 1941–1956* (Lawrence, Kansas, 1979), 85–94; Lawson interview. While management showed no intention of acquiring modern lightweight passenger equipment, area residents hoped to see it eventually. For example, the *Oelwein Daily Register* of October 2, 1951 reported that a local minister in his Sunday sermon "envisioned returning to Oelwein in 1975 and stepping down from 'the City of St. Paul' on the Chicago Great Western's new streamlined passenger line."

11. Unidentified clipping, Olmstead County Historical Society, Rochester, Minnesota; Chicago Great Western Railway Company public timetable, January 18, 1948; March 3, 1949; *Oelwein Daily Register,* July 27, 1950; *Rochester* (Minnesota) *Post-Bulletin,* August 17, 1950. The Clarion-Oelwein McKeen car, M-1003, built in 1910 and acquired in 1928, was perhaps the last piece of this type of rolling stock still serviceable in the United States. Instead of going to a museum, it soon became scrap.

12. Chicago Great Western Railway Company public timetable, October 21, 1951; *Reports of the Public Service Commission of the State of Missouri* (Jefferson City, 1953), 65. By the time William N. Deramus III, left the Great Western in January 1957, Oelwein to Chicago train service was merely a memory. On November 1, 1953, the Post Office Department discontinued its mail contract between these two terminal cities, and the company began to reevaluate these runs. Through trains ended on August 12, 1956, although they temporarily continued to run between Oelwein and Dubuque. But the Iowa Commerce Commission finally allowed these trains to stop on September 30, 1956. The Great Western cogently argued that the runs were an unfair burden: they had lost the mail contract and carried an average of less than one revenue passenger daily westbound and only 1.6 on the eastward trip. See *Oelwein Daily Register,* October 25, 1953; April 18, May 17, August 31, September 19, 1956.

13. Interview with James L. Rueber, Clear Lake, Iowa, April 14, 1982; *Oelwein Register,* October 18, 1894. The official symbol for the Chicago Great Western also changed. Deramus dropped the familiar Corn Belt Route herald and motto that had been used since the early days of the Felton administration. In its place he selected the "Lucky Strike" logo with "Chicago" and "Railway" in smaller type than "Great Western." Indeed, the CGW head sought to end "Chicago" from regular usage. It was, after all, "just another word . . ."; the idea being that one less word meant economy, Deramus interview.

14. Lawson interview; interview with Thomas J. Lamphier, St. Paul, Minnesota, April 15, 1982; letter from D. Keith Lawson to author, August 2, 1982.

15. "History of the Chicago Great Western Railway Company"; *Oelwein Daily Register,* January 13, 1950; Finance Docket, No. 17594, Interstate Commerce Commission, February 8, 1952.

16. *Oelwein Daily Register,* August 12, 1950; March 15, November 3, November 7, 1952; Philip R. Hastings, *Chicago Great Western: Iowa in the Merger Decade* (Newton, N.J., 1981), 63; *Twelfth Annual Report of the Chicago Great Western Railway Company* (1952), 10; interview with Marlin Lincoln, Kansas City, Missouri, October 15, 1980 (hereafter cited as Lincoln interview); *Modern Railroads,* October 1954.

17. Deramus interview; Lincoln interview.

18. *Oelwein Daily Register,* November 3, 1952; *Modern Railroads,* October 1954.

19. Letter from Lawson to author, May 10, 1980; John B. Hoverson, "The Chicago Great Western Railway Company: 'Maple Leaf Route,' September 1, 1884–June 30, 1968," unpublished manuscript, in possession of the Kansas City Southern Railway Company, Kansas City, Missouri, 43.

20. Hoverson, "The Chicago Great Western Railway

Company," 43; letter from D. Keith Lawson to author, June 17, 1982.

21. *Ninth Annual Report of the Chicago Great Western Railway Company* (1949), 1; *Thirteenth Annual Report of the Chicago Great Western Railway Company* (1953), 4; Keith L. Bryant, Jr., *History of the Atchison, Topeka and Santa Fé Railway* (New York, 1974), 290; John F. Stover, *History of the Illinois Central Railroad* (New York, 1975), 541.

22. Interview with William S. Hunter, Des Moines, Iowa, August 25, 1980; Lawson interview.

23. *Ninth Annual Report of the Chicago Great Western Railway Company* (1959), 3; Reynolds & Co. report; *Rochester Post-Bulletin,* May 10, 1950.

24. *Oelwein Daily Register,* July 7, 1950; *Ninth Annual Report of the Chicago Great Western Railway Company* (1949), 3; *Tenth Annual Report of the Chicago Great Western Railway Company* (1953), 8, 10.

25. *Oelwein Daily Register,* February 2 and February 6, 1953; Lawson interview.

26. Lawson interview; 77 (S. Ct.) 635 *Supreme Court Reporter* (St. Paul, 1957).

27. Lawson interview.

28. Letter from W. N. Deramus III to author, October 4, 1982.

29. Ibid.; letter from D. Keith Lawson to author, August 2, 1982; *Oelwein Daily Register,* March 9 and March 10, 1953.

30. Letter from D. Keith Lawson to author, August 26, 1981.

31. Ibid.

32. Ibid.; Hoverson, "The Chicago Great Western Railway Company," 51.

33. Hoverson, "The Chicago Great Western Railway Company," 46; interview with Charles Finch, Dubuque, Iowa, January 8, 1980; Hawkinson interview; letter from V. Allan Vaughn to C. D. Foster, July 10, 1956, personal possession.

34. Lawson interview.

35. *Great Western Safety News,* January 1955. Interestingly, Deramus suspended publication of the Katy's monthly employee's magazine soon after he assumed control of that road in 1957.

36. *Modern Railroads,* August 1957; *Great Western Safety News,* October 1955; October 1956; *Oelwein Daily Register,* September 19, 1955; September 24, 1956. As Deramus recalls, "The company-sponsored annual picnic was merely taking up what the KCS had done years before"; letter from W. N. Deramus III to author, October 4, 1982.

37. *Thirteenth Annual Report of the Chicago Great Western Railway Company* (1953), 4; *Fourteenth Annual Report of the Chicago Great Western Railway Company* (1954), 4; *Fifteenth Annual Report of the Chicago Great Western Railway Company* (1955), 2; *Sixteenth Annual Report of the Chicago Great Western Railway Company* (1956), 2; Hawkinson interview; *Oelwein Daily Register,* March 29, 1950; *New York Times,* Junes 30, 1948; December 30, 1956.

38. *Fifteenth Annual Report of the Chicago Great Western Railway Company* (1955), 2; "History of the Chicago Great Western Railway Company," unpublished manuscript, 18; letter from W. N. Deramus III to author, October 4, 1982.

39. Deramus interview; *Fifteenth Annual Report of the Chicago Great Western Railway Company* (1955), 7; *Safety News,* March 1957; *Oelwein Daily Register,* October 18, 1955.

40. *Railway Age,* April 29, 1957; *Oelwein Daily Register,* January 8 and January 11, 1957; letter from W. N. Deramus III to author, October 4, 1982. Soon after William N. Deramus III arrived at the Katy, he cut costs to the bone. The agenda included his order to move secretly the corporate headquarters from St. Louis to Denison, Texas, a decision designed to slash overhead expenses but one that generated an enormously bad press reaction. All Katy executives were instructed to stay away from the office. Terse, printed notices advised the 115 displaced employees that they faced unemployment unless they reported to the Texas community within forty-eight hours. The road offered them transportation and a week's lodging aboard vintage Pullman cars, plus a small food allowance. About sixty-five workers made the trip; the others, some with forty years' service, got two days' salary as their severance pay. This outraged St. Louis leaders, and the city's august Chamber of Commerce even expelled the Katy from its ranks. See *St. Louis Post-Dispatch,* April 1 and April 2, 1957.

41. Lawson interview; Hawkinson interview. Deramus questioned the Reidy statement. "I merely told him, not what you say here, but that it would be in his [Reidy's] best interests to remember that the only way to success on the Milwaukee Railroad was to be a Catholic and on the Southern Pacific to be a Mason. It was my thought and I so expressed to him, that it was not a very good way to keep up the morale of one's own organization," letter from W. N. Deramus III to author, October 4, 1982.

CHAPTER EIGHT

1. Letter from Leonard H. Murray to author, January 10, 1983; Russell F. Moore, ed., *Who's Who in Railroading in North America* (New York, 1959), 527; *Oelwein* (Iowa) *Daily Register,* January 26, 1961.

2. *Minneapolis Star,* January 11, 1957; *Chicago Great Western Railway Company Annual Report, 1961,* 4.

3. *Chicago Great Western Railway Company Annual Report, 1963,* 12; *Chicago Great Western Railway Company Annual Report, 1966,* 5, 10; *Chicago Great Western Railway Company Annual Report, 1964,* 13.

4. *The Mixed Train,* 12(March 1963):3, 13(April 1964):2; *Chicago Great Western Railway Company Annual Report, 1960,* 4–5; *Chicago Great Western Railway Company Annual Report, 1963,* 14; *Safety News,* January-February 1963.

5. Philip R. Hastings, *Chicago Great Western Railway: Iowa in the Merger Decade* (Newton, N.J., 1981), 15.

6. CGW Minute Book 16; *Oelwein Daily Register,* November 14 and December 29, 1961; April 12, 1962.

7. *Chicago Great Western Railway Company Annual Report, 1965,* 8; *The Mixed Train,* 10(April 1961):3, 14(October 1965):5, 31(May 1982):4; *Safety News,* September-October 1965. In a footnote to the passing of Great Western varnish, one rider, Edward M. Langemo, an 84-year-old resident of Minneapolis, was on number 14 when it rolled into his home city's Great Northern station on September 30, 1965. Eighty years before Langemo had also been aboard the first train; he had participated in the initial run ceremonies on September 23, 1885, between Kenyon, Minnesota, and St. Paul.

8. CGW Minute Book 16, Chicago & North Western Transportation Company, Chicago; CGW Minute Book 17; *Chicago Great Western Railway Company Annual Report, 1964,* 6; CGW Minute Book 19; *Safety News,* March-April 1967.

9. *Chicago Great Western Railway Company Annual Report, 1964,* 2; *Chicago Great Western Railway Company Annual Report, 1967,* 1.

10. See *Chicago Great Western Railway Company Annual Reports, 1957–1967.*

11. Richard Saunders, *The Railroad Mergers and the Coming of Conrail* (Westport, Conn., 1978), 87.

12. Ibid., 85–86, 92–93, 95–18; *New York Times,* January 16, 1968.

13. Saunders, *The Railroad Mergers and the Coming of Conrail,* 82; Lawson interview.

14. *Oelwein Daily Register,* February 4 and June 8, 1946; Lawson interview.

15. Lawson interview; Hawkinson interview.

16. Hawkinson interview; CGW Minute Book 16.

17. *Oelwein Daily Register,* October 18, 1962; CGW Minute Book 17; *Chicago Great Western Railway Company Annual Report, 1962,* 6. President Murray later recalled that the Soo and the Great Western were really two quite different roads: "Soo was & is a granger road in the west and a service road in the east especially between Mpls. & Chicago. At that time the operating concept on the CGW was to hold for tonnage & move heavy tonnage trains. Soo could not have survived nor could a merged company using the operating policies of the CGW. It worked well for them but it would not for a different transportation unit such as unification would create." Letter from Leonard H. Murray to author, January 10, 1983.

18. CGW Minute Book 17.

19. Ibid.

20. *Oelwein Daily Register,* November 12, 1963; Lawson interview.

21. Hawkinson interview.

22. CGW Minute Book 17. The C&NW had long thought about entering the Kansas City gateway. In 1915, for example, the road pushed southwest from the mining camp of Buxton (Miami), Iowa, into the nearby coal fields of western Monroe County. This sparked talk of the extension's being a springboard to the Missouri metropolis.

23. CGW Minute Book 17; *Modern Railroads,* September 1964.

24. CGW Minute Book 17.

25. Ibid., *Chicago Great Western Railway Company Annual Report, 1964,* 14; Hawkinson interview.

26. CGW Minute Book 17; *Chicago Great Western Railway Company Annual Report, 1964,* 2.

27. *Chicago & North Western Railway Co. — Merger — Chicago Great Western Railway Co. Finance Docket No. 23388* (Washington, D.C., 1967), 14, 15 (hereafter cited as *ICC Merger Report*); CGW Minute Book 18.

28. Letter from Harold O. Moe to Interstate Commerce Commission, February 3, 1965, Finance Docket No. 23388, Folder F1A, Interstate Commerce Commission Papers, Washington, D.C. (hereafter cited as ICC Papers).

29. Letter from Richard O. Shirk to Harold D. McCoy, ICC Papers; *ICC Merger Report,* 15–16.

30. *ICC Merger Report,* 23–24; *Petition of Soo Line Railroad Company for Reconsideration of the Commission's Decision Approving Merger and for Further Hearing as to Condition for Soo Line's Protection* (Chicago, 1967), 6 (hereafter cited as *Soo Line Petition*).

31. *ICC Merger Report,* 13, 30–37; *Minneapolis Tribune,* April 28, 1967.

32. *Soo Line Petition,* 1–27; *Wall Street Journal,* May 29, 1967; CGW Minute Book 19.

33. CGW Minute Book 19; *Oelwein Daily Register,* March 29 and April 19, 1968.

34. *Safety News,* June 30, 1968.

AFTERWORD

1. Philip R. Hastings, *Chicago Great Western: Iowa in the Merger Decade* (Newton, N.J., 1981), 63; letter from

James L. Rueber to author, August 28, 1982. At the time of the merger the North Western put most of the former Great Western into its Missouri Division, with headquarters at Oelwein. Then in January 1974 the C&NW decided to eliminate that organizational structure and to fuse it with its Central Division, based in Mason City, and with the Iowa Division, located in Boone. Trackage north of the North Western's Chicago to Omaha main line joined the Central Division; mileage south entered the Iowa Division. The C&NW argued that terminating the Missouri unit increased efficiency since it reduced the number of operating divisions from nine to eight and ended situations "where rights-of-way of different divisions criss-cross repeatedly, as [is] common in Iowa." Another explanation centers on the North Western's attitude toward Great Western employees. Initially, the new owners planned to call the former Corn Belt Route the "CGW Division" but quickly changed their minds when they remembered their unpleasant experiences with the Minneapolis & St. Louis. When the C&NW acquired that road in 1960, it called the former property the "M&StL Division." Eventually the company altered the name to the Central Division. Unmistakably, the C&NW management wanted to obliterate all vestiges of the Chicago Great Western. Naming the property the Missouri rather than the CGW division was not enough; the "Great Weedy" must be fully integrated into the larger corporation. See *North Western News,* January 16, 1974.

2. *New York Times,* December 31, 1963; December 31, 1967; Interview with V. Allan Vaughn, Chicago, Illinois, December 4, 1980; *Railway Age,* July 28, 1980.

3. As of January 1983 the following former CGW lines remained: Carroll to Harlan, Iowa, 40 miles (not in service); Cedar Falls, Iowa branch, 7 miles (not in service); Elmhurst to Fox River, Illinois, 20 miles; Mason City to Somers, Iowa, 88 miles; Oelwein to Coulter, Iowa, 80 miles; Oelwein to Kansas City, 353 miles (the 45-mile Marshalltown to Bondurant segment is to be abandoned); Randolph to Northfield, Minnesota, 9 miles; Randolph to Red Wing, Minnesota, 27 miles (Cannon Falls to Red Wing not in service); St Paul to Randolph, Minnesota, 32 miles.

4. Interview with Galen L. Vargason, Chicago, Illinois, December 3, 1980; *Dubuque* (Iowa) *Telegraph-Herald,* March 31, 1981; *Oelwein* (Iowa) *Daily Register,* November 7, 1981; *Waterloo* (Iowa) *Courier,* November 1, 1981.

5. *Oelwein Daily Register,* November 6, 1981; *Post-Bulletin* (Rochester, Minnesota), December 19, 1982; letter from James L. Rueber to author, August 28, 1982.

6. Letter from Robert F. McAteer to Chairman, Interstate Commerce Commission, May 4, 1967, Interstate Commerce Commission Papers, Washington, D.C.

7. Richard Saunders, *The Railroad Mergers and the Coming of Conrail* (Westport, Conn., 1978), 263–335; *New York Times,* August 1, 1982.

BIBLIOGRAPHY

NOTE ON SOURCES

As mentioned in the Preface, the bulk of the corporate records of the Chicago Great Western disappeared at the time of the merger. Yet some have survived. The Chicago & North Western Transportation Company has in its Chicago headquarters building minute books from the Minnesota & Northwestern and the Great Western for scattered years. The firm also possesses miscellaneous papers of the CGW and various predecessor roads, including construction contracts, leases, and general correspondence.

Three archival collections likewise proved especially valuable. The James J. Hill Papers, housed in St. Paul's James Jerome Hill Reference Library, contain extensive materials on the Mason City & Fort Dodge Railroad and on the closeness between Hill and A. B. Stickney. The Illinois Central Railroad Papers, located in the Newberry Library in Chicago, cast light on the obscure Dubuque & Dakota Railroad and on the IC's relationship with the Stickney road. Last, the Samuel M. Felton Papers at the Baker Library of the Harvard University Graduate School of Business Administration, while modest in size, furnish important insights into the career of the Great Western's second president.

Various reports also offer superb, specialized information. In 1920, the company produced for the Interstate Commerce Commission its "Corporate History of the Chicago Great Western Railroad Company as of the Date of Valuation June 20, 1916." While some factual errors mar this study, it gives a fine skeletal framework of the CGW's corporate past. Twenty years later the United States Senate published its *Investigation of Railroads, Holding Companies, and Affiliated Companies . . . Control of the Chicago Great Western and . . . Chicago Great Western Dividends . . . Kansas City Southern Stock Transaction.* These documents tell the seamy story of the Bremo Corporation and the financial escapades during the Patrick Joyce regime.

Much of the saga of the Corn Belt Route is described in the scores of newspapers from on-line communities. I have made an effort to read most of these publications. One paper stands out: the *Oelwein* (Iowa) *Register,* later the *Oelwein Daily Register.* From the 1880s through the 1960s, the "Hub City" organ chronicled with care local Great Western happenings and frequently reprinted or reported other company news. Early in the century the *Register* featured a regular railroad "gossip" column that is particularly rich in equipment and personnel information.

Finally, I have relied on annual reports, employee

magazines, state regulatory publications, trade journals, and interviews. The footnotes and selected annotated bibliography provide the pertinent details. Copies of some of these sources are in my extensive collection of Chicago Great Western materials.

ANNOTATED BIBLIOGRAPHY OF SELECTED BOOKS AND UNPUBLISHED MANUSCRIPTS

Adler, Dorothy R. *British Investment in American Railways, 1834–1898*. Charlottesville, 1970.
The leading work on the subject of investments made by British individuals and institutions in railroads of the United States. Includes discussion of the CGW.

Athearn, Robert G. *Rebel of the Rockies: A History of the Denver and Rio Grande Western Railroad*. New Haven, 1962.
This superb history of the D&RGW provides coverage of promoters' dreams to cross the Rocky Mountains.

Brown, Henry L. *Steam Locomotives of the Chicago Great Western 2-8-0 Consolidated Type*. Minot, N. D., 1977.
A largely pictorial work, this title offers technical coverage of one type of steam locomotive commonly used by the CGW.

Bryant, Keith L., Jr. *History of the Atchison, Topeka and Santa Fe Railway*. New York, 1975.
Bryant's work is the leading history of a road that generally was an ally of the CGW.

Bryn-Jones, David. *Frank B. Kellogg: A Biography*. New York, 1937.
This biography is the standard account of the life of this well-known lawyer-diplomat and CGW legal adviser.

Carlson, Norman, ed. *Iowa Trolleys*. Chicago, 1975.
While primarily a pictorial work, this rail fan publication also contains helpful sketches of individual Iowa interurbans.

Chandler, Alfred D. *The Visible Hand: The Managerial Revolution in American Business*. Cambridge, 1977.
In perhaps the most significant recent study of American business, Chandler examines the growth of the nation's railroad system.

Chicago Great Western. "Corporate History of the Chicago Great Western Railroad Company as of the Date of Valuation, June 20, 1916." Chicago, 1920.
The CGW prepared this detailed outline of its history and those of two affiliated companies, the Mason City & Fort Dodge and the Wisconsin, Minnesota & Pacific, for the ICC in order to satisfy, in part, the mandate of the Valuation Act of 1913.

Chrysler, Walter P. *Life of an American Workman*. New York, 1950.
This autobiography relates the automaker's brief career with the CGW in its motive power department.

Cleveland, Frederick A., and Fred Wilbur Powell. *Railroad Promotion and Capitalization in the United States*. New York, 1909.
Although largely an overview of the development of nineteenth-century American railroading, this book includes material on local financing of the CGW's DeKalb, Illinois, extension.

Craig, Marshall B. "The Chicago Great Western's Oldest Miles." Unpublished manuscript.
This short, typed essay focuses on the Dubuque & Dakota Railroad, a future component of the CGW, and can be found in the manuscript collection of the State Historical Society of Iowa.

Daggett, Stuart. *Railroad Consolidation West of the Mississippi River*. Berkeley, 1933.
This examination of the general topic of railroad

consolidation in the Midwest and West during the 1920s reveals how the CGW fit into the Ripley plan of 1921 and the ICC unification proposal of 1929.

Donovan, Frank P., Jr. *Gateway to the Northwest: The Story of the Minnesota Transfer Railway.* Minneapolis, 1954.
The Donovan booklet provides historical treatment of the major Twin Cities switching firm, one in which the CGW owned an interest.

———. *Mileposts on the Prairie: The Story of the Minneapolis & St. Louis Railway.* New York, 1950.
A popular history of the Minneapolis & St. Louis, a CGW neighbor, this work is the only full-length study of this company.

Dubin, Arthur D. *More Classic Trains.* Milwaukee, 1974.
This heavily illustrated work about passenger service on a wide variety of railroads features a chapter entitled "The Great Trains of the Great Western."

Farrington, S. Kip, Jr. *Railroads at War.* New York, 1944.
Written near the close of World War II, this work chronicles efforts by the nation's railroads to keep the war-machine running.

Felton, Samuel M. "Report on the Chicago Great Western Ry., March–1909." Unpublished manuscript.
Located in the Samuel Felton Papers at the Baker Library, Harvard University, this report is a careful analysis of the CGW made for J. P. Morgan & Company.

Finch, C. W. "The Winston Tunnel." Unpublished manuscript.
Former CGW station agent C. W. Finch, presently of Dubuque, Iowa, offers a short account of the Winston Tunnel located near Galena, Illinois.

Fuess, Claude Moore. *Joseph B. Eastman: Servant of the People.* New York, 1952.
This full-length biography of federal bureaucrat Joseph Eastman is especially rich on the relationship between government and railroads during World War II.

Gardner, Ed. *Chicago Great Western Scrapbook.* Mountain Top, Pa., n.d.
Privately printed, this booklet contains a compilation of photographs, mostly from old postcards and public timetables.

Haberman, Ian S. *The Van Sweringens of Cleveland: The Biography of an Empire.* Cleveland, 1979.
More than a biography of brothers O. P. and M. J. Van Sweringen, this work traces the growth and ultimate collapse of the Van Sweringen railroad empire.

Hastings, Philip R. *Chicago Great Western: Iowa in the Merger Decade.* Newton, N.J., 1981.
Concentrating on the CGW during the 1960s, this small paperback portrays much of the system pictorially.

Hayes, William Edward. *Iron Road to Empire.* New York, 1953.
This journalistic account of the history of the Chicago, Rock Island & Pacific offers the only specialized coverage of this major CGW competitor.

Hilton, George W., and John F. Due. *The Electric Interurban Railways.* Stanford, 1960.
In the foremost study of the interurban phenomenon, Hilton and Due note the CGW's cordial relations with several Midwestern electric roads.

"History of the Chicago Great Western Railway Company." Unpublished manuscript.
Anonymously prepared and in possession of the author, this several-page typescript provides uneven yet valuable material on the saga of the CGW. 47:

Hoogenboom, Ari and Olive. *A History of the ICC: From Panacea to Palliative.* New York, 1976.
This brief, trenchant examination of the shifting fortunes of the ICC since its founding in 1887 is a provocative case study of how the regulatory idea rose, flourished, and eventually deteriorated.

Hoverson, John B. "The Chicago Great Western Railway Company: 'Maple Leaf Route,' September 1, 1884–June 30, 1968." Unpublished manuscript.
More a collection of primary source documents, this typed manuscript in the possession of the Kansas City Southern Railway Co. nevertheless contains interesting narrative material, especially for the twentieth century.

Keilty, Edmund. *Doodlebug Country: The Rail Motorcar on the Class I Railroads of the United States.* Glendale, Calif., 1982.
One section of this profusely illustrated work features the ubiquitous self-propelled passenger cars found on the CGW.

Kerr, K. Austin. *American Railroad Politics, 1914–1920: Rates, Wages, and Efficiency.* Pittsburgh, 1968.
This work deals with the role of various interest groups, mainly shippers, workers, managers, and investors, in formulating and implementing federal railroad policy during the World War I era.

Lamb, W. Kaye. *History of the Canadian Pacific Railway.* New York, 1977.
The most complete history of the Canadian Pacific includes coverage of A. B. Stickney's activities in the company's construction in Manitoba during the early 1880s.

Leonard, William Norris. *Railroad Consolidation under the Transportation Act of 1920.* New York, 1946.
Leonard's book provides a thoughtful review of the ramifications of the ill-fated merger provisions of the Transportation Act of 1920.

Martin, Albro. *Enterprise Denied: Origins of the Decline of American Railroads, 1897–1917.* New York, 1971.
Arguing that the political reformers ruined the railroad industry with unreasonable regulations, Martin provides an excellent framework in which to examine carriers during the progressive era.

———. *James J. Hill and the Opening of the Northwest.* New York, 1976.
This sympathic yet balanced biography of James J. Hill offers useful insights into the relationship between Hill and A. B. Stickney.

Middleton, William D. *North Shore: America's Fastest Interurban.* San Marino, Calif., 1964.
Middleton's extensively illustrated history of the North Shore gives a good picture of an innovative Midwestern interurban.

———. *South Shore: The Last Interurban.* San Marino, Calif., 1970.
This popular account of the South Shore contains a discussion of the road's development of the modern concept of hauling truck trailers on flatcars.

Miles, R. E. *A History of Early Railroading in Winona County.* Winona, 1958.
In this local history of railroad development in one southeastern Minnesota county, coverage is included on the Winona & Western, a CGW predecessor company.

Miller, Paul E. "A Financial History of the Chicago Great Western Railroad Company," 1924.
This Northwestern University M.A. thesis centers on the CGW's original financial structure and the 1909 reorganization.

Olmsted, Robert P. *Six Units to Sycamore: Chicago Great Western in Illinois.* Woodridge, Ill., 1967.
An attractive pictorial essay on the CGW in the 1960s, this modest publication deals with freight-train movements in the greater Chicago area.

Olson, Russell L. *The Electric Railways of Minnesota*. Hopkins, Minn., 1976.

This review of Minnesota traction companies also includes discussion of CGW friend, Minneapolis, Northfield & Southern, a road proposed as a "juice" line but operated with internal combustion equipment.

Overton, Richard C. *Burlington Route: A History of the Burlington Lines*. New York, 1965.

One of the best railroad company histories ever published, *Burlington Route* is a comprehensive study of the CGW rival, the Chicago, Burlington & Quincy and its affiliated properties.

Report of Emergency Board: Chicago Great Western Railroad Company. Washington, D.C., 1937.

This federal government report contains the findings of the three-member emergency labor board created by President Franklin D. Roosevelt to investigate worker unrest on the CGW.

Sandeen, Ernest R. *St. Paul's Historic Summit Avenue*. St. Paul, 1978.

One of the nation's most architecturally significant residential streets is Summit Avenue in St. Paul, Minnesota, along which A. B. Stickney's mansion once stood.

Saunders, Richard. *The Railroad Mergers and the Coming of Conrail*. Westport, 1978.

In a brilliant and pathbreaking study on railroad mergers in the 1950s and 1960s, Saunders emphasizes the limitations of what many railroad and business leaders thought was a panacea for the industry's growing financial problems.

Shaw, Thomas W. "Oelwein's Italian Neighborhoods: Italian-Americans of Oelwein, Iowa, 1901 to the Present," 1978.

An unpublished M.A. thesis completed at the University of Northern Iowa, this comprehensive analysis of the Oelwein, Iowa, Italian community tells of its close relationship with the CGW.

Splawn, Walter M. W. *Consolidation of Railroads*. New York, 1925.

A detailed examination of the Transportation Act of 1920, this tome reviews the measure and examines its advantages and disadvantages.

Stickney, A. B. *Omaha as a Market-Town*. St. Paul, 1903.

This pamphlet shows how CGW president Stickney boosted communities along his railroad.

———. *The Railway Problem*. St. Paul, 1891.

In one of the most important works ever penned by an Amreican railroad executive, Stickney explains the industry's competitive shortcomings and suggests the value of meaningful federal regulation.

———. *A Western Trunk Line Railway without a Mortgage: A Short History of the Finances of the Chicago Great Western Railway Company*. New York, 1900.

Stickney explains in this booklet how his company adopted the "English System" of railroad financing.

Stover, John F. *A History of the Illinois Central Railroad*. New York, 1975.

This foremost study of the Illinois Central includes an examination of the company's lines in the CGW service territory.

[U.S. Senate]. *Investigation of Railroads, Holding Companies, and Affiliated Companies: Chicago Great Western Dividends; Chicago Great Western Purchases of Its Own Stock; Control of the Chicago Great Western; Kansas City Southern Stock Transaction. . . .* Washington, D.C., 1940.

These four Senate reports vividly describe the nefarious activities of CGW President Patrick H. Joyce and the Bremo Corporation.

White, John H., Jr. *The American Railroad Passenger Car*. Baltimore, 1978.

White's monumental work on the evolution of the railroad passenger car includes comments on the Mann Boudoir equipment that the CGW operated early in its history.

INDEX

Court cases, name trains, publications, and steam railroads are listed in italics.